D1608982

Garden Witch's
HERBAL

True ecstasy hails neither from spirit nor from nature,
But from a divine union of these two.

MARTIN BUBER

About the Author

Ellen Dugan, also known as the Garden Witch, is a psychic-clairvoyant who lives in Missouri with her husband and three children. A practicing Witch for over twenty-four years, Ellen also has many years of nursery and garden center experience, including landscape and garden design. She received her Master Gardener status through the University of Missouri and her local county extension office. Look for other articles by Ellen in Llewellyn's annual *Magical Almanac*, *Wicca Almanac*, and *Herbal Almanac*. Visit her website at:

www.ellendugan.com

ELLEN DUGAN

Garden Witch's
HERBAL

Green magick,
herbalism & spirituality

FROM THE AUTHOR OF
GARDEN WITCHERY

Llewellyn Publications
WOODBURY, MINNESOTA

Book design and editing by Rebecca Zins
Cover design by Ellen Dahl
Cover image and interior illustrations © Jennifer L. Meyer

Llewellyn is a registered trademark of Llewellyn Worldwide, Ltd.

ISBN 978-0-7387-1429-5

Llewellyn Worldwide does not participate in, endorse, or have any authority or responsibility concerning private business transactions between our authors and the public.

All mail addressed to the author is forwarded but the publisher cannot, unless specifically instructed by the author, give out an address or phone number.

Any Internet references contained in this work are current at publication time, but the publisher cannot guarantee that a specific location will continue to be maintained. Please refer to the publisher's website for links to authors' websites and other sources.

Llewellyn Publications
A Division of Llewellyn Worldwide, Ltd.
2143 Wooddale Drive, Dept. 978-0-7387-1429-5
Woodbury, MN 55125-2989

Printed in the United States of America

OTHER BOOKS BY ELLEN DUGAN

Garden Witchery: Magick from the Ground Up
(Llewellyn, 2003)

Elements of Witchcraft: Natural Magick for Teens
(Llewellyn, 2003)

Cottage Witchery: Natural Magick for Hearth and Home
(Llewellyn, 2005)

Autumn Equinox: The Enchantment of Mabon
(Llewellyn, 2005)

The Enchanted Cat: Feline Fascinations, Spells & Magick
(Llewellyn, 2006)

Herb Magic for Beginners: Down-to-Earth Enchantments
(Llewellyn, 2006; also available in Spanish as *Magia con las hierbas*)

Natural Witchery: Intuitive, Personal & Practical Magick
(Llewellyn, 2007)

How to Enchant a Man
(Llewellyn, 2008)

FORTHCOMING BOOKS BY ELLEN DUGAN

*Book of Witchery: Spells, Charms & Correspondences
for Every Day of the Week*
(Llewellyn, 2009)

Acknowledgments

For my friends—you know who you are. To my coven-mates, who cheered me on. Thanks for listening and for all your support. "Love ya— mean it!" A special thank-you goes to Mickie, Christy, and also to Jen, who gave up an entire Sunday afternoon to help me get the index together. We started out with soft drinks and switched to margaritas after an hour of listing items in alphabetical order—at least there were no quizzes this time, but we did have fun.

With appreciation to Becky Zins, my editor. For acquisitions editor Elysia Gallo, who challenges me to improve and grow as a writer. Also a word of thanks to Nanette Stearns for her technical assistance and kindness, and to Lynne Menturweck for her superb art direction.

Finally, to my husband, Ken, and to our three children, Kraig, Kyle, and Erin, with love.

Contents

Chapter 2

GREEN WITCHERY IN THE CITY, 23

Contents

Chapter 3

MAGICKAL PLANTS OF THE SOUTHWEST, 47

Contents

Contents

~ Contents

Contents

Illustrations

Introduction

New Lessons from the Oldest of Magick

But there are higher secrets of culture,
which are not for the apprentices but for proficients.
These are lessons only for the brave.

RALPH WALDO EMERSON

What is it about plants, trees, flowers, and the idea of green magick that continues to fascinate and bewitch us? Perhaps it is their timeless appeal or their captivating qualities. Magickal herbalism is a perennially popular magickal topic. Folks just can't seem to get enough of that old green magick. Every spring when gardening season begins, Witches, Pagans, and common folk alike flock to the local greenhouses and garden centers, looking for the perfect additions to their magickal gardens. Perhaps they are searching for something new to try, or they are on the lookout for a prized variety of botanical that has eluded them for years. It is the thrill of the hunt and the spirit of the quest that inspires us all. I honestly believe that a deeper, more advanced study of green magick and magickal herbalism is a brilliant way to discover what new lessons the oldest magick can teach us.

I define green magick as a practical, nature-based system of the Craft that focuses on a reverence for the natural world, the individual's environment, and the plants and herbs that are indigenous to the practitioner's own area. Herbal and natural magick are essential to green magick.

No matter how long you have practiced your craft, be it months, years, or decades, there is a real need to deepen the connection to the earth—to dig further, to expand your magickal skills, and to learn more. With this in mind, *Garden Witch's Herbal* came to be. In this, my tenth book, I thought it was time to return to where my journey as an author began, for here is where my heart truly lies. Let's take a return trip to the Witch's garden to revisit herbal enchantments and green magick and search further into the mysterious, magickal world of plants.

By further exploring this green path of magick and by listening to our own hearts, we gain a deep and meaningful sense of connection to nature and have the opportunity to advance and expand our level of spirituality. This sense of reverence is but a tool and another enchanting lesson to be learned.

GREEN MAGICK AND SPIRITUALITY

Nature is the symbol of spirit.

RALPH WALDO EMERSON

Green spirituality holds that all of life is a magickal experience. A green practitioner is well known for their connection with their living and working environment, by their ethics, and by their affinity to the powers of the natural world. This is an intensely personal path of magick, as it takes into consideration the actual physical climate and location of where you live along with your relationship with the energy that is available within your own individual environment.

Witchcraft traditionally uses the energies that are naturally within the elements of earth, air, fire, and water and combines them together with the practitioner's personal power to create positive change and to accomplish a magickal goal. In green magick and green spirituality, the Witch becomes a link between the energies and magick of the natural world and the world of humanity. A Witch carries information back and forth between these two worlds, becoming a sort of bridge. This connection allows love and knowledge to flow back and forth between the magickal world and the mundane, bringing hope, peace, healing, and positive energy to each world.

This is, in fact, an ancient magickal practice. According to folklore, Witches were referred to as "hedge jumpers." This term highlights their knowledge of the green world and their ability to "jump the hedge," or boundaries, between the two worlds. Hedge Witches, as they are more commonly called, were thought to be able to travel back and forth between the physical world and the spirit world at will. However, it wasn't that they were leaping back and forth between the different planes so much as they stood and practiced their craft with one foot firmly planted in each world, creating that spiritual bridge. They then became walkers between the worlds, and today this description is still a common one to illustrate the path of the Green Witch.

However, balance between these worlds cannot be reestablished by separating yourself far out in a little enchanted cabin in the woods. We have to balance our magickal selves with the natural world in one hand, along with the reality of urban life in the other. Green Witchcraft is a sacred relationship with the world on all its many planes of existence.

A Green Witch is not defined by what he or she does for a living or by whatever label society or the Pagan community sticks on them. They are not just one, they are all; they are at one with everything; they simply flow between. They may identify themselves as a Garden Witch, Cottage Witch, Kitchen Witch, Celtic Witch, a self-taught Eclectic, or even a Traditional Witch—meaning a person that has taken formal training in a specific tradition, such as Gardnerian, Alexandrian, Feri, Dianic, or Cabot. The mantle of green magick slips easily over all these practices. Green magick is not so much of a tradition as it is a magickal way of life.

Today's green practitioners are clever and adaptable. They are very likely to live in the city or be tucked into the suburbs, but their physical location does not define them. These green folks choose to work with the magickal energies of nature as they find it, no matter what their lifestyle, magickal title, profession, location, or climate.

The Green Path:
No Matter Where You Live

Her green mind made the world around her green.
WALLACE STEVENS

The green path of magick is a paradox: while it is a time-honored variety of Witchcraft, it is also an eclectic one—meaning while the oldest of techniques and time-honored Craft practices are used, there is still plenty of room for personalization and adaptation for the environment where the Witch happens to live. This is a path that closely follows the cycles of natural life, the Wheel of the Year, herbalism, the groves, and the garden. Whatever part of the world the Witch calls home is the fundamental key to their own individual magickal practice.

Let's say you happen to live in the upper East Coast or Midwest of the United States; then you would incorporate the climate variations, flora, fauna, and four classic seasons that you are familiar with. If you made your home in the Deep South, the West Coast, or the Southwestern states, however, then you would obviously incorporate into your practices the flowers, trees, cycles of the seasons, and native plants and wildlife that are indigenous to your area.

For instance, a Witch living in the Deep South may never have the opportunity to work with snow or ice magick; however, they have access to plant life and flowers growing outside their back door in January that someone living farther north could only dream about.

Honestly, this is as simple as going with what you've got, for skilled Witches easily adapt to their surroundings. They improvise when necessary and study their own environment so they know which earthy, natural supplies are available to them. Finally, they overcome any obstacles in their lives by using a clever combination of knowledge, personal power, love, and sheer force of will.

To effectively use this green magick, you must know that it springs from two sources: the heart and the mind. You have to feel it in your heart, and you have to know that if you believe change is not only possible, but factual, then so shall it be. A Witch using green magick will work to create and to preserve balance within themselves, to find harmony with their own mundane and magickal communities, and to celebrate their connection with the natural world. Sounds like a tall order, doesn't it? Never fear, it can be done, and it can be done beautifully. In the chapters that follow, you will discover many new bewitching ideas and techniques that can show you how.

No matter where you live, what your experience level, or what variety of magickal tradition you observe, you will find something here that will complement your own magickal practice—which in turn will enable you to create a deeper connection to your earth religion.

It takes a brave soul to travel the green and natural path of the Witch. To study and practice a religion that is often misunderstood or scoffed at takes courage. This daring and determination will serve you well as you expand and advance your studies of green magick, herbalism, and spirituality. Because it is a personal expression of your magickal skills, much of this type of magickal work is performed solo.

By standing on your own, you will gain some quality one-on-one time with the natural world. This gives you the opportunity to discover your own unique connection to nature and all the herbs and botanicals in the plant kingdom. Your success depends on your willingness to get in there and experiment. Plan on tracking your spells and carefully watching and recording the outcome of your magick. For those who possess the predisposition for green magick, the rewards can be great, and the magickal results are most impressive.

Plants are intricately intertwined into all magick and earth religions. For those who know how to open their hearts and listen, they offer us supplies, inspiration, and lessons. So come and join me for a time as we explore the enchanted groves and dig deeper into the magickal gardens of the green world. Let's discover together the wonder and magick that the natural world can offer us.

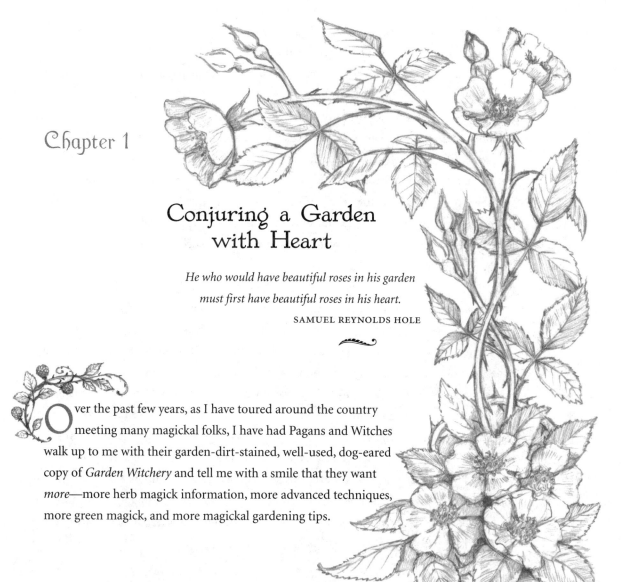

Chapter 1

Conjuring a Garden
with Heart

*He who would have beautiful roses in his garden
must first have beautiful roses in his heart.*

SAMUEL REYNOLDS HOLE

O ver the past few years, as I have toured around the country
meeting many magickal folks, I have had Pagans and Witches
walk up to me with their garden-dirt-stained, well-used, dog-eared
copy of *Garden Witchery* and tell me with a smile that they want
more—more herb magick information, more advanced techniques,
more green magick, and more magickal gardening tips.

I have been promising you all that I was indeed working on it; for those of you who have been waiting, here you go. Let's dig in, shall we?

As a magickal gardener who has delved deeply into the mystical world of plants, I know firsthand that there is a real connection to divinity to be gained here and an earthy sense of empowerment that comes from working with the soil, growing and tending to your own plants, and getting your hands dirty. This is the ultimate in grounding and centering.

When we garden, we create an intimate relationship with the five fundamental elements of the natural world. These five elements are recognized by many magickal traditions and cultures, even though the final element may vary. Wiccan traditions identify these magickal elements as earth, air, fire, water, and spirit. To the Chinese, the five elements are wood, fire, metal, earth, and water. To be rooted firmly in nature's magick, all of the elements must be honored within the magickal garden.

If you step outside for a moment, you will become intimately linked with these elements immediately, so let's do that right now. Close your eyes for a moment, and search your heart. What does it tell you? Now look around you; what do you sense? Step out of your shoes and onto the grass somewhere. Feel the grass tickling your feet? Be thankful for the support and the grounding energy that the element of earth is lending you.

Open your eyes, and look around. Notice any birds flying about? Do you feel the breeze as it rushes past? If so, then greet the element of air as it brings forth inspiration and change. The sun shining down on you can symbolize fire, as can landscape lighting that illuminates the garden path. The feminine, fertile element of water can be represented in many guises: a natural body of water, such as a nearby creek or pond; a garden fountain; a birdbath for our feathered friends to splash about in; the rain that falls or dewdrops dangling on the leaves of the plants—all are representations of this element. Becoming more viscerally aware of these magickal elements and the very foundations of nature makes us all part of something greater and more magickally meaningful.

When we work our green magick in harmony with the elements and the natural world, we share something far older than just gardening. Here, we touch an ethereal connection to the basic harmonies of creation. This act then actually allows us to connect with the final element of spirit. As Witches and Green Magicians, we come into contact with the powers of creation and divinity every day, no matter where we live. Our lives become enriched by the deities of the earth, the powers of the changing seasons, and the truly awesome force of nature. It is important to grasp that this intimate connection to the earth over time will help our spirituality become deeper, more personal, and more meaningful. On the most basic level, our spellcraft becomes more powerful as we become more in tune with the earth.

Since most of us live in the cities or in the suburbs, not snuggled into a cottage deep in the woods, we experience a greater challenge when we wish to renew or expand our connection to the natural world. But fortunately, you can find traces of this primal magick just about anywhere. It's much easier than you think. The first place to look is within. Make up your mind, here and now, to search for and to find the energies of nature, no matter where you live. Then you can turn your attention to the trees and plants that share your surroundings. You'll discover the magick within a small copse of trees whether it is in the yard or the public park. Within the world of the urban grove and garden, the force of nature is very much alive and present, for here lives a smaller version of the wild places and the great woodlands.

In my book *Garden Witchery*, I showed you that magickal plants are all around you and easy to grow in the home landscape. I encouraged you to live a little and to surround your- self with these charming plants and to link back into the enchantment of nature. *Garden*

Witchery taught you how to practically incorporate both gardening and herbalism into your magickal practices.

This book of more advanced green magick techniques is written for the Witch, for the magickal herbalist, and for those who search for the sacred and the divine in nature. In our return visit to the Witch's garden, I want to show you how the local groves of trees and your very own gardens can influence more than your magick. They can, in reality, influence your green spirituality.

Magickal Inspiration and Garden Design

Gardeners are like landscape painters.
Their canvas is the soil, their paints the vast array
of living flowers, trees, and shrubs.
DONALD NORFOLK, *THE SOUL GARDEN*

When people set out to create a magickal garden, they are, in fact, expressing their own personalities in the overall design. As we transform our yards and personal spaces into magickal, secret gardens and sacred groves, we begin to appreciate these areas as places of growth not only for the assorted plants and trees but for ourselves as well. Gardening is good for the mind, body, and spirit.

If a garden is to reflect the mystical and the sacred side of nature, then it has to be diverse, just like us. There are many different types of trees, herbs, and flowers—and magick—to incorporate into your spiritual plan. Now is when you begin to fine-tune things, for the

Witch's garden is a tangible symbol of your commitment to making time for magick and spirituality in your everyday life.

The rest of this chapter will discuss the foundations of good magickal gardening design—a discussion on style, space, and how to get a little enchanted garden atmosphere going. This is green magick at its most basic and elemental. There are even pointers on how to correctly work with color schemes in the garden. And you can bet your watering can that these principles are important in every garden, no matter if it's a clever container garden on a patio or deck or a rambling flower bed that fills up the entire yard. This is good practical knowledge to have because the design helps to set the magickal mood and the overall atmosphere in the Witch's garden.

CREATING MAGICKAL GARDENS WITH ATMOSPHERE

Nature uses human imagination to lift her work
of creation to even higher levels.
LUIGI PIRANDELLO

Whenever I teach a class on herbs and gardening, be it to magickal folks or mundane, I typically get questions about how to create a "mood" or "theme" in a garden. The ambiance of a garden is everything. Even those of us who've been gardening for a while realize that there is more to gardening than just sticking the plants in the ground. After a while, you want your garden to flow together and to set an atmosphere or theme. For magickal practitioners, that theme is likely going to be an enchanted one.

One of the most popular garden themes today is a faerie garden. That's always a hot topic, no matter what type of group I am lecturing or teaching (even at the community college where I teach adult continuing education classes on flower gardening). As a Witch, this always makes me chuckle. If you mention faerie gardens even to the most sedate crowd, the whole room perks up. Questions start being fired off, and everyone gets enthusiastic.

So let's get motivated! What type of garden are you dreaming of? What would you do if you could just go crazy in the garden? Perhaps you'd plan a theme garden devoted to one specific deity, or design a faerie-tale garden, or even a tranquil feng shui-style of meditation garden. Maybe you wish to plant a bigger enchanted herb garden full of magickal plants for spells and charms. How about a handy Kitchen Witch garden full of veggies and culinary herbs?

The choice is completely up to you. No matter what magickal mood you are trying to invoke in the Witch's garden, design and color will come into play. By applying these advanced techniques and by tweaking the design a bit further, you can conjure up the atmosphere that you want. Have fun incorporating these practical ideas and tips into your garden of witchery. Dare to turn a simple garden into one that inspires you spiritually and transforms your dreams into something spectacular.

Make no mistake, the fastest way to turn a pedestrian flower bed into an enchanting garden is to get a little atmosphere going. There must be something here that captures people's imaginations and tugs at their heart. We make use of the basic elements of design not only to beautify but to increase our perception of the environment. This helps us to open up and to receive the messages and secrets that are inherent in the natural and the magickal world.

The Enchanting Elements of Design

All of nature wears one universal grin.

HENRY FIELDING

Creative design is what turns a collection of trees, herbs, perennials, and flowers into a garden. The clarity and color schemes found in your magickal garden give focus to your goals and intentions. The complexity in your plant forms, such as texture and pattern, will make for a sensual garden that begs to be touched, sniffed, and enjoyed. Create a refuge, add a sense of mystery, and be conscious of the flow of energy when creating a magickal garden.

No matter what type of garden you are planning, you'll enjoy better results if you incorporate the design tips that are discussed in this chapter. Don't forget to look at the magickal garden with an eye toward design. Pay attention to your intuition, and work on improving the mood and the overall aura, or atmosphere, that you are attempting to achieve in your landscape. The best gardens all share a few main qualities, even though the styles and themes may be radically different. These design qualities are clarity, complexity, mystery, and refuge. Without these traits, a garden doesn't enchant us or invite us in.

Clarity

This defines the perimeter of the garden and the use of pathways. Where does your magickal garden begin? Where does it lead, and where does it end? The clever use of a clearly defined entrance, or threshold, into the garden makes it special and welcomes you in. A good garden threshold area is like a welcoming embrace. The threshold into a garden is an in-between place that is full of possibilities and enchantment. In fact, a gate can be a symbol of a spiritual doorway, or passage, that separates one reality, or one world, from the next.

Once inside the garden, you should be drawn along a pathway to its heart; the heart of the garden is a place you feel compelled to approach. It's fascinating and irresistible. Also, the heart of the garden defines its use. This is where your magickal intentions are centered and visitors' attentions will be focused.

Complexity

In the simplest of terms, this is *variety*. You can achieve this with the magick of color. (Color in the garden will be discussed in detail in our next section.) Now, it's true that color shouldn't be so overwhelming that the eye can't rest. However, keep in mind that even in a shady hosta garden, for example, there are dozens of varieties and different shades of green available, and all those hues of green can harmonize with each other beautifully—anything from lime green to blue green to white stripes and edges and yellow hues. Play on that, use your imagination, and see what you can create. Look at the pattern of the foliage and the texture of leaf and flower. Pay attention to patterns and any symbolism that may be meaningful to you.

Mystery

Give your Witch's garden something that will inspire curiosity. Here, you balance what is known with what is unexpected. The garden should captivate you and lure you in, in some subtle way—that tantalizing promise of *more*. For example, a path that turns the corner into an unexpected surprise. A hidden water feature that you can hear but have to search to find. Wind chimes hanging from a tall tree that sing out in a breeze. A statue of a goddess or faerie tucked into a shady nook or grotto. A small, secret place to leave offerings to the elementals and faeries of the garden. Mystery is vital in a magickal garden, because that feeling of stumbling upon a secret garden is such a delicious one. Use your imagination, and see what you can do to add some mystery and magick to your garden.

Refuge

Refuge is best described as a feeling of welcome relaxation and reflection; in other words, a place where you can "sit a spell." Your garden should include a place to sit and to relax. This can be as simple as a concrete or wooden bench, a tire swing, a boulder, a glider, or a curvy metal chair. Wherever you choose to make your refuge, offer some type of seating, and make the area special. In my garden, this area is under the rose arbor. Tucked under there is a small bistro table and chair set. It's shady and private, and when the roses bloom in May, it is filled wall-to-wall with hot pink roses. Incorporating a resting place in your magickal garden offers you a chance to relax, contemplate, and enjoy—and perhaps creates a serene spot to even work a spell or two.

COLOR MAGICK IN THE GARDEN

Green is the fresh emblem of well-founded hopes.
In blue, the spirit can wander, but in green it can rest.
MARY WEBB, *THE JOY OF SPRING*

Working successfully with color in the garden is one of the more important lessons that I have taught to Master Gardener interns over the years, and it is necessary knowledge for budding landscape and magickal garden designers too. That being said, you'll need to ask yourself a few questions before deciding on your color scheme. Do you prefer a subtle blending of colors that complement each other, or do you prefer contrasting colors? Magickal gardeners can certainly apply these basic principles when they choose the colors of their plants and create absolutely charming effects. Do you have a favorite color that you'd like to dominate in the garden all year, or would you like to see diverse colors all working together?

If you think color is not important in the garden, think again. The clever use of color can set the mood and make a space seem larger or even cozier. Color can warm up a shady spot or cool down a sunny one. Color is often used to create a specific atmosphere in the garden. It can draw attention to a particular feature, create an impression of spaciousness, or help make a large area seem cozier. The trick is to learn what colors harmonize, or work well together, and how to identify them. Here are a few color schemes for you to consider.

Complementary Colors

You remember your complementary colors from elementary school, don't you? These are pairs of colors that are directly opposite from each other on the color wheel. They are the tried and true color combinations such as red and green, blue and orange, and yellow and purple.

Analogous Colors

Also called "harmonious colors," these are colors that are next to each other on the color wheel—e.g., the warm tones of yellow, yellow orange, and orange, or the cooler hues of blue violet, violet, and red violet. An analogous color combination of lavender, blue, and cool pink appeals to many people and is a lovely way to get a flower bed to flow together and create a sense of unity.

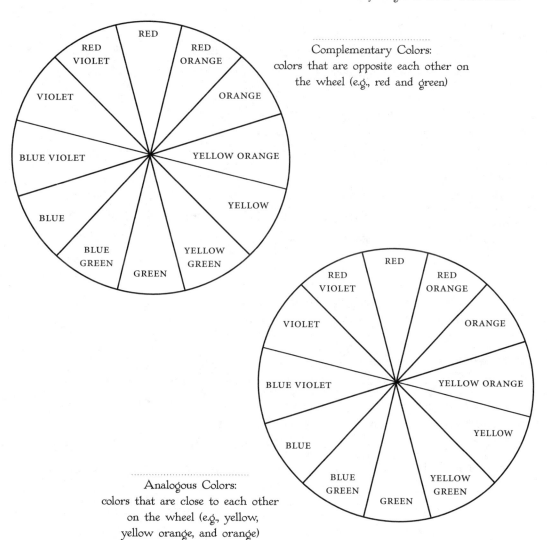

Complementary Colors:
colors that are opposite each other on
the wheel (e.g., red and green)

Analogous Colors:
colors that are close to each other
on the wheel (e.g., yellow,
yellow orange, and orange)

11

Triadic Colors

These color combinations result from drawing an equilateral triangle inside the color wheel, such as red, yellow, and blue, or green, violet, and orange.

Monochromatic Colors

These are sometimes referred to as "single-color gardens." This is the simplest kind of color scheme and one of the easiest for novice gardeners to work with. This type of color scheme is built on varying shades of one basic color—for example, the lighter and darker shades of red, such as medium pink, pale pink, purple, and reddish purple. These types of single-color gardens give a sense of openness and space to even the smallest of gardens.

It also can really make a shady garden pop. Imagine an all-white garden tucked in a shady spot. You could turn it into a moon goddess garden, if you wanted. Imagine how gorgeous a creamy white hydrangea, white-edged hostas, and white impatiens would be. Each would play well off the other and show to their best advantage, since with a monochromatic garden, the plant's form and texture will take center stage.

Neutral Colors

These are the blending colors in the garden: grey, silver, and white. True green may also be used as a neutral feature in the garden. These neutral colors tone down the effects of sharply contrasting or clashing colors that may seem harsh to the eye if placed next to each other. Want an example? Let's say you have orange nasturtiums and purple pansies side by side; they will clash. Tuck in some silver dusty miller, and it will soften the look so that it won't seem so visually jarring.

Bright Colors

The warm, vibrant colors of red, hot orange, and bright yellow draw attention to themselves and make large areas seem smaller and cozier. They create the illusion of warmth, invoke the element of fire, and cast a festive atmosphere.

Dark Colors

Dark colors such as purples and blues will create an impression of more space. These are soothing, calming colors that invoke the element of water. Plus they will weave the illusion of coolness in hot, full-sun-exposure gardens, no matter what the temperature.

Pastel Colors

These soft shades of white, pale yellow, and pink will stand out in twilight gardens and shady areas. You may employ these colors to invoke the element of air. Also keep in mind that these colors will light up during twilight and are good color choices if the evening hours are the ones you are most able to enjoy in the garden. Consider pastels if you are planning a witchy nighttime garden.

Seasonal and Multi-Season Color

Part of the fun of choosing colors for your magickal garden is deciding when those colors will appear. Remember to choose plants for all of the seasons—choose plants for spring, summer, and the fall months, and try to plan for a little bit of winter interest too. This way, your garden shifts seamlessly from one season to the next.

Your Magickal Garden's Style, Structure, and Space

More things grow in the garden than the gardener knows.

SPANISH PROVERB

Now we move along to our next decision: finding your style and deciding what is best suited for your own enchanted garden space. At this point, you have to follow your heart (and, of course, indulge in your own magickal personality). The best style of garden for you is always the one you prefer. No, I'm not being overly simplistic here; it's true. It might be a mixture of styles—formal, cottage, woodland, or Oriental—but hey, the sky's the limit!

Still not sure where to begin? Try looking through some books on garden design, and then go visit a public garden and see what style tugs at your heart. Reading about garden styles isn't enough. You must go out and experience the gardens in person. Feel the texture of the leaves, see the colors of the blossoms, and smell their fragrances. Get your senses involved; they will lead you in the right direction.

Perhaps you have a hankering to try an Oriental approach, with bamboo, rounded pebbles, pine trees, and simple water features. Maybe you are crazy for cottage style, with blooming herbs, perennials, and vegetables all growing jumbled together. What about a mysterious and shady garden with lots of perennial ferns, hostas, and impatiens for color?

Some magickal folks go for the structured and proper look of a formal knot garden or an Elizabethan sun dial garden full of herbs. There are those of us who get pleasure from the more formal setting—just for fun. It's so traditional and precise. My formal herb beds even have a neat row of boxwood hedges outside of their fence that I just adore. I suppose it's because all my other beds are cottage style, so wild and unstructured.

And if you are wondering, no, the styles don't clash. They are simply different, and I might add that they are located in separate parts of the yard. After strolling through all the cottage gardens, the formal one really jumps out at you, beckoning visitors for a closer look. And this is exactly what I was going for. I use the entire yard—both front, sides, and back—and successfully blend several styles together.

Which brings us to the consideration of space. I do realize that not everyone has a large, open area in which to plant. Your garden bed options may be limited due to a lack of space or restricted to flower beds that are already established—and that's okay, too. I know many gardeners, both magickal and mundane, who happily tend their herbs and plants in small raised beds. Typically these are created in a rectangular or square shape and built with land-scaping timbers or stone. For gardeners who have disabilities, who are older, or who have problems bending over and kneeling, or simply have the challenge of gardening in a limited space, these simple square raised beds are the most practical way to go.

While it's true that soft curves and flowing lines do mimic nature, they are not always practical in small spaces. Your witchy garden style does not have to be defined by the area you plant in. Just because you garden in a square-shaped bed doesn't mean you have to be strictly formal. You can still achieve that casual and cottage look if you wish. In fact, one of my largest cottage-style gardens has straight edges. It has to, as it hugs one side of my house and is set off by a brick path to lead people deeper into the garden. But do I run screaming because it doesn't have, as one gardening book says, "the undulating lines of nature"? Nah. I let the plants do the work of softening the straight lines for me.

To achieve a wild and natural appearance, I allow the foliage of the plants and flowers to grow and drape over the straight edges of the beds. This softens the look and creates a more natural and carefree atmosphere. It also breaks up that rush of energy shooting straight through the side yard, and it allows my visitors to stroll along the brick path, checking out all the plants as the path pulls them deeper into my enchanted gardens.

So why are these softer edges and curves so important in garden design, anyway? Because they mimic the natural world and the wild places. Remember that nature is irregular, random, and untamed. Cities and houses incorporate straight lines, but nature does not, and you don't have to in your gardens either. This line of thought and garden design actually coordinates beautifully with the Chinese practice of feng shui.

In feng shui, straight lines are often avoided in the garden because they break up the flow of the life force, called *chi*. As Witches and natural magicians, we should all be very familiar with working with and manipulating elemental energies. Adding some positive chi into your personal magickal garden design is a subtle and very clever way to create a garden with heart—one that will encourage wealth, health, and happiness to its caretakers and visitors alike.

FENG SHUI IN THE MAGICKAL GARDEN

He who plants a garden plants happiness.
CHINESE PROVERB

Garden feng shui is a design philosophy that places garden items such as plants and lawn furniture in a beneficial way. Feng shui translates to "wind and water." These two universal forces are necessary for life and carry energy, or chi, that brings balance into your life. When your natural environment is harmonious, according to feng shui practices, it makes you feel more comfortable and welcome. Adding a touch of feng shui in the garden is an easy way to manifest positive intentions into your life. I tried it myself, and it's fun.

I've been gardening for twenty-five years, and I only recently began to apply some feng shui practices into my own gardens. While reading up on this one weekend, I discovered to my dismay that while our garden gate (the main entrance to the garden) was great, the clutter we had on the outside—the garbage cans—was considered a feng shui no-no. And since they were sitting close to the house and by the windows, all that garbage energy was swirling straight in the house—and into our bedroom, no less!

Hmmm … feng shui book in hand, I stalked outside and took a critical look at the garden gate area. (You know, the whole threshold area we talked about before.) Well, damn. Not even an inkling of a welcoming hug at this Witch's garden gate. I had several mistakes out there: the aforementioned garbage cans, a tired-looking metal wind chime, and, to my shame, weedy flowers growing under the privacy fence on either side of the gate.

Once you stepped through the gate and into the side gardens, everything was fine. But the entrance, the threshold area, really needed some work. I found my husband and dragged him out there with me as well. Even though explaining the concept of feng shui earned me a incredulous look, he did agree with me that, as our entrance into the garden, the top of the driveway area looked less than welcoming.

As a result of my discovery, we got to work. We arranged the garbage cans on the far left side of the driveway away from the house and opened up the right side of the fence and gate area. There are simple ways (called "cures" in feng shui) of deflecting negative chi at entrances, such as hanging up wind chimes, using garden path lighting, or adding pots of plants, so I worked with what I had—and, much to my husband's relief, didn't spend any money either.

I took that old metal wind chime and freshened it up with some verdigris-looking paint and completed it with a weatherproof sealer. Amazing what a little paint and time can accomplish! Then I blessed the chime to ring out bad vibes and to ring in positive chi. We hung that chime on the privacy fence to the right of the gate. Next, we moved a pot of mixed annuals and placed it also to the right of the gate and next to the house, which looked much more inviting than the garbage cans had. I dug out an old grapevine wreath and hung that on the outside of the gate and tucked in a few yellow heads of dried yarrow.

Now, while I'll be the first to admit that the wreath isn't exactly feng shui, it certainly did help make the gate look more inviting. Since yarrow is the wise woman's herb and a wreath can be used as a symbol for the Wheel of the Year, I was satisfied that I had combined a few feng shui cures along with a little witchy symbolism.

A half-hour's worth of work, pulling a few weeds, moving the garbage cans, sprucing up an old wind chime, and hanging a simple wreath made a huge difference out there. In fact, my husband was so impressed with the change in the feel of the garden gate area that the next day he decided the pot of annuals wasn't big enough. Off we went to look for a large tropical potted plant that could take the summer heat and still look inviting. We picked up a coral-colored flowering hibiscus. This addition made us feel pretty pleased with ourselves, as according to feng shui, the color red or orange at a tall gate can help stimulate positive chi—which only goes to prove that you *can* teach an old Garden Witch a new trick.

MAKING THE FIVE ELEMENTS
OF FENG SHUI WORK TOGETHER

Nature has four seasons and five elements;
in order to grant a long life, the four seasons and
the five elements store up the power of creation…
NEI CHING

~~~)

Now that I've gotten you in the mood to try a little feng shui, let's get down to the specifics. There are five elements in feng shui: wood, fire, earth, metal, and water. Incorporating a bit of something from each of these will bring balance into your garden. No matter what style or design for your landscape that you ultimately choose, this will augment the atmosphere and create a feeling of harmony and welcome. Here is an uncomplicated list of the feng shui elements and their correspondences. Add a bit of each of these into your witchy garden plan, and see what develops.

Wood

This element is associated with garden objects such as wooden fences, decking, bamboo, and wicker. The natural materials are plants, trees, and flowers. (Yes indeed, your garden is already full of wood energy because of all the plants!) The color is green, and the direction is east. Wood enhances growth and creativity. It is flexible and strong.

Fire

This element is associated with garden objects such as landscape lighting, candles, tiki torches, and a fire pit or grill. Natural materials are crimson, cone-shaped flowers and candle flames. The color is red, the direction is south. This passionate element brings enthusiasm and will energize you.

Earth

This element is associated with garden objects such as ceramic tile, terra-cotta pots, and brick pathways. Natural materials are the soil and pebbles, as well as rectangular flower beds and straight-edged lawns. You may also add stone or terra-cotta statues to the garden space to bring in even more of the earth element. The color is yellow and earthy tones of orange and brown. The direction is referred to as "the center." This element, just as you'd expect, grounds and centers you. It is also nurturing and rich.

Metal

This element is associated with garden objects such as metal accent pieces, a trellis, or even curvy wrought-iron lawn furniture. Try metal garden lighting too. Work in circular shapes when you can, as this figure also coordinates with the element of metal. Natural materials are white flowers and silver foliage plants. (For silver-colored plants, try lamb's ears, mullein, or dusty miller.) Colors are white, grey, and pastels; the direction is west. This dense element brings power, strength, and action.

Water

This element is linked to such garden objects as water features, fountains, ponds, and birdbaths and also glass, crystals, and mirrors. Blue flowers will naturally add a splash of water energy as well. A quick way to add the element of water into a garden where a water feature can't easily be added is to hang a crystal from a tree branch. You can also use a glass-topped table. The colors for this element are dark, such as black and deep blue; the direction is north. This flowing element relaxes and revitalizes you.

A Feng Shui Color Guide for the Garden:
An Enchanting List of Color, Hue, and Tone

According to feng shui traditions, these plant and flower colors encourage the following emotions. You will notice, however, that these are almost identical to the traditional color correspondences of the Witch and the magickal practitioner.

BLACK: enigma, enchantment

BLUE: peace, healing, relaxation

COBALT BLUE: connecting to a higher purpose

GREEN: growth, prosperity, tranquility

LIGHT GREEN: relief, tranquility

LIME GREEN: awakens the spirit

MAGENTA: higher emotional and spiritual processes

ORANGE: energy, fusion, conversation, mysticism

PALE BLUE: mystery, contemplation

PINK: friendship, affection, romance

PURPLE: spirituality, magick, divinity

RED: power, exhilaration, passion, warm feelings

SILVER AND GREY: goddess colors, moon magick

WHITE: purity, innocence, new beginnings

YELLOW: clarity, mental illumination, intuition

Chapter 2

Green Witchery in the City

The city is a powerful landscape of magick,
filled with secrets and energy
for those who know where to look.

CHRISTOPHER PENCZAK,
CITY MAGICK

A true Witch is in sync with the environment, no matter where it is they happen to call home. A modern Witch rarely lives in a secret cottage at the edge of the woods, surrounded by lush garden beds and trees. They can and do live and practice their craft quite successfully in the city. If they are in tune with the rhythms of their surroundings and the flow and beat of the town or city, this is an easy task. It's not where you live and practice your craft and green magick that matters, it's how you work with what you have.

Green magick and herbal enchantments are an integral part of all witcheries. This chapter will show you ways to apply a touch of that old green magick regardless of where you live and practice your craft. No matter where you dwell—in the city, the suburbs, or the country—it is possible to create a Witch's garden. Over the years, I have fielded many questions from Witches and magick users all asking about growing plants, flowers, and herbs in a city environment. Be assured, it can be done—and it can be done beautifully.

I have seen apartment-dwelling Witches turn front porches, balconies, and decks into mini gardens with the clever use of containers and window boxes. I know one couple who took a small patch of unused ground, no larger than three feet by six feet, and turned that into a fabulous magickal garden. This spot was directly across from their front door, and they were itching to do something with it instead of just watching the weeds grow. So they checked with their landlord first and asked if there would be any objections to them gardening in that little weedy patch. The landlord didn't mind, as long as they kept the sidewalk area clear.

So, armed with gardening tools and shovels, they pulled the weeds, turned the earth, amended the soil with compost, and planted away. What this couple pulled off was amazing. Sandwiched between a sunny sidewalk and an old privacy fence, this tiny city garden was stuffed full of flowering herbs, culinary herbs, a few tomato plants, and a Green Man statue. The garden was the talk of the apartment complex. Even the landlord raved about how cleverly the couple had used the space. Where there is a will, there is a way … or I should say, where there is a Witch, there is always a way to garden.

City-dwelling Witches, take heart. It is possible to successfully grow herbs and magickal plants while living in the city. You can indeed surround yourself with the elemental energies of green magick. Container gardens are the answer to your problems, and lush little city nooks filled with colorful plant-filled containers are everywhere, popping up in the most unusual places—rooftop gardens, flower-filled balconies and decks, a row of terra-cotta pots bursting full of herbs lined up on fire escapes. Sunny patios and decks are filled with magickal and culinary herbs and produce even as we speak. Secret shady gardens delight their owners in alleys behind apartment buildings, and dainty window boxes add enchantment to many a metropolitan windowsill.

Many herbs and magickal plants will flourish in pots and containers. You can grow just about anything in a pot, including veggies, flowers, and herbs. The best part about container gardening is that you have control over weeds, the size of the plants, and your color combinations. Container gardens are mobile, adjustable, and suitable to everyday life. If you grow tired of the arrangement, it is easy to shift things around. With container gardening, city Witches have the opportunity to create a private, magickal outdoor sacred space all of their own. In these magickal gardens, they can dream, relax, and stay connected to nature.

SARAH'S CITY WITCH GARDEN

Learn of the green world what can be thy place,
In scaled invention or true artistry.
EZRA POUND

A dear friend and coven-mate of mine lives deep in the city of St. Louis. She lives in Soulard, which has a reputation for clubs, bars, and one of the larger Mardi Gras celebrations in the country. Behind Sarah's old brick four-family flat, she has an amazing magickal city garden that is a mixture of a small garden beds and several strategically placed container gardens.

On her back porch, there are containers, hanging baskets, and pots bursting with color and scent. As you move down the steps and onto the brick path, she has carved out a small magickal garden planted with herbs, perennials, and cottage-style flowers.

When our coven went to her home for Beltane this past year, we got a chance to see her little Witch's garden in all its glory. Sarah was excited to show me her garden, and it was phenomenal. In a small garden bed, rosemary and tarragon were in a race to see who could grow taller, while terra-cotta pots filled with a bewitching assortment of annuals, herbs, and flowers were tucked along the front of her tiny city garden like a border.

Behind the rosemary and tarragon, stately red hollyhocks and silver artemisia grew side by side while phlox crept along the old brick walkway. For a touch of whimsy and magick, Sarah had added decorative garden stakes. One was a painted metal sun and moon, and there was a stained-glass star; metal and glass candleholders were strategically placed in her garden space.

Against the building, opposite the garden bed, she had benches for her large houseplants that she moved outside for the warmer weather. Here, another multileveled container garden happily thrived. Tucked between the two large potted houseplants were more colorful containers of flowering annuals in every shade imaginable. Some were elevated on old concrete blocks and some were on decorative columns. Purple, pink, and white petunias, yellow daisies, tall snapdragons, blue lobelia, geraniums in every color, and culinary herbs were thriving here and mixed with abandon. Even an old metal child's wagon, filled with more pots of flowering plants, was pressed into gardening service. A metal watering can stood guard, and a large metal star hung from a plant hook off the side of the building. There was even a small, cheerful sign tucked into the potted ficus tree announcing "The Witch Is In!"

I was impressed. Sarah and her boyfriend had taken an old, neglected spot and turned it into a place filled with magick and atmosphere. Deep in the city, green magick does flourish. It's simply up to the Witch to make it so.

Growing a Witch's garden in the city is a creative process of trial and error. City living can be stressful on plants. They have to manage pollution and an artificial habitat. Design your own magickal city garden with plants that will thrive on the strengths, weaknesses, and quirks of your particular growing conditions. Experienced urban gardeners like Sarah know that they can find a balance between those plants that they want and those plants that they can successfully grow.

But let's face it, not all of us are pros at this sort of thing. To help you with your urban magickal gardening, here are some practical pointers that will help you achieve growing success.

YOUR URBAN WITCH GARDEN SITE

Blows the wind to-day,
and the sun and the rain are flying…
ROBERT LOUIS STEVENSON

The site where you choose to create a container garden will become your own mini climate. A mini climate includes such things as the amount of sun and wind you will receive, wind

27

exposure, and moisture levels. You must also take into consideration that neighboring buildings can affect sun and shade patterns by cutting off sunshine or reflecting more of light and heat back to you due to light-colored walls. The trick to discovering your site's mini climate is observation. Keep a sharp watch on how much sun your balcony or deck receives and at what time of day, if any, that you have shade. The key thing here is when you have shade—if you have early morning shade and full sun from noon on, your site probably faces west. That is a sunny garden, and it will require heat-tolerant plants that need full sun.

There are varying degrees of shade, too: full shade, dappled shade, and part shade. But which one do you have? Well, to help you sort that out, here are some basic guidelines for determining what type of sun exposure or shade you have. To begin, draw a simple diagram of your area. Then, beginning at sunrise, take notes on where your shade and sun patterns fall. Then at various times of the day—about every two hours—note the changes with dashed lines for sun and solid lines for shade. Make a little note alongside your drawings to mark the time. Yes, this will take all day, but it is important to do, so stick with it.

You will also want to note where the shade patterns fall during the different seasons, so plan to make shade maps in spring, summer, and fall. For example, a sun-loving rose will require full sun—at least six hours a day—to look its best, so you'll need to plan accordingly. These seasonal shade maps may be your most valuable tools in determining which plants you will be able to grow successfully.

SUN AND SHADE PATTERNS

Leaves of the summer, lovely summer's pride,
Sweet is the shade below your silent tree.
WILLIAM BARNES

⌒⌒⌒⌒

Less Than 2 Hours of Sunlight = Full Shade. Plant suggestions are bugle, columbine, dead nettle, ferns, hostas, ivy, lily of the valley, monarda, mints, periwinkle, Solomon's seal, tansy, and violets. Consider that light-painted walls will help to reflect sunlight and warm up your shady garden.

2-6 Hours of Sunlight = Partial Shade. These plants should thrive: angelica, astilbe, betony (aka lamb's ears), black cohosh, catmint, coral bells, ferns, foxglove, heliotrope, hostas, lady's mantle, mallows, mint, pansy, soapwort, and sweet woodruff.

6-12 Hours of Sunlight = Full Sun. Look for heat-tolerant plants such as rosemary, lavender, coneflowers, sunflower, santolinas, and scented geraniums. You will also have great luck with culinary herbs and roses if you do not allow them to dry out. Exposed sites, such as rooftops, penthouses, terraces, and balconies, often receive six to twelve hours of sunlight per day and perhaps indirect sunlight as well.

WIND AND RAIN PATTERNS

Rain is grace; rain is the sky condescending to the
earth; without rain, there would be no life.
JOHN UPDIKE

Too much of a good thing may create its own challenges. Full sun and steady winds can cause problems. Plants can bake in strong summer heat. Excessive winds strip moisture out of plant leaves, which is known as transpiration. Transpiration is the process in which a plant loses water, primarily from the leaf stomata (the pores in the epidermis of leaves and stems).

There are four main factors that affect transpiration. These factors are light, temperature, relative wind, and humidity. How do you avoid this little situation? With regular watering and with mulch, my friend. Try adding an inch-deep layer of natural mulch to your planters. Also consider providing a little shade and/or a windbreak for those full-sun gardens with awnings, pergolas, and trellises.

The next time it rains, you will also want to keep an eye on how precipitation falls on your chosen site and how the water drains. Some spots may stay completely dry, some areas may take in a bit of water, and some will receive a good soaking—so plan accordingly. Together, these growing conditions of shade, sun exposure, and rainfall patterns will help you determine what you can and cannot achieve in your urban Witch's garden.

Don't panic now; go ahead and make your drawing. Find out how much shade or sunlight, wind and rain you will receive. Another quick method is to check out which direction your site is oriented to; use a compass if necessary. Here is an easy directional plant list with annual and perennial plant suggestions for color and structure. (This is a general rule of thumb only; remember those other site considerations that were discussed earlier. For more plant options, check out the plant list on page 29 as well.)

> South Facing. This is sunlight all day, which can be described as full sun. You should have success with the widest selection of plants and culinary herbs. Also try annual purple fountain grass, sunflowers, roses, geraniums, and petunias.

> East and West Facing. This is around six hours of sunlight, also considered full sun, but in the morning and evening respectively. East facing: hydrangeas, day lilies, morning glories, impatiens, and azaleas. West facing: geraniums, coreopsis, clematis, coneflowers, lavenders, and sunflowers.

> North Facing. This could be as little as two hours of sunlight per day. If you receive upwards of three to five hours of sun, this can be described as partial shade. Two hours or less of sunlight would be full shade. North-facing plants include begonias, bleeding hearts, hostas, ferns, hellebore, lily of the valley, and rhododendrons.

No matter what your sun exposure, make the most out of the space you do have by arranging containers in groups that complement each other. Today, container gardening is one of the most popular forms of gardening. If you take a look around, you can discover myriad magazine articles and books devoted to the topic.

Conjuring Container Gardens

I know a little garden-close
Set thick with lily and red rose,
Where I would wander if I might
From dewy dawn to dewy night.
WILLIAM MORRIS

Keep in mind that when you place large containers on decks, balconies, or rooftops, check the strength of the structure first. Find out if your building has weight limits or rules about heavy objects on balconies, as containers filled with soil can be very heavy. Conversely, small containers may be easily blown away. Find yourself a happy medium—try an intermediate-sized, lightweight container or use window boxes and fasten them down securely. You can also make use of hanging baskets. As you set up these containers, remember to utilize gravel or small rocks for the bottom two inches of the container to aid in drainage. Work with a high-quality potting mix and add lots of sterile compost to enrich your soil. Invest in some water-soluble fertilizer, and get ready to garden!

You will notice that I have included various annuals, herbs, and perennials in these mixed pots for added color, height, and scent. As you assemble your individual containers, place the taller plants either in the back or center of the pot. Then place the medium-sized plants in front or around the tallest ones, with the shortest or trailing varieties around the outside edges. A trick that professionals use when designing pots and containers for sale is to plant them very full. Don't scrimp on the plants! There is nothing sadder than a scrawny container that has to wait for two months of growth to fill in.

Mix and match these suggested combinations however your Garden Witch's heart desires. Just remember to coordinate the shade or sun tolerances of the plants. Plant many containers or a few large ones—whatever you have space for or would prefer. Now, here are some bewitching combinations that I have conjured up just for you. The sun requirements are listed first and then the plants.

PRACTICAL MAGICK CONTAINER GARDENS

He could walk, or rather turn about in his little garden, and
feel more solid happiness from the flourishing of a cabbage or
the growing of a turnip than was ever received from the most
ostentatious show the vanity of man could possibly invent.
SARAH FIELDING

Moonlit Magick
(Part shade) Mugwort, nicotiana, betony, alyssum, and white petunias for scent and nighttime sparkle. Tuck in white zinnias to attract the butterflies.

Sorcery in the Shade
(Shade) Pansies, violas, ferns, hostas, ivy, and trailing mints. Look for chocolate or orange mint to add some fragrance. Plant variegated ivy to add some visual interest to the pot. Also, you can switch out the spring cool-weather-loving pansies with a colorful, shady annual like impatients for the hot summer months.

Faerie Garden

(Shade to part shade) Columbine, pansy, viola, foxglove, fern, periwinkle, ivy, annual blue lobelia, alyssum.

Fragrant Fascinations

(Full to part sun) A standard tree rose, lavender, alyssum, sage, pineapple sage, catmint, scented geraniums, coordinating shades of begonias and petunias for color. Add spicy dianthus (pinks) for color and more scent.

Hedge Witch Hanging Basket

(Sun to part sun) Look for prostrate varieties of herbs such as rosemary and thyme, the type of variety that "creeps" or trails. Nasturtiums make a nice trailing plant, as does scented bacopa. Strawberries make great hanging basket plants and require full sun. Try an everbearing variety of strawberry for plants that will produce fruit for a longer season.

Kitchen Witchery

(Full to part sun) Plant some of the classic Witch's garden herbs: rosemary, basil, dill, parsley, bronze fennel, thyme, and tricolor sage.

Faerie/Butterfly Garden

(Sun) Yarrow, coneflowers, brown-eyed Susans, daisies, miniature roses, lavender, parsley. Parsley is a host plant for caterpillars.

Silver Sorcery

(Sun) Artemisia and lamb's ears; add lavender, santolina, and heliotrope for scent. Let the silver and fuzzy licorice plant (*Helichrysum*) dangle over the sides of the container.

COLORFUL & ELEMENTAL
THEME CONTAINERS

Colors, like features, follow the changes of the emotions.
PABLO PICASSO

~~~♪

This is fun to try: create container gardens to honor the colors of the four elements. These next four container gardens are a bewitching mixture of annuals, ornamentals, perennials, and herbs. Remember to put the tallest plants in the center and to work outwards, planting the containers full. Use a good potting mix, and make sure your pots and containers all have drainage holes.

Earth

Green (full to part shade). With lots of textured foliage, this is perfect for a mysterious, shady garden. Try ferns, lady's mantle, hostas, varieties of 'Wizard' coleus, licorice plant (*Helichrysum*), and mints for fragrance. Add white begonias or impatiens for sparkle. Variegated white and green ivy will attractively spill over the edges of the pot.

Air

Yellow (full sun). Plant shorter varieties of the sunflower in the center. Add yellow cockscomb, white daisies or feverfew, marigolds, lemon-colored snapdragons, yellow calendulas, yellow zinnias, and santolina. Variegated vinca vine or prostrate rosemary have foliage that will spill gracefully over the sides of the container and add fragrance and style.

Fire

Red (sun to part shade). For the center of the arrangement, try annual purple fountain grass; its botanical name is *Pennisetum setaceum* 'Rubrum'. Or use perennial Japanese blood grass for height and visual interest. A miniature red rose or a standard tree rose in red would be gorgeous as well. Plant bright red annual sage (salvia), red geraniums, and scarlet petunias so that they dangle over the sides of the pot. Try deep purple, annual sweet potato vines to flow over the edges and to add more flair. In the autumn, switch out the spent annuals with russet- and red-colored chrysanthemums.

Water

Blue (shade to part shade). Plant tall blue delphiniums in the center of this pot for height. For fragrance, add heliotrope, streptocarpella, and bacopa, a trailing herb that has become popular in the past few years. Bacopa has a wonderful scent and tiny white flowers. Tuck bacopa into hanging baskets and pots to spill and drape over the sides of the pot. Finish out this theme container with purple- and blue-colored pansies, blue lobelia, and forget-me-nots. Switch out the pansies with pale violet and white-colored impatiens when the cool-weather-loving pansies fade in the summer heat.

CULINARY HERBS
OF A DIFFERENT COLOR

I think it pisses God off if you walk by the color purple
in a field somewhere and don't notice it.

ALICE WALKER

For added interest in the garden or in your containers or pots, look for varieties of culinary herbs with different-colored foliage. These will add even more color to the garden as they grow and bloom. Here is a colorful list to choose from. The herb is listed first, then the variety of the name (if applicable), and lastly, the color of the foliage.

BASIL 'DARK OPAL': deep purple leaves and stem

BASIL 'HOLLY'S PAINTED': purple-splotched leaves

BASIL 'PURPLE RUFFLES': dark purple leaves and stem

BAY 'GOLDEN BAY': golden leaves

FENNEL 'BRONZE': brownish green leaves and stems

LEMON BALM: variegated gold-splashed leaves

MARJORAM, GOLDEN: gold-splashed to golden yellow leaves

MINT, GINGER: gold-splashed leaves

MINT, ORANGE BERGAMOT: purple- to bronze-tinged leaves

MINT, PINEAPPLE: cream-edged leaves

SAGE 'ICETERINA': yellow variegated leaves

SAGE 'PUPURASCENS': purple leaves

SAGE 'TRICOLOR': purple, deep pink, and white leaves

SORREL 'RED': red-veined leaves

THYME, LEMON 'ARGENTEUS': silver-edged leaves

THYME, LEMON 'AUREUS': gold-edged leaves

Windowsill Culinary Herb Garden

Parsley—the jewel of the herbs,
both in the pot and on the plate.
ALBERT STOCKLI

~

Herbs that are grown indoors add fresh aroma to your home, and because they are so close at hand, they encourage you to make use of them for seasonings and in food preparation. Basically, indoor-grown herbs require a sunny growing area (five to six hours of sunlight per day), water, and humidity. They will need protection from cold drafts and extreme temperatures. Also, turn your pots occasionally to promote even growth of the plants.

Interested in the magickal associations of these herbs? Please refer to the list beginning on page 39.

Here are a few bewitching culinary herbs that are suited to growing indoors:

BASIL (*OCIMUM BASILICUM*): Great indoor plant. Pinch off the flowers to encourage leaf production. Basil's culinary uses are numerous. Adds a nice flavor to Italian foods, red sauces, and tomatoes.

BAY (*LAURUS NOBILIS*): Add a leaf to savory dishes, chili, or stews.

BORAGE (*BORAGO OFFICINALIS*): Use these pretty and edible blue flowers to garnish food and beverages.

CHIVES (*ALLIUM SCHOENOPRASUM*): Cut off the flowers for improved leaf production. Chives are a versatile cooking herb. Season potatoes, eggs, salads, stews, etc.

MARJORAM (*ORIGANUM MAJORANA*): May be added to salads, eggs, or cheese dishes, or to meat in the last few moments of cooking.

OREGANO (*ORIGANUM SPP.*): Popular in Italian dishes, red sauces, and meat dishes.

PARSLEY (*PETROSELINUM CRISPUM*): Parsley is underappreciated until you start to learn to cook with it when it is fresh. Adds great color and freshness to many dishes.

ROSEMARY (*ROSMARINUS OFFICINALIS*): Great with chicken, pork, or beef. Do not overwater this plant.

TARRAGON (*ARTEMISIA DRACUNCULUS*): These thin aromatic leaves have a distinctive flavor. Tarragon is becoming popular once again as a seasoning in cooking, especially in French dishes.

FEATURED PLANTS' MAGICKAL ASSOCIATIONS

For the advantages which fashion values are plants
which thrive in very confined localities…
RALPH WALDO EMERSON

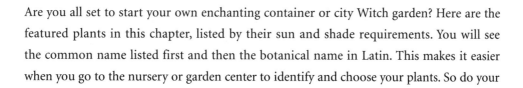

Are you all set to start your own enchanting container or city Witch garden? Here are the featured plants in this chapter, listed by their sun and shade requirements. You will see the common name listed first and then the botanical name in Latin. This makes it easier when you go to the nursery or garden center to identify and choose your plants. So do your homework—figure out what your sun and shade patterns are, then choose the best enchanting plants for your balcony, rooftop, deck, or patio. Happy magickal gardening!

Please note: These flowers, plants, and herbs are not intended to be taken internally or to treat medical issues. Some are toxic. This listing of magickal associations is for spells and charms only.

Shade Plants

BEGONIA (*BEGONIA* SPP.): a warning, encourages premonitions

BUGLE (*AJUGA REPTANS*): health, healing

COLUMBINE (*AQUILEGIA CANADENSIS*): courage, love

FERNS: faerie magick, invisibility

FORGET-ME-NOT (*MYOSOTIS SYLVATICA*): improves memory, aids in finding lost treasures

HOSTA (*HOSTA* SPP.): mystery, devotion, health

IMPATIENS (*IMPATIENS* SPP.): also known as "Busy Lizzies" and used in spells and charms to bring a speedy outcome

IVY (*HEDERA* SPP.): fidelity, love, protection, grace

LILY OF THE VALLEY (*CONVALLARIA MAJALIS*): happiness, protection, faerie magick, wisdom (*note:* mildly toxic)

MINT (*MENTHA* SPP.): prosperity, health (*note:* edible culinary herb)

PERIWINKLE (*VINCA MINOR*): protection, utilized in bindings (*note:* toxic)

RHODODENDRON (*RHODORA* SPP.): welcome, loving homes

SAGE (*SALVIA OFFICINALIS*): wisdom, protection, helps to make wishes come true

SOLOMON'S SEAL (*POLYGONATUM OFFICINALE*): protection, banishing unwanted spirits

TANSY (*TANACETUM VULGARE*): vigor, long life

VIOLET (*VIOLA ODORATA*): faerie magick, love, protection from enchantment

Part Sun/Shade Plants

ANGELICA (*ANGELICA ARCHANGELICA*): inspiration, protection

BACOPA (*BACOPA MONNIERI*): soothes, brings peace, calms the nerves

BERGAMOT (*MONARDA DIDYMA*): success, prosperity

BETONY (*STACHYS* SPP.): also known as lamb's ears; used in protection and children's magick

BLACK COHOSH (*CIMICIFUGA RACEMOSA*): A shade-loving herb that imparts courage to its bearer. This herb is a wonderful addition to spells that will encourage love and increase sexual potency.

CATMINT (*NEPETA CATARIA*): sacred to the goddess Bast; used for cat magick, affection, beauty, playfulness, and cheer

FOXGLOVE, COMMON (*DIGITALIS PURPUREA*): This biennial plant's enchanting blossoms may be used in charms and spells for faerie magick and protection. When foxgloves are grown in the garden, it's like putting out a sign to attract both the elementals and the Fae. (*Note:* toxic)

FOXGLOVE, YELLOW (*DIGITALIS LUTEA*): A perennial foxglove that is dainty and blooms yellow. Use in spells for protection and to get the attention of the faeries. (*Note:* toxic)

HELIOTROPE (*HELIOTROPIUM ARBORESCENS*): This herb has the scent of vanilla and cherries, which explains the folk name often ascribed to this plant of "cherry pie." Magickal associations to this flowering herb are invisibility and faerie magick. *Garden Witch Tip:* If you have sensitive skin, you may wish to wear gloves while handling this plant, as it can cause contact dermatitis.

LADY'S MANTLE (*ALCHEMILLA VULGARIS*): love, romance, women's mysteries

LOBELIA (*LOBELIA ERINUS*), ANNUAL BLUE VARIETY: protects against gossip, and as a true blue flower it is sacred to Venus/Aphrodite

MALLOW (*MALVIA* SPP.): love, protection, banishing

MUGWORT (*ARTEMISIA VULGARIS*): sacred to the goddess Artemis; moon magick, women's mysteries (*note:* mildly toxic)

NICOTIANA (*NICOTIANA TABACUM*): Use flowering tobacco for moon magick, healing, and cleansing; it is a good herbal substitute for more baneful herbs. (*Note:* toxic)

PANSY (*VIOLA TRICOLOR*): This popular annual flower comes in a rainbow of colors and color combinations. The folk name for the pansy is "heartsease," which is appropriate because this flower is worked into love spells, love divinations, and, according to flower folklore, will help to heal a broken heart.

SALVIA, RED (*SALVIA*): This popular annual bedding plant may be used for strength and wisdom.

SOAPWORT (*SAPONARIA OFFICINALIS*): This lovely flowering herb is perfect for cleansing spells.

SWEET WOODRUFF (*GALIUM ODORATUM*): This shade-loving groundcover encourages protection and safe homes. It is also worn or carried as a protective charm for athletes.

Sun Plants

BAY (*LAURUS NOBILIS*): protection, health, promotes psychic abilities

BORAGE (*BORAGO OFFICINALIS*): courage, psychic abilities

CALENDULAS (*CALENDULA OFFICINALIS*): health, sunshine

CHIVES (*ALLIUM SCHOENOPRASUM*): protection, absorbs negativity

COCKSCOMB (*CELOSIA* SPP.): promotes energy, protection, healing

COREOPSIS (*COREOPSIS LANCEOLATA*): cheer, sunshine, chases away the blues

DAISY (*CHRYSANTHEMUM LEUCANTHEMUM*): innocence, sweetness

DELPHINIUM, BLUE (*DELPHINIUM GRANDIFLORA*): love; these blue flowers are sacred to Venus/Aphrodite

DIANTHUS/CLOVE PINKS (*DIANTHUS CARYOPHYLLUS*): promotes energy, beauty, and health

DILL (*ANETHUM GRAVEOLENS*): protection, prosperity

FENNEL (*FUNICULAR VULGARE*): health, purification

FEVERFEW (*TANACETUM PARTHEIUM*): protection, health, safe travel

FRENCH TARRAGON (*ARTEMISIA DRACUNCULUS*): The word *dracunculus* is French for "little dragon." Tarragon fights fatigue. It is suggested that you slip a few leaves in your shoe.

GERANIUM (*PERLAGONIUM* SPP.): Red for protection, pink for love, coral for energy, and white for fertility.

LAVENDER (*LAVENDULA OFFICINALE*): protection, counteracts the evil eye

MARIGOLDS (*TAGETES PATULA*): power of the sun, protection, promotes wealth and glory

MARJORAM (*ORIGANUM MAJORANA*): joy, love, serenity

MORNING GLORY (*IPOMOEA HEDERACEA*): power, protection, love bindings, banishing (*note:* mildly toxic)

OREGANO (*ORIGANUM* SPP.): relieves anxiety, encourages peace

PARSLEY (*PETROSELINUM CRISPUM*): protection, prosperity, astral projection

PETUNIAS (*PETUNIA* SPP.): power, cheer

ROSE (*ROSA* SPP.): love, power (Rose petals add an extra boost of power and will encourage a speedy outcome to your spells.)

ROSEMARY (*ROSMARINUS OFFICINALIS*): remembrance, cleansing, love, health

SAGE (*SALVIA OFFICINALIS*): wisdom, healing, protection

SANTOLINA (*SANTOLINA CHAMAECYPARISUS*): Also known as cotton lavender. This herb is sacred to Mercury and is actually a part of the daisy family. Try using this herb for communication and to speed up the outcome of your spellwork.

SNAPDRAGONS (*ANTIRRHINUM MAJUS*): protection, breaks negative energy, repels manipulative spells

STRAWBERRIES (*FRAGARIA VESCA*): sacred to Freya; promotes perfection, love, and health

SUNFLOWER (*HELIANTHUS ANNUUS*): affluence, confidence, grandeur, helps you to stand out in a crowd

SWEET POTATO VINE (*IPOMOEA BATATAS*): This is a non-edible annual vine. Sweet potato vines come in some fabulous colors, like lime green and deep purple. Magickal associations for the lime green vines include luck and prosperity; for purple-colored vines, passion and power. This plant is part of the morning glory family and is mildly toxic.

THYME (*THYMUS VULGARIS*): new projects, love, romance, psychic powers, cleansing

YARROW (*ACHILLEA MILLEFOLIUM*): This plant brings seven years of marital happiness and is worked into healing spells. Also, this is a classic Witch's herb and is considered an all-purpose magickal herb.

ZINNIA (*ZINNIA SPP.*): In the language of flowers, it symbolizes "thinking of you." May be used in friendship spells and to promote sunny dispositions.

wild yarrow

The Fascination of Flowers

Each flower is a soul opening out to nature.
GÉRARD DE NERVAL

⌒

I know you will find plenty of ways to put all the information in this chapter to good practical use, for no matter what climate you live in, herbal magick is available and waiting for you. Working with herbs, flowers, and botanicals is one of the most rewarding varieties of Witchcraft, and it is also integral to the practice of green magick. May you enjoy your time spent with the plant kingdom; allow your soul to bloom, and absorb all the lessons the plants can teach you.

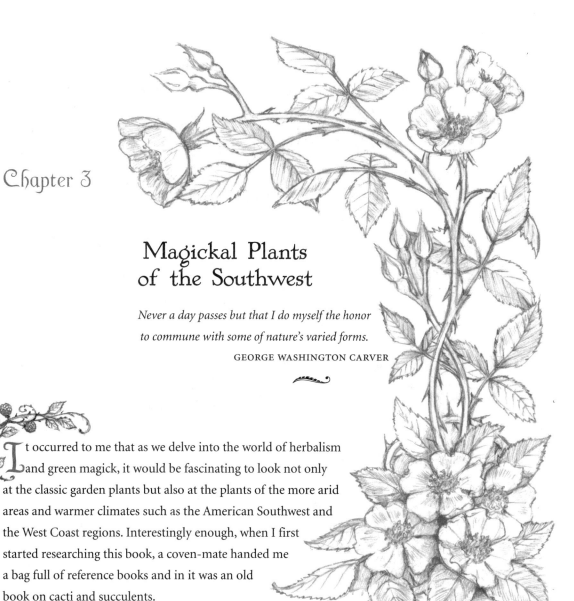

Chapter 3

Magickal Plants
of the Southwest

Never a day passes but that I do myself the honor
to commune with some of nature's varied forms.

GEORGE WASHINGTON CARVER

It occurred to me that as we delve into the world of herbalism
and green magick, it would be fascinating to look not only
at the classic garden plants but also at the plants of the more arid
areas and warmer climates such as the American Southwest and
the West Coast regions. Interestingly enough, when I first
started researching this book, a coven-mate handed me
a bag full of reference books and in it was an old
book on cacti and succulents.

The book had belonged to her family, and apparently her mother had used it when they gardened and lived in New Mexico when my friend was a little girl. At first, I ignored the book, and then after a while it started to tickle my imagination. Then when another friend suggested that I include a chapter on the plants of the Southwest and not leave out the western gardening Witches, I really got inspired. So I dug into that bag and pulled out those books. Then I hit the library and was amazed and frankly envious at the number of plants that were so well suited to gardeners in warmer climates.

century plant

And as I sat in my office on a bitterly cold January day, I researched those gorgeous plants and dreamed a little. I was captivated at the variety of plants, many with magickal associations that are popular with and readily available to southwestern gardeners today. I drooled over gorgeous varieties of sage, willow, privet, cacti, wildflowers, and grasses. Like any other gardener, magickal or mundane, I am always on the lookout for new varieties of plants and fresh gardening information. As I happily took reams of notes, I could feel my enthusiasm firing up. So I rubbed my Garden Witch's hands together, started writing, and conjured up some fresh herbal magick, Wild West style.

Magickal Associations for Thirteen Plants of the West and Southwest

The West of which I speak is but another name for the Wild; and what I have been preparing to say is, that in Wildness is the preservation of the World.

HENRY DAVID THOREAU

There are so many plants to pick from that eventually I decided to write on the most common, popular plants that were readily available to gardeners in the West Coast and southwestern regions. When it comes to the local varieties of magickal plants, such as the popular California poppy, the New Mexico sunflower, or the desert willow, simply apply the classic magickal associations for the common poppy, the sunflower, and the willow tree. No matter where it grows, the plants will have basically the same magickal uses as their botanical cousins.

However, as I always stress, your knowledge and experience is vitally important here. Follow your instincts, and see what the plants tell you about their elemental correspondences. You may decide that for you, personally, they differ. And if that is so, then keep notes and simply go with what works best for you. Here are thirteen fascinating plants for you to incorporate into your own herbal magick.

Century Plant (*Agave Americana*)

Also known as agave. This native plant of Mexico is now grown worldwide. It is a succulent plant and is described as "half hardy." The leaves are grey green, sword-shaped, and can grow to be six feet in length. The plant got its common name due to the belief that it only flowered once every one hundred years—not true, but the plant does only bloom once in its lifespan. The century plant bears a tall panicle, or bundle, of tubular-shaped, light yellow flowers up to twenty-five feet in height. The average life span for this plant is twenty-five years, and it dies shortly after flowering.

There is also a beautiful variegated variety of agave called 'Marginata' with yellow and green striped foliage, which would be an enchanting addition to a warm climate garden. The leaves of the century plant yield a papyruslike fiber called *pita*, which can be made into rope, matting, and even a crude cloth. Because it is so versatile, it was an important plant to the pre-Columbian civilizations. Please note that while the century plant is sometimes called American aloe, it is not even related to the aloe plant.

There are no classic magickal associations for this stately beauty, so I would imagine the century plant could be worked into spells for endurance and strength and the rare blossoms for miracles. In my opinion, the astrological association would be the sun, and the elemental correspondence would be fire.

Desert Four o'Clock (*Mirabilis multiflora*)

This variety of four o'clock grows well in southwestern gardens and grows wild in piñon-juniper woodlands or in shrublands. Four o'clocks are herbaceous perennial plants, meaning they die back to their roots every year. The plants grow in clumps with many stems and may reach up to three feet in height. The leaves are deep green and are described as "egg-shaped" or sometimes heart-shaped. The cuplike magenta flowers are borne in small clusters. Interestingly, four

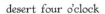

desert four o'clock

o'clocks do not have petals—they have sepals, which are petal-like in look but in reality are fused together, creating a funnel-shaped blossom. The Native Americans used this plant as a sedative. Some tribes created a pale brown or purple dye for wool from this plant as well.

In the language of flowers, the four o'clock symbolizes shyness. And just as their name suggests, four o'clocks bloom in the late afternoon, remaining open throughout the night. It should be noted that sometimes on a cloudy day they may be fooled into opening in the morning. Four o'clocks will draw in hawkmoths in the evening, which are the main pollinators of this flower. A charming and very appropriate folk name for four o'clocks is "Beauty of the Night." Due to their nocturnal blooming habitats and their sedative properties, I would ascribe the magickal association of the moon to this lovely flower. The suggested elemental correspondence is water. Magickal uses would be lunar magick, overcoming shyness, sleep, and dreams.

Gayfeather/Liatris (*Liatris spicata*)

Also called prairie gayfeather, blazing star, or button snakewort, this gorgeous blooming herb is from the aster family. It has rosy purple or mauve flower spikes that are covered in florets. The flowers are described as being the shape of a bottlebrush and open from the top of the stem down. The gayfeather has tiny, thin leaves that get smaller in size as they grow closer to the flowering top. The plant is described as having a haylike scent. The foliage of this plant will repel moths. Liatris is a popular flower in floral design as it lasts for days when it is cut. This is also a striking specimen plant when grown in the garden. It will attract bees and butterflies.

gayfeather/liatris

In the language of flowers, this purple beauty stands for gaiety and cheer. Magickally, you may use the gayfeather to bring some happiness and brightness into your life. The planetary correspondence is Venus; the elemental association is water.

A Flower Fascination with Liatris

Arrange some of these pretty purple spikes in a water-filled vase with other enchanted flowers from your garden. Now either give them as a gift to someone who is down in the dumps or keep them for your own family and soak in the positive vibrations that they can offer to all of you.

Here is a little floral fascination that you can add to boost the power and magickal energy of your floral arrangement. Once you have the flowers arranged to your liking, hold your hands over the blossoms and repeat the following spell verse:

Liatris is a blazing star, also called gayfeather,

Bring sunshine, cheer, and joy to my/their home, in any weather.

Add your natural power to mine, and swirl about this/their place,

With a touch of herbal magick, I'll put a smile on your face.

This cheerful herbal spell is spun straight from the heart,

Worked for the good of all with a Green Witch's art.

Once you have finished the spell, either give the arrangement as a gift right away or set it in a place of prominence in your home so the whole family can enjoy it.

Jacob's Ladder (*Polemonium foliosissmum*)

This herbaceous perennial may grow up to two feet tall and is a late spring to early summer bloomer. The sky blue flowers are borne in clusters and are a beautiful bell shape with distinctive golden yellow stamens. The plant got its name from the unique foliage: the leaves are arranged in pairs and grow straight across from each other on the stems in a ladderlike style. There are other varieties of Jacob's ladder that bloom in white as well. One European variety of Jacob's ladder is also known as Greek valerian, and its botanical name is *Polemonium caeruleum*.

In the language of flowers, Jacob's ladder tells its recipient to come back to earth and to let go of their pride. Magickally, you may work this plant into charms and spells designed to quickly restore peace, serenity, and a sense of calm. According to *Culpeper's Herbal*, this flower's ruling planet is Mercury. The suggested elemental correspondence is air.

jacob's ladder

Lupin/Lupine (*Lupin* spp.)

There are many varieties of the lupin that grow beautifully in drier, warmer climate gardens. This plant can be a herbaceous perennial, and there are also a few varieties of lupin that are annuals. (Check your local nursery for plants that are best suited to your garden and your climate.) Classically, this plant has long, narrow leaf stems with a circle of narrow leaves at the top. Leaves are composed of several leaflets that branch out from a central point. The eye-catching flowers blossom in June and are classically described as being "arranged in dense or open whorls on an erect spike, or raceme." While blue is the most common flower shade, lupins may come in a variety of colors such as yellow, purple, dark pink, or white.

A pretty variety of lupin that is recommended for western gardens is the silvery lupine (*Lupinus argenteus*). This is a perennial plant that has silvery-grey foliage and grows up to two feet in height. The flowers bloom in midsummer and look like sweet peas. The blossoms are lilac to violet in color.

In the language of flowers, lupines symbolize imagination and voraciousness. Magickal uses include increasing your personal power and attraction. Classically, the lupin has the planetary association of Mars, but as many wild lupines are deep blue, including the annual Texas bluebonnet (*Lupinus texensis*), you might also consider the planetary influence of Venus. The suggested elemental correspondence is water. According to flower folklore tradition, all blue flowers are sacred to the goddesses of love, Aphrodite and Venus.

> **Garden Witch Tip:** It is important to note that there are several varieties of wild lupins that are considered poisonous to livestock. In fact, there are some sobering articles online from the USDA (United States Department of Agriculture) on the problems wild lupins can cause to grazing sheep and cattle.

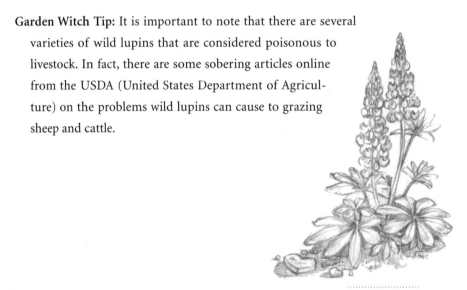

lupin

Moss Rose/Portulaca (*Portulaca grandiflora*)

This annual flower has a high heat and drought tolerance and grows up to eight inches in height. It comes in a variety of colors such as rose, pale pink, orange, yellow, and white. This annual has succulent-looking foliage and comes from the purslane family. Moss rose flowers can be found in double or single varieties, and the petals close up in the afternoon. Portulaca is one of my favorite annuals for late summertime containers, as they thrive in full sun and love the heat. I can only imagine how gorgeous they would be in a garden that was typically warm and dry.

Magickal associations for this flower are sleep, love, good luck, and protection. Scatter the flower petals in the four corners of your home to increase its protection and to repel negativity. Try tucking a pale white blossom under your pillow at night to rid yourself of nightmares. To encourage love, work with the pink-colored flowers. To give your spells a boost of energy, work with the yellow- and orange-colored flowers. The moss rose/portulaca is ruled by the moon (as are all plants in the purslane family), and its elemental correspondence is water.

moss rose

Prickly Pear (*Opuntia phaeacantha*)

This cactus represents about a dozen species of the *Opuntia* genus of cactus in North American deserts. Prickly pear cactus can have yellow, red, or purple flowers, even among the same species. They vary in height from less than twelve inches to up to six to seven feet in height. The red fruits of the prickly pear are edible. Prickly pears have flat, fleshy pads that look like large leaves. The pads are, in reality, adapted branches, or stems, that provide several purposes, among them water storage, photosynthesis, and flower production.

The spines of this cactus are described as "modified leaves" that grow out from a small "wart" on the pad of the plant. There is another type of spine on the prickly pear as well: tiny barbed spines called *glochids*. These are located just above the cluster of regular spine, are yellow or red in color, and remove easily from the pads of the cactus. However, those tiny, colored spines are tougher to see and are more difficult to remove from the skin, should you be unfortunate enough to discover this the hard way.

To make your herbal magick even more unique and personal, you could also work color magick with the blossoms of the prickly pear: yellow for wisdom and red for protection and to shield your loved ones. Finally, you may use the purple-colored prickly pear blossoms for added power in any protection spell.

In the language of flowers, the prickly pear symbolizes satire. The planetary ruler for all cacti is Mars, and the elemental association is fire. On an interesting note, in the language of flowers, a cactus symbolizes endurance. The magickal association for all varieties of cacti is protection.

prickly pear

Protecting Your Property with Cactus

To add a bit of magickal protection to your property, you may wish to plant a cactus at each corner of your home's foundation, or you may decide to plant them at the outer four corners of your property to mark the area as a protected and sacred space. (If you do this, it is recommended that the cacti all be the same species.)

As to astrological timing, if you work this spell during a waning moon, then focus on removing all negative influences from your property. Conversely, if you happen to work this spell during a waxing moon, then concentrate on increasing the protective vibrations of your home and yard. Select your plants, and then dig all four holes. Then, one at a time, starting in the east, plant the first cactus. Move clockwise and plant the remaining cactus, moving from the south to the west and ending in the north. As you set the final cacti in place, say:

> *As above, now so below;*
>
> *Around my home protection grows.*
>
> *At the four corners I've set in place*
>
> *These spiny plants that will guard my space.*

To close up this green magick, I would pat the soil down firmly but gently, and water all the plants well to avoid transplant shock. Then hold your hands over the plants one at a time and say:

> *This protective cactus spell is spun from the heart,*
>
> *Worked with my love and trust in my Green Witch's art.*

Repeat these closing lines at each cactus, moving clockwise around the home or property. When you are finished, put away your gardening tools, and go relax and enjoy the rest of your day.

Garden Witch Tip: Here is another magickal idea: cactus spines are often incorporated into Witch jars for protection and security. (It's a more natural component as compared to pins, needles, or broken glass.) Just be careful when you gather the spines from the cactus. Remember not to take too much and to leave the plant in good condition. A spine or two will suffice.

Sagebrush (*Artemisia tridentata*)

This small tree or shrub is described as vigorous and bears pungent and spicy-scented, grey green, wedge-shaped leaves; it is the state flower of Nevada. The leaves are covered in fine silvery hairs, which help the plant protect itself from transpiration, or water loss. The sagebrush blossoms in late summer/early fall and bears yellow flowers that are arranged in long clusters. Varieties of sagebrush cover large areas of the high, dry plains of the West. There are five subspecies of sagebrush, including the popular California sagebrush (*Artemisia californica*). The Native Americans valued the sagebrush plant for its healing properties and considered the smoke from dried, burning sagebrush a sacred purifier.

According to flower folklore, all types of sage symbolize both wisdom and skill. According to *Cunningham's Encyclopedia of Magical Herbs*, the sagebrush is classified as a plant that carries feminine energies. Its magickal uses are purification and exorcism.

sagebrush

Burning dried sagebrush and waving the fragrant smoke around is a simple way to purify, or "smudge," a place or person. The planetary association of sagebrush is Venus, and the elemental correspondence is earth.

Shrubby Cinquefoil

In the West, this enchanting herb is identified as *Potentilla fruticosa*; however, shrubby cinquefoil has recently been reclassified as *Dasiphora floribunda*. Shrubby cinquefoil is a beautiful blooming shrub in the wild, but to the delight of gardeners, it has been cultivated extensively and is readily available at western nurseries. This deciduous shrub is multi-branched and described as possessing a spreading and upright habit. The shrub grows from one to three feet in height. The bark is reddish brown, and this plant has short and thin leaves. This variety of cinquefoil blooms from June through August. The five-petaled flowers are bright yellow and shaped like large buttercups.

In the language of flowers, the blossoms of the cinquefoil represent a beloved daughter and maternal love. Conversely, this is thought to be a plant with masculine energies. The five points on the leaves represent the magickal uses of the plant: love, power, prosperity, health, and knowledge. The cinquefoil, in all of its varieties, is an excellent hex-breaking plant. The blossoms and the foliage may be worked into charm bags or magick to break or neutralize a manipulative spell that another may have cast upon you. The planetary ruler for cinquefoil is Jupiter, and the elemental association is fire.

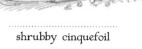

shrubby cinquefoil

A Cinquefoil Charm Bag Recipe

Supplies

- Cinquefoil foliage and blossoms (fresh or dried)
- One silver- or grey-colored sachet bag, or a three by three-inch square of grey fabric and a coordinating twelve-inch ribbon (the silvery grey color will help neutralize discordant energy)

Directions: Work this spell in a waning moon to help make the situation decrease or on a Saturday to tap into that day's banishing properties. To begin, gather together fresh cinquefoil foliage and blossoms. (You may use dried cinquefoil in a pinch.) Place the botanicals into a silver- or grey-colored sachet bag. You can easily find little organza bags in a rainbow of colors at an arts and crafts store; look in the bridal section. If you use the fabric square, then place the botanicals in the center and gather up each corner. Tie the fabric closed with the ribbon. Now hold the herb-filled bundle in your hands, and repeat the following charm:

> Grey is the color of neutrality,
> I banish any spells cast against me.
> By the cinquefoil's hex-breaking power,
> I am free from you, as of this hour.
> This protective charm bag is conjured from the heart,
> Worked with my love and trust in my Green Witch's art.

Keep the herbal charm bag with you, tucked in your pocket or purse, for one week. Afterwards, open up the charm bag and neatly dispose of the herbs. Add them to a compost pile or to your yard waste. Gently hand wash the sachet bag or fabric, allow it to air dry, and you may use it again if you wish.

Wild Hyssop (*Agastache cana*)

Also commonly called a hummingbird plant or a hummingbird mint. Wild hyssop is a bushy perennial that grows up to three feet in height. It bears dark pink to rosy purple tubular flowers in summer that are about one inch long. This plant is stunning and blooms from June through September. It can grow up to two to three feet in height and approximately eighteen inches in width. This beautiful plant is heartily recommended for mixed borders and herb gardens. The foliage is sweetly scented and is attractive to butterflies, bees, and hummingbirds. It is also said to deter mosquitoes when the crushed foliage is rubbed on the skin.

> **Garden Witch Tip:** I would test how you or anyone else reacts to this plant on a small patch inside the elbow first. Then wait several hours, and see how your skin reacts. (This way, you can make sure you are not allergic to this foliage before you go crazy and rub it all over any exposed skin.)

Another beautiful variety of hyssop that also thrives in the Southwest is the purple hyssop (*Agastache pallidiflora*). This plant bears purple flower spikes that are two feet long. Many varieties of hyssop are very popular with gardeners as they typically bloom for long periods of time in the garden. Hyssop flowers are also popular for arrangements both as a freshly cut and as a dried flower.

wild hyssop

In the language of flowers, the hyssop signifies cleansing. Magickally, hyssop is worked into purification rituals and protection charms. You can tuck the foliage and blossoms into charm bags or add them to a candle spell. The fragrance of hyssop blossoms is often used in aromatherapy to heighten your spirituality. Hyssop is considered to have masculine energies. Its planetary correspondence is Jupiter; the elemental association is fire.

Wild Plum Tree (*Prunus americana*)

This tree is the only plum native to the Southwest. In the wild, you will find it growing in mountain fields and along ditches and fences. In the garden, it is often grown as a shrub but can be grown as a tree. If grown in the garden and left unpruned, it will grow into a tall, bushy shrub, with thicket-forming, thornlike, spreading side branches and a broad crown. This tree thrives with neglect, so leave it be and allow it to grow naturally in the garden. At maturity, the wild plum may range from twelve to twenty feet in height.

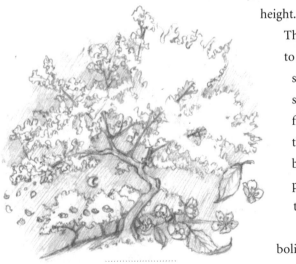

wild plum tree

The leaves of the wild plum are described as three to four inches in length and simple, with an oval shape with pointed tips. The wild plum tree blossoms in early spring. It bears white five-petaled flowers, and the leaves appear at the same time as the flowers. The fruit is classified as a drupe and is borne in mid to late summer. The fruit of the wild plum is edible, can vary in color from purple-red to golden, and measures about an inch across.

In the language of flowers, the plum tree symbolizes independence, valor, happiness, matrimony, and perseverance. Magickally, the plum tree brings joy and cheer to anyone who grows the tree on their property. It will attract bees and butterflies. The plum is considered a feminine plant. It is ruled by the planet Venus and has the elemental correspondence of water.

Wild Yarrow (*Achellia millefoil*)

Also called milfoil, this herb is a hardy perennial that bears large, flat clusters of small white or pink flowers at the top of erect downy stems. The plant blossoms heavily at the beginning of summer and then off and on throughout the fall. Yarrow dries well and can be worked into various magickal arts and crafts. Yarrow has aromatic, ferny, green foliage that can grow to above twelve inches in height. The larger leaves of the yarrow plant make pretty fillers in floral arrangements. However, the fresh foliage may cause skin irritation in some individuals.

According to herbal lore, this plant was named after Achilles and is associated with healing, as Achilles used this herb to help heal his soldiers who were wounded in battle, giving it another folk name of "wound wort." The straight, dried stems of yarrow were also once used for divination by I Ching masters and also the Druids.

Personally, I often consider the yarrow flower to be the herbal equivalent of the white spell candle; it is truly an all-purpose magickal herb. This herb is also rumored to keep a married couple happily together for seven years. In the language of flowers, yarrow announces that it is a cure for all sorrows and heartaches.

A classic Witch's herb, there are many varieties of yarrow, both as wildflowers and garden perennials. There are many types and

wild yarrow

cultivars of yarrow available at the garden center or nursery today. Yarrow can range in colors from yellow, white, pink, and red to purple. The magickal associations of this feminine plant will be the same no matter if it is the wild variety or a cultivar that you selected from the nursery. Yarrow is ruled by the planet Venus, and its elemental association is water.

Here is an all-purpose herbal blessing that you can use as you gather your botanicals for magickal use. Oh, and yes: this gathering charm will work for you beautifully no matter where you live.

All-Purpose Herb Gathering Charm

I gather this herb for a magick spell,

Bringing harm to none, may it turn out well.

By the powers of earth and air, fire and water,

I conjure up love, safety, money, health, and laughter.

By all the power of three times three,

As I will it, then so must it be.

Yucca (*Yucca filamentosa*)

Also known as needle palm. There are forty to fifty species of yucca worldwide, and they can be classified as perennials, shrubs, or trees. The yucca plant is part of the agave family. The needle palm variety of yucca may reach heights of thirteen feet and has stiff, narrow, and swordlike evergreen leaves that fan out from the base. The greenish white, tuliplike flowers are borne on long, narrow spikes that may reach up to four feet in height. The flowers of the yucca slowly open in the evenings. On an interesting side note, the flower of the yucca is the state flower of New Mexico.

Yuccas are widely grown as ornamental specimens in gardens. Many yuccas also bear edible parts, including fruits, seeds, flowers, flowering stems, and roots. Yucca fiber was once used to make rope, and the leaves can be woven into baskets. All the yuccas contain saponin, a natural hair cleanser that is used today in cosmetics and soap.

Magickal uses for this masculine plant include protection, purification, and setting boundaries. Twisting the fibers of the yucca plant into a solar cross and then displaying it on the wall of the home was thought to protect those who dwelled within. I would suggest adding fresh yucca flowers into red charm bags to help rid a person of negative energy. They will also work nicely to protect against emotionally toxic work or living environments.

You may also plant four yucca plants at the corners of your house, as was suggested in the prickly pear section. (See the "Protecting Your Property with Cactus" spell on page 57.) I would simply adjust the words of the spell accordingly. The planetary ruler for the yucca is Mars, and the elemental association is fire.

yucca

65

WALKING ON THE WILD SIDE

Nature knows no difference between weeds and flowers.

MASON COOLEY

I hope that you found the botanical information in this chapter to be interesting. Most of all, I hope that it sparked ideas for you and inspired you to work with the plants that are indigenous to your neck of the woods. I can only imagine how incredibly smug Witches who can garden year-round feel while some of us are sitting cooped up inside and scowling at the barren landscapes, leafless trees, and snow and ice of the winter months. So if you live in a more temperate zone, lucky you.

Keep notes on your Witch's gardens and your magickal plants no matter where you live, and see what the plants are willing to teach you. Pick up a spiral notebook or start a gardener's journal. As you keep your notes and log in your gardening successes and experiences each season, you will gain a treasured keepsake of your garden and your life. Take photos of the plants and of your landscape. Try scrapbooking the journal—make it gorgeous and make it personal. Have some fun and be creative.

In our next chapter, we are really going to get a little wild. Sound intriguing? Let's be daring and walk on the wild side—of flowers, that is. Get ready for wildflowers and witchery!

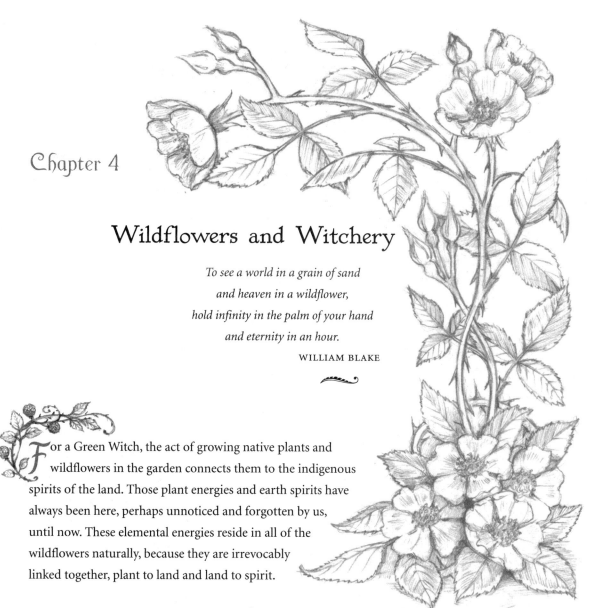

Chapter 4

Wildflowers and Witchery

To see a world in a grain of sand
and heaven in a wildflower,
hold infinity in the palm of your hand
and eternity in an hour.

WILLIAM BLAKE

For a Green Witch, the act of growing native plants and wildflowers in the garden connects them to the indigenous spirits of the land. Those plant energies and earth spirits have always been here, perhaps unnoticed and forgotten by us, until now. These elemental energies reside in all of the wildflowers naturally, because they are irrevocably linked together, plant to land and land to spirit.

When you bring wildflowers and native plants into your garden, you are introducing and inviting those harmonious energies and local spirits back into your own enchanting garden space or local sacred grove. Once you've acknowledged their powers or reacquainted them back into your life, the earth spirits are contented, and all their magickal blessings are showered upon you.

Working with wildflowers as a part of your green magick practices can be accomplished by one of two means: either with homegrown native plants (many varieties are readily available at your local nursery center these days) or with the wildflowers found blossoming outdoors. If there is a variety of wildflower that you have growing at home in your own gardens, then you may certainly gather a bit from your gardens for your spellwork. If, however, the plant is growing wild in nature, then leave the plant as you find it.

Do not gather, dig up, or cut wildflowers! Some of our native species are protected. In fact, if you are caught gathering flowers from the wild, you may face a hefty fine from your local conservation department. Gathering a single leaf or fallen twig from a common tree is one thing, but please leave the wildflowers that you encounter in the woodlands alone. Think of it this way: if you pick all of the plants blooming in the meadows and woods, then no one else is able to enjoy the wildflowers. In keeping with that theme, none of the spells in this particular chapter require you to harvest the wildflowers, only for you to work with them where you find them—be it in the garden or in the wild.

As you rediscover the magick of wildflowers, our little jewels of nature, stop and acknowledge their tenacity and beauty. If, for example, you should stumble across a little butterfly weed plant happily growing alongside the woods, then feel free to stop and admire it. Hunker down and take a good look at it. Stroke a finger gently over its orange flowers. Then, while you are there, ask the plant to lend its healing energy to your spellwork. Now, go ahead and be spontaneous: work a quick spell for healing.

The intuitive spellcrafting of the Natural Magician or Green Witch is an art that is almost forgotten. It requires no tools other than the sound of your voice, your personal magickal energies, and your own two hands. In other words, *just do it.*

To seal the spell and to signify that you have performed magick with the plant, take a small twig and trace a circle in a clockwise direction gently around the plant on the ground. The circle does not have to show; this is a symbolic gesture. Leave the area as you found it, with no traces that you were even there. The phrase "walk gently upon the earth" means just that. This is a basic tenant of working magick in the wild. As a Witch, you are a protector of the wild places. All Witches, Pagans, and Green Magicians know better than to disturb, deplete, or harm our natural resources.

The idea of green magick in the wild places was meant to encourage and inspire you. I want to persuade you, the reader, to work your magick quietly and intuitively in nature— whether this happens to be in the glades, meadows, woods, or in a quiet and secret space that you have created in your own yard is up to you.

If you think that you'd like to try growing a wildflower garden to add a little "wild" to your backyard Witch's garden, then check seed catalogs and local nurseries for native plants. You can also check out these websites for wildflowers, native plants, and seeds:

- www.mowildflowers.net
- www.grownative.org
- www.mobot.org/default.asp

In the following Garden Witch's dozen of wildflowers, I have given you both the common name and the botanical name (in italics). In this listing, you will find plant descriptions, approximate bloom times, and the folklore and magickal associations of the wildflower. There will also be an accompanying spell with each featured plant. Now, again, you may either work this in the garden or spontaneously, wherever you find the flower growing. Try picking up a local wildflower identification guide to have on hand, and start to appreciate and recognize your own native flora that are indigenous to your area.

Then write up a few of your own spells and flower fascinations for the wildflowers that grow in your neck of the woods. Dare to embrace the unsung art of the Green Witch. Be spontaneous and intuitive; create your own green witchery and natural magick.

Bewitching Wildflowers

First flower of their wilderness, star of their night,
Calm rising through change and through storm.

SAMUEL GILMAN

Please take a moment and look over these directions for the wildflower spells. The following spells require no more supplies than the plants themselves, your voice, and your intentions. This is as basic and as practical as you are going to get. Oh, I imagine somewhere somebody is clutching their chest in horror and sputtering in disbelief. "Heavens above, there isn't even a mention of astrological timing! No charm bags, no candles, no accompanying crystals … is she actually suggesting that no magickal tools be used at all?"

But perhaps there is an excellent reason for what I am teaching here. Do you have an inkling of what that might be? I am instead promoting the use of the most powerful "tools" that any Witch possesses. These tools would be your heart and your mind. After all, the most powerful accessories that any Witch owns are their intention and a desire to create a positive change.

Here is where you are going to stretch your wings a bit: the sky will not fall if you work magick without fancy wands and accessories, I promise you. Instead, I want you to sit down next to the chosen magickal plant, and spend some time with it. Hold your hands over the wildflower and see what sort of energy you experience from the plant. Then ground and center yourself. Next, you should raise your energy high and then repeat the spell verse.

As was suggested previously, in order to close these wildflower spells and to signify that you have performed magick with the plant, take a small twig and trace a circle in a clockwise direction gently around the plant on the ground. The circle does not have to show; this is a symbolic gesture. Ground any extra energy back into the earth, and leave the area as you found it, with no traces that you were even there. Trust that your green magick will work. And now, on to the wildflower spells.

Prairie Anemone (*Anemone caroliniana*)

This plant grows about twelve inches tall. The flowers are borne singly on a stem. Typically the five petals may be tinged with pink or pale purple. The leaves are deeply divided into sections about halfway up the stem. Its habitat is prairies and fields, where it prefers to grow in acidic soils. Bloom time is March through May.

A folk name for this flower is the windflower, from the Greek word *anemone,* which means "wind." In the language of flowers, the anemone signifies truth, honesty, and faith. Magickal associations are health and hope. The anemone is also associated with the planet Mars and the element of fire. If you grow anemones at home in the garden, they will protect your property and your family.

prairie anemone

71

A Windflower Protection Spell

The anemone is often called the windflower,

Now surround my home with your protection and power.

A Witch's wildflower and magickal tool,

Aligned to fire and Mars so strong and true.

Close the windflower spell with these lines:

This protective wildflower spell is spun from the heart,

Worked for the good of all with a Green Witch's art.

Note: You can easily change the words in the second line to "now surround me with protection and power" if you so choose.

Bluebell (*Mertensia virginica*)

These fleshy, showy plants can grow to two feet in height. Flowers are arranged in clusters, hanging bell-like, and are about one inch long. The buds start out pink and then change to blue as they open. The leaves of the bluebell are a bluish green in color and oval shaped. They grow in both sun and shade in bottomlands and hillsides of woods. Bloom time is April through May. The plant goes dormant in the month of June.

Flower folklore tells us that the bluebell stands for constancy and declares that "I am faithful." It was, at one time, the national flower of England. The English variety of the bluebell is identified as *Hyacinthodes non-scripta*. It was also known as the wild hyacinth and grew abundantly in the medieval woodlands of England.

The bluebell is a faerie flower, and if you make an unselfish wish when you spot the first bluebells of the spring, the faeries are sure to grant your request. Magickal associations are good luck and truth. The astrological correspondence is Venus. Plus, it's good to note that all true blue flowers are sacred to Venus and Aphrodite, the Greco-Roman goddesses of love and desire. If a person wears a bluebell, they are compelled to tell you the truth.

> **Garden Witch Tip:** A friendly warning—working magick with the bluebell will show you the truth in any matter. Just remember you are asking for the truth, and you may discover more than you wish. With this spell, you are not asking to see what you want, you are asking for the truth, so keep that in mind.

Bluebell Spell to Know the Truth

Bluebell, bluebell, lend your power to mine,
Please show me the truth, here, now, at this time.
A Venus flower, you are faithful, constant, and true,
May I use this knowledge wisely in all that I do.

Close the wildflower spell with these lines:

This seeker's wildflower spell is spun from the heart,
Worked for the good of all with a Green Witch's art.

bluebell

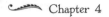

Butterfly Weed (*Asclepias tuberosa*)

Butterfly weed can grow up to three feet in height. Its flowers are displayed at the top of their stalks in clusters. Flowers are found in several shades of orange to red. They bloom from midsummer to fall. The leaves are fuzzy, narrow, and lance shaped. Butterfly weed is part of the milkweed family, so expect the pods and the pretty floating seeds to come in late summer–early fall. It can and will reseed itself quite easily. The plant's habitat includes just about anywhere that has disturbed soil such as upland fields, prairies, glades, and the edges of woods. It prefers sun to light shade. It is also readily available as a nursery plant. Scout out a plant or two from your local nursery to add to your butterfly and magickal gardens.

butterfly weed

This plant has many folk names such as swallow-wort and pleurisy root. Sacred to the Greek god Apollo, the name of this wildflower is taken from the Greek Asclepias, who was thought to have been both a physician and a god of healing. In the language of flowers, the butterfly weed stands for joy and gaiety. This plant's magickal uses are health and energy. Its astrological influence is Jupiter, which also ties into healing and health issues.

A Healing Spell with Butterfly Weed

The bright orange butterfly weed bestows energy to spare,
Grant me health by the powers of water, fire, earth, and air.
By Apollo's and Jupiter's grace, help me to be strong,
May I live a charmed life that is happy, healthy, and long.

Close the wildflower spell with these lines:
This healing wildflower spell is spun from the heart,
Worked for the good of all with a Green Witch's art.

Goldenrod (*Solidago gigantea*)

This is the state flower of Nebraska, and it has strong stalks that can reach two to seven feet and curve near the top into flower-bearing little branches of a bright golden-yellow. The leaves are narrow and resemble willow leaves. The leaves are longer at the bottom and shorter toward the top of the plant. Goldenrod lives in sunny spots, prairies, rocky woods, and along wet places such as rivers and ponds and blooms from July through October.

Goldenrod will sometimes volunteer into your garden. The birds often drop the seeds. Finches enjoy goldenrods, so let a little patch of goldenrod grow wild in your garden; it will bring good luck to your home. Rumor has it that if you hold a stem of the plant in your hand, the flower head will bend toward lost items. In Colonial America, goldenrod had several folk names, including blue mountain tea and woundwort.

In the language of flowers, goldenrod calls for caution, while other floral languages say it means encouragement. This is the bloom to work with if you want your secret love to remain undiscovered. Magickally, goldenrod has the association of prosperity and prophecy. Its astrological influence is Venus, and its associated element is air.

My Secret Love Spell with Goldenrod

> *This golden herb of Venus lend your power to mine,*
> *May our love stay a secret between us for a time.*
> *This flower means caution, but it encourages too.*
> *Encourage my love and I to stay faithful and true.*

Close the wildflower spell with these lines:

> *This lovely wildflower spell is spun from the heart,*
> *Worked for the good of all with a Green Witch's art.*

goldenrod

Hedge Bindweed (*Calystegia sepium*)

Also known as the wild morning glory, this is a creeping, viney, and climbing plant. Its flowers are large and funnel shaped; they are usually white blushed with pink in the center, or they may be a pale pink with white stripes inside the throat. Bindweed flowers close up by noon on sunny days, just like their cousin, the blue morning glory. Bindweed's leaves are described as being arrow-shaped with two squarish lobes. It is found in sun to part shade in fields, waste places, and roadsides. Bloom time is summer through early fall.

In the language of flowers, the wild morning glory promises to be "reassured by your affections." Magickal uses for morning glory blooms include happiness and peace. If you grow the climbing flowers in your garden, you may also use the vines for bindings and protection. Stuff the vines in a jar along with dark-colored glass pebbles and pins to repel intruders and thieves. Bury the Witch jar on your property at a full moon.

The wildflower spell below is designed to use wherever you happen to find the wild morning glory growing—along your fence or up a sturdy perennial in the garden. (At the moment, I have bindweed growing up a decorative celestial metal and glass plant stake.) The bindweed's astrological influence is Saturn, and the elemental correspondence is water.

Garden Witch Tip: Morning glories of all varieties are mildly poisonous. Make sure that you keep them out of reach of small children.

hedge bindweed

Banish Troubles with Bindweed

I banish my troubles with the help of hedge bindweed,

These vines will bind up trouble with all possible speed.

Climbing where they may, these wildflowers are lovely and sweet.

Any problems are bound by the power of three times three.

Close the spell up with these lines:

This protective wildflower spell is spun from the heart,

Worked for the good of all with a Green Witch's art.

Scarlet Indian Paintbrush (*Castilleja coccinea*)

The scarlet Indian paintbrush grows anywhere from eight to fifteen inches tall. The flowers are inconspicuous and greenish yellow, hidden within the axils of brightly colored bracts, which can vary in color from red, orange, and yellow. The leaves are short and oblong with rounded ends. The stems are hairy and can vary in height. It lives in sunny spaces, fields, prairies, glades, and wet areas. This plant can tolerate both very dry and wet conditions. Bloom time is April through July.

The scarlet Indian paintbrush is a flower traditionally used to attract love. If this is grown in your garden, then carry a flower with you to promote loving vibrations. If you discover the flower in the wild, then do as suggested earlier and be sure to leave the plant for others to enjoy. Go ahead and work your magick with the plant then and there. A gentle touch or two of the plant won't hurt anything. Please thank the plant for lending

scarlet indian paintbrush

you its energies. Remember to seal the spell as suggested previously by drawing a clockwise circle around its base. Its astrological influence is Venus; its elemental association is water.

Attracting Love with Indian Paintbrush

With your colorful bracts, attract a new lover to me,

With a touch of magick and the power of three times three.

May my love spell be blessed by the element of water,

By Venus, may they be filled with passion, life, and laughter.

Close the spell with these lines:

This loving wildflower spell is spun from the heart,

Worked for the good of all with a Green Witch's art.

Mullein (*Verbascum thapsus*)

This prominent plant takes over disturbed land and can reach up to seven feet in height. The giant stalks of mullein are hard to miss. The flowers are yellow, and they will bloom from the bottom up on that long spike. Bloom time is May to September. The leaves of this plant look like gigantic lamb's ears. They are oblong, silvery green, soft, and fuzzy. This plant is considered a biennial, which means that it will not produce a flower stalk until its second year. Mullein favors dry, sunny conditions in fields, waste areas, and embankments. Mullein is available as a nursery plant and makes a great addition to a children's garden. The first year, the leaves are soft, huge, and a fuzzy silver. The second growing year, the flower stalk shoots straight up, so give it room. (I have had the flower stalks grow as tall as eight feet in my gardens.) Let mullein reseed itself if you want it to make another appearance in your garden for a third year.

Folk names include Aaron's rod, hag's tapers, hag's torch, graveyard dirt, flannel plant, and velvet plant. In medieval times, the flower stalks were dipped in tallow and lit for torches (which explains the name hag's tapers). Also on an interesting note, the early American settlers used the large, soft mullein leaves for diapers.

The astrological influence of mullein is Saturn, and the elemental correspondence is fire. Magickally, mullein was thought to ward off evil spirits. Mullein leaves are often dried and ground up for various spells. The dried leaves also can be used as a substitute for graveyard dirt.

> **Garden Witch Tip:** This wild herb is a strong protection against evil, negativity, bad mojo, and astral nasties. With the term "astral nasties," I'm not trying to sound cute—I literally mean random elementals, spirits, or thoughtforms that are hanging around and causing you grief. Maybe they were created by you—and maybe they were not. Want them gone? Here's how.

Banishing Astral Nasties with Mullein

With mullein's magick power, I ward and protect me,
I now push away all spirits, evil, and astral nasties.
With the strong influence of Saturn, this will never occur,
By the element of fire, I banish you forever.

Close the spell with these lines:

This protective wildflower spell is spun from the heart,
Worked for the good of all with a Green Witch's art.

mullein

Prairie Rose (*Rosa setigera*)

Also called the climbing wild rose. In the Rosaceae (rose) family, there are over 3,300 varieties worldwide. The prairie rose climbs or forms sprawling bushes with arching, thorny canes. The flowers are soft pink, heavily scented, and usually three inches across. The blooms are single with five petals and many bright yellow stamens. Bloom time is May through July. The leaves are set up into three leaflets on older stalks and in groups of five on newer growth. These roses do produce hips that will turn a beautiful red in the fall. Find this plant in sun and part shade, moist fields, prairie thickets, streamside, and along roads and fence rows.

> **Garden Witch Tip:** If you'd like to grow some of these care-free beauties in your yard, look for roses that are called landscape roses or "nearly wild." These modern varieties of roses will produce the same kind of old-fashioned blooms as the prairie rose.

The old flower folklore suggests that the wild rose symbolizes maidenly beauty. It says that the recipient of this wildflower is "as bonny and virginal as this pure bloom." In natural magick, the rose and its petals are used quite often for various spells and charms, including love, healing, and protection. (Please refer to my book *Garden Witchery* for more information on the magick of all the various colors of roses.) It is important to note that the five-petaled

prairie rose

wild rose is an ancient symbol of the Goddess. The astrological correspondence for the wild rose is the same as the hybrid rose: it is Venus, and the elemental association is water.

A Fragrant Call for the Goddess's Blessings

May the Goddess and all her blessings shine down on me,

Whether I am on land, in the sky, or on the sea.

A five-petaled rose is a symbol of her power,

May my life be as sweet as this magickal flower.

Close the Goddess blessing with these lines:

This fragrant wildflower spell is spun from the heart,

Worked for the good of all with a Green Witch's art.

Skullcap (*Scutellaria incana*)

Hoary skullcap grows two to three feet in height and is part of the mint family. This particular variety of skullcap grows from the midsections of the country to the eastern coast of the United States. Hoary skullcap grows as far south as Texas and as far north as New York state (and all the states in between, all the way to the East Coast). The stems of the hoary skullcap are short, branched, and covered in fine grey hair. The flowers are purplish blue and clustered together in an oblong grouping.

There is also another variety of wild skullcap that is common throughout the United States and Britain, and it is called *Scutellaria galericulata*. Known as the Common Skullcap, it is often called Marsh Skullcap or Hooded Skullcap. This plant grows one to three feet in height and is common in meadows, marshes, and wet shores. All of the skullcap's purple-blue flowers are a half-inch long and start to bloom from the bottom up from June through

September. The plant's leaves are oval shaped with pointed ends. This plant likes full sun to partial shade in wooded slopes, alongside streams, and in rocky, open woods.

> **Garden Witch Tip:** In the home garden, skullcap performs best in rich, fertile, and moist soil. Skullcap has to have lots of sun and moist soil for the best growing success.

Magickally, skullcap is used to promote relaxation and peace. The astrological association is Saturn; the elemental correspondence is water. It is also said to protect your man from the wiles of other women. Here is a wildflower spell to use for just such an occasion.

Skullcap Spell to Keep a Good Man

They say that a good man is hard to find,
So stay far away from this man of mine.
By the banishing powers of Saturn, you will move along,
You shall not ruin our love, for it is faithful, true, and strong.

Close the spell with these lines:

This loving wildflower spell is spun from the heart,
Worked for the good of all with a Green Witch's art.

skullcap

Spiderwort (*Tradescantia longipes*)

Also known as the wild crocus, spiderwort is a low-growing plant six to eight inches tall, with bright purplish blue trilobed flowers. There are also some varieties that are magenta, but blue is the most common. The flower petals are arranged in the shape of a triangle and often bloom together in small clusters. Bloom time is April and May. The leaves are grasslike with a wide crease, or vein, down the center. This plant likes acidic soils and shade to part shade in wooded slopes and valleys. Spiderwort is another easy to find and popular wildflower at most nurseries. Nursery varieties may grow taller than their wild cousins.

Spiderwort adds a little mystery and wildness to your part-shade gardens. They got their name (*wort* being an old word for "herb") because they were mistaken for another plant that was thought to cure the bite of a poisonous spider. In reality, they do not cure spider bites—and they don't attract spiders either.

In the language of flowers, the spiderwort confesses that it feels "respect but not romantic love." Magickally, spiderwort is associated with both the planet Venus and the goddess Venus/Aphrodite (as are all true blue flowers), and the

spiderwort

tripetaled spiderwort flower may be easily worked into spells for friendship and to help you gain respect from others, which can come in handy when you are applying for a new job or looking to be accepted by a new group.

Winning Acceptance from a New Group

By the three blue petals of the spiderwort plant,
I'll be accepted by this group/job that I so want.
A triangle of magick the little petals do form;
In the best possible way, their feelings toward me shall warm.

Close the spell with these lines:

This simple wildflower spell is spun from the heart,
Worked for the good of all with a Green Witch's art.

Thistle (*Cirsium vulgare*)

The thistle is part of the daisy family. This particular variety is commonly known as the bull thistle, plumed thistle, or the roadside thistle. Thistle may grow up to seven feet in height. The upper stems and branches are covered in thorns and prickles. The flower heads are pale lavender to a rose color. Bloom time is from June through September. There are many varieties of thistles, and they are easy to spot, as the spines grow right up to the flower-heads. The leaves are deeply lobed, silvery green, and hairy and spiny as well. Find these plants in fields, waste places, and roadsides.

The thistle is a common wildflower throughout North America, Europe, Asia, and North Africa. Another thistle variety, *Onopordum acanthium*, commonly called the Scotch thistle, is the national flower of Scotland. In the language of flowers, the thistle symbolizes simplicity and independence. If you grow thistles in the garden, you will encourage protection, strength, and healing.

Magickally, these plants are used to break hexes and to ward off negativity and evil. Their astrological influence is Mars, and they are aligned with the element of fire.

> **Garden Witch Tip:** Thistles do tend to volunteer in the garden from time to time. As long as you don't have small children running around, I would encourage you to let one or two grow wild in an out-of-the-way place and enjoy the protective qualities of this herbal wildflower. These wildflowers also attract goldfinches and butterflies. Thistles brought into the house from the garden are used to break spells and malevolent charms.

Breaking Hexes with Thistle

By the protective magick of thorns and prickles,
I break all hexes with the help of the thistle.
By fire's bright power all evil must flee,
And as I do will it, then so must it be!

Close the spell with these lines:

This protective wildflower spell is spun from the heart,
Worked for the good of all with a Green Witch's art.

thistle

Tickseed Coreopsis (*Coreopsis lanceolata*)

The coreopsis is part of the daisy family, and its several stems, up to three feet in height, make for a noticeable glade species. The flowers are bright yellow, with large heads about two inches across, and the ends of the petals are jagged. Bloom time runs from April through June. Leaves are narrow, undivided, and mostly arranged at the bottom of the stems. Coreopsis loves the sun, and you can find it growing in prairies, glades, and along roadsides.

Tickseed coreopsis is now widely available as a nursery plant. This perky little golden perennial attracts butterflies and brightens up many a flower garden. It is also drought tolerant, and it is the official state wildflower of Florida. When grown in the garden, they make great cut flowers, and they are not too fussy about soil types. At home in my gardens, the coreopsis blooms off and on through September, while the heaviest blooming occurs in late May through June.

In the language of flowers, the coreopsis is a symbol for a person who is always bright and cheerful. Astrological association is the sun, and the elemental association is fire. Magickally, you could work with the coreopsis for antidepression spells and to bring about good luck and better days.

tickseed coreopsis

Banishing the Blues with Coreopsis

May these bright yellow flowers brighten up my days,

Banishing the blues and chasing sadness away.

Now encourage good cheer, smiles, and laughter,

May I be content forever after.

Close the spell with these lines:

This cheerful wildflower spell is spun from the heart,

Worked for the good of all with a Green Witch's art.

Yellow Lady's Slipper (*Cypripedium pubescens*)

The yellow lady's slipper is part of the orchid family. They are rare and exotic wild orchids and can grow up to two feet tall. These flowers have brown-bronze, twisting flags, one upright and the others on either side of the yellow "slipper." There are also pink and white varieties of lady's slippers as well. Other common names for this romantic wildflower include whippoorwill's shoe, yellows, slipper root, and Indian shoe. Bloom time for this beauty is April through June. The leaves are bright green and prominently veined; the stem is long, sharply tapered, and fuzzy. The lady's slipper prefers acid soil in part shade to shade and in upper and middle elevations of north- and east-facing wooded slopes.

According to old folklore, wherever Cinderella dropped her shoe, that's where lady's slippers will grow. (Apparently Cinderella was running amok in the forests and woodlands in her ball gown.) In the language of flowers, the lady's slipper sweetly stands for a beautiful, whimsical person or capriciousness. Magickally, the energies of the lady's slipper are often worked with protection magick.

If you should find such a rare flower growing wild, consider yourself very fortunate indeed. Do not disturb the area, and leave the lady's slipper be. Just quietly enjoy the experience. The nature spirits surely must be watching over you to have given you such a gift. The lady's slipper's astrological influence is Saturn, and the elemental association is water.

Faerie Blessing with the Lady's Slipper

A rare wild orchid is the lady's slipper,

May the nature spirits hear me and come hither.

Please bless me now, with good fortune and wisdom true.

I'll always have respect for nature and for you.

Close the spell with these lines:

This faerie wildflower spell is spun from the heart,

Worked for the good of all with a Green Witch's art.

yellow lady's slipper

CLOSING THOUGHTS ON
WILDFLOWER WITCHERY

Where Cinderella dropped her shoe,
'Tis said in fairy tales of yore,
T'was there the first lady's slipper grew
And there its rosy blossom bore…

ELAINE GOODALE EASTMAN

Remember to walk softly upon the earth as you work your green magick with wildflowers. These flowers are intricately connected with the spirits of the land, and those nature spirits will be watching you carefully to see how you treat the wildflowers as you work magick with them. They are indeed little natural treasures, so value them, respect the land, and harm nothing in nature as you work your green magick to create a positive change.

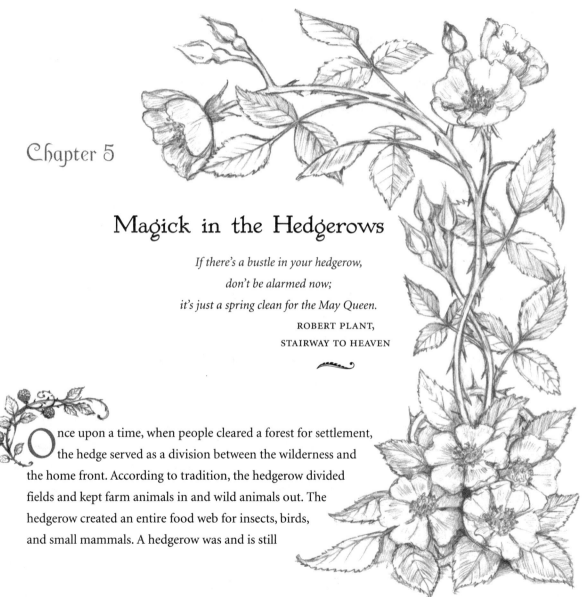

Chapter 5

Magick in the Hedgerows

If there's a bustle in your hedgerow,
don't be alarmed now;
it's just a spring clean for the May Queen.

ROBERT PLANT,
STAIRWAY TO HEAVEN

Once upon a time, when people cleared a forest for settlement, the hedge served as a division between the wilderness and the home front. According to tradition, the hedgerow divided fields and kept farm animals in and wild animals out. The hedgerow created an entire food web for insects, birds, and small mammals. A hedgerow was and is still utilized as a living boundary. The terms *hedge* and *hedgerow* come from the Anglo-Saxon words *haga*, *hege*, and *hegeroewe*, which is defined as a fence or boundary formed from a thick row of shrubs or smaller trees. Anglo-Saxon estate boundaries were usually marked with hedgerows, many of which, hundreds of years later, still designate the borders of some parishes today in Britain. There are some hedgerows that are thought to be a thousand years old.

The old hedgerows were not only planted to surround farmland and to denote the boundaries of a landowner's property, they also protected the crops and livestock and kept deer, bears, and wolves out. These hedges of shrubs, plants, and small trees were also used cleverly along waterways and wetlands to protect the fish by keeping the destructive hoofs and waste of farm animals away from shorelines, which improved the water quality for the community as well as the surrounding areas.

Now, for many of us, holding wolves and bears at bay or keeping livestock out of our water supply is not a pressing issue. However, the hedgerow is very suitable for the urban magickal gardener and for those who own small rural properties. Planting a hedgerow gives you the opportunity to work with your own native plants and to encourage biodiversity. Here is your chance to encourage wildlife such as birds and beneficial insects to come in. A hedgerow can, in fact, make a living green privacy fence with four-season interest. If your hedgerow plants are correctly chosen to work well with your particular growing conditions, such as your cold hardiness zones, and incorporate native plants, shrubs, and smaller trees, you will have a winning combination. Native plants tend to be more drought tolerant, and once established, the classic hedgerow needs very little maintenance.

Magickal Plants of the Hedgerows

The fair maiden who, the first of May,
Goes to the fields at the break of day
And washes in dew from the hawthorn tree
Will ever after handsome be.

OLD ENGLISH RHYME

Traditionally, a Witch's property or garden was thought to contain at least one hawthorn hedge. Hawthorn was not only a magickal plant of many powers, it was and is still today highly valued as the foundation plant of the hedgerows. The blackthorn, wild rose, and gorse were all popular plants that were typically utilized in the hedgerows also, as was the elder tree, the hazel, apples of several varieties, and the bramble, otherwise known as the wild blackberry.

Now, you will notice as you read farther along that all of these featured plants produce fruit, whether for human consumption or for bees, birds, and other small game. A greater variety of plants in the hedgerows only encourages and supports a broader diversity of local wildlife. The hedgerow is like a miniature ecosystem. I should also mention that native trees such as the oak, ash, and maple were also utilized in the structure of hedgerows, as were hundreds of varieties of wildflowers that volunteered or were purposefully planted to increase the hedgerow's biodiversity. The majority of the featured hedgerow plants are also full of thorns, which helped keep larger livestock and other problem animals at bay—not to mention making it tough for an adversary to get through the thorns and onto your property without injury.

As in the wildflower sections, the hedgerow plants will also be listed first by their common name, with the botanical name in italics. Why do I list the botanical names, you wonder? Well, as a gardener and magickal herbalist, botanical names are key, as they make identification exact, and in the long run, they make working with the plants easier.

> **Garden Witch Tip:** It is important to note that some of the classic hedgerow species such as the gorse and the alder buckthorn are considered noxious weeds in certain parts of the world. Check with your local conservation department or a reputable nursery for other native plant suggestions that will benefit the ecosystem. There are many options available to you.

Each of the following traditional hedgerow plants will feature a description of the leaves and fruits, a bit of folklore, any astrological correspondences, and, of course, the plant's magickal information as well. Happy spellcasting!

FEATURED HEDGEROW PLANTS

And still the dog rose shines in the hedge.
JOHN MONTAGUE

Alder Buckthorn (*Rhamnus frangula* 'Asplenifolia')

Also called the glossy buckthorn or the fern-leaf buckthorn, this European variety is an upright, spreading deciduous shrub that usually grows six to twelve feet tall and spreads six to ten feet wide. The buckthorn's glossy green leaves are quite unusual in that they are extremely narrow with irregular margins; they are often described as "long and lacy." This shrub resembles a willow and has a weeping effect in its growth characteristics. The fall color of the leaves is yellow. Clusters of tiny white-green flowers appear in the leaf axils in May. The alder buckthorn's flowers are attractive to bees but are classified as "ornamentally insignificant." These tiny flowers give way to green drupes (the fruit) that measure about a quarter of an inch in diameter. The fruit starts out green but turns red and finally black over the months of July to September. This shrub is prized for its foliage and is often utilized today as a specimen plant or grown together as a screen. The alder buckthorn is often recommended in the landscape for use as a bird-friendly hedge.

Magickally, the buckthorn was incorporated into spells for protection, and folklore states that it was also used in full moon charms cast so the Witch could be visited by the elves. Carrying a few buckthorn leaves in a charm bag is also thought to bring you good luck in court. Finally, placing buckthorn branches above your doorways and windows is supposed to render the home spellproof from outside influences. The astrological influence of this hedgerow plant is Saturn; the elemental correspondence is water.

A Buckthorn Charm Bag for Good Luck

This hedgerow charm will work best if cast during a waxing moon. As the moon grows fuller, so too will your good luck grow.

Place the fresh alder buckthorn leaves inside of a green sachet bag or use a six-inch square of green cotton fabric. Put

alder buckthorn

the leaves in the middle, pull up each corner, and tie it closed with a green ribbon for prosperity and luck. Now hold the charm bag in your hands and enchant it with the following verse:

> *These fresh green buckthorn leaves will create a charm,*
>
> *Bringing good luck in court and causing no harm.*
>
> *This good-luck hedgerow spell is spun from the heart,*
>
> *For the good of all and with a Green Witch's art.*

Tuck the charm bag in your pocket, and keep it with you for good luck.

Apple (*Pyrus malus*)

The apple tree is a tree of the Goddess. In Norse mythology, Freya dispensed golden apples to the gods so they could share in the magickal gifts of this fruit. The Celts believed that the apple tree was a good omen and that it grew in Paradise and was the keeper of all knowledge. The apple was known as the fruit of the gods, the fruit of the underworld. The old rhyme "An apple a day keeps the doctor away" comes from the belief that the apple was a magickal cure-all.

It is thought that cultivated varieties of the apple were probably introduced to Britain by the Romans. During medieval times, monastic gardens increased the varieties of apple trees by grafting shoots of the trees onto established rootstock. The wild apple is native to Europe and western Asia. It has a short trunk and can grow from twenty to forty feet high. The bark is described as grey, broken, and

apple

scaly. The apple may be found growing wild in rural and sub-rural areas, typically wherever humans have lived. The leaves of the apple are classically described as broad, flat, simple, and being of the same size. The apple tree bears clusters of five-petaled white flowers that are blushed with pink. Some modern varieties of apple trees do bear a reddish pink blossom. The blossoming time is typically April through June but will vary widely depending on the particular variety of apple. Apple blossoms represent youth, love, fertility, and enchantment. Also, apple blossoms are the state flower of Arkansas.

The fruit matures in summer and is larger than that of the crab apple. From a botanical standpoint, the fruit of the apple is called a pome. The fruit of wild apple trees average three and a half inches across, while modern varieties and cultivars measure much larger. The apple was a favorite medieval fruit, and as you would imagine, they were mainly used as a food source, eaten cooked or raw, made into sauces and jams, and included in a variety of dishes.

Inside the apple is a natural star. Slice an apple crosswise to reveal the star-shaped arrangement of the seeds. The apple fruit is often used in magick and rituals as a natural pentagram. In the language of flowers, the fruit symbolizes healing, preference, and appeal. The apple is sacred to many magickal cultures, and the wood was preferred for magickal wands and staffs. Also, it is good luck to grow an apple tree in the garden, as it marks a sacred space and will attract nature spirits and land elementals. The astrological correspondence of the tree is Venus. It is associated with the element of water.

The ABC Charm

According to folklore, if you have a sick plant in the garden, take a "perfect" apple and charm it to restore vitality to the ailing plant. Then, after you have enchanted the apple, dig a hole next to the plant and bury the apple. Legend states that as the buried apple decomposes, the other plant will be restored to health. Try working this charm during a waning moon: as the moon grows smaller, the plant's illness will diminish. To perform this charm, hold the apple in your hands, and then repeat the verse:

> *A is for the apple, so rosy, round, and fair,*
> *B is for blessing, as I speak it in the air.*
> *C is for charm, may you restore vitality,*
> *This spell is spun by the power of three times three.*

Now bury the apple; gently pat and smooth out the ground. Mark the area by drawing a pentagram in the dirt on top of the apple. Pat the soil three times, and then close the spell with these lines:

> *This plant-healing apple spell is spun from the heart,*
> *Worked for the good of all with a Green Witch's art.*

Blackthorn or Sloe (*Prunus spinosa*)

From a botanical standpoint, the blackthorn is a large shrub or a small tree of the genus *Prunus*. It is a native plant to Europe, Western Asia, and North Africa. The common name, "blackthorn," comes from the small tree's dark bark and skin and from the thorns, or spines, that it bears. The blackthorn is covered in white blossoms in early spring and is often the first tree to flower in the wild. The flowers will appear before the leaves, and the leaves are followed by the purple fruit. The blackthorn bears a dark purple fruit called the sloe.

This bitter, edible fruit is used in jellies, jams, and wines. Today, the sloe is frozen first before cooking or eating to make it more palatable. In the past, it would have been cooked into preserves, and folks would not have eaten it raw. The fruit of the blackthorn was also used to make sloe gin.

In medieval times, this was a prized "tree" for planting in hedgerows, as the thorns kept sheep and roaming cattle out of gardens. The blackthorn is still a popular plant today for hedging and for cover for game birds. Some forms are grown as ornamental specimens and of course for their flowers and bird-friendly fruits. The blackthorn blossom also draws butterflies and provides a good source of nectar for the birds in the spring.

In Irish myth, the Lunatishees—the blackthorn faeries—guard blackthorn bushes. This is a healing and a protective plant, and its astrological correspondence is Saturn.

The Blackthorn Reversal Candle Spell

If you believe that a spell was cast against you or that negative thoughtforms from an unknown person may be influencing you detrimentally, then this is the spell to help reverse the effects. This candle spell is creative and just a bit nasty. (Yes, feel free to twiddle your fingers à la Mr. Burns and purr, "Ah, excellent…") In this spell, you will be using the thorns of the blackthorn tree and inserting them into a white, unscented pillar candle.

blackthorn

This spell would be the most successful if cast in a waning moon phase on a Saturday. We are using the waning moon to diminish the effects of the other caster's negative spells, while Saturday is the day associated with Saturn and karma, and it's perfect for spell-busting. As you cast this spell, you will be calling upon the Crone Goddess and asking her to dispense her justice as she sees fit—not as you imagine it but as she deems necessary.

Take three thorns from the blackthorn tree and carefully insert the first of the three into the candle. As you insert the first thorn, speak the first line of the spell. Then intone the second line of the spell as you put in the second thorn. The third line is repeated as you insert the third thorn in the candle. Finally, light the candle and say the fourth line.

Here is the spell:

May this thorn prick your conscience and cause you to regret,

This thorn will teach you a lesson you'll never forget.

The third thorn now breaks all spells that were cast against me,

The Crone protects her children with the power of three.

Close the spell with these lines:

May this spell work out in the best possible way

With the wisdom of the Crone Goddess, come what may.

The three thorns and candle will create a reverse

Keeping me free from harm and any other curse.

Allow the candle to burn out in a safe place. When finished, dispose of any leftover wax and the thorns neatly and away from your property.

Garden Witch Tip: Should you be unable to locate a blackthorn tree, you could substitute the thorns from another hedgerow tree or plant such as the hawthorn for this reversal spell. If possible, though, work with the blackthorn.

Wild Blackberry or Bramble
(*Rubus fruticosus*)

The term *bramble* refers to thorny plants of the genus *Rubus* of the rose family (*Rosaceae*). Brambles include blackberries, raspberries, loganberries, and other similar plants. Technically, bramble fruit is the fruit of any plant of the genus *Rubus*. In the UK, the term *bramble* typically refers to the blackberry bush only, while in Scotland and the north of England, it refers to both the blackberry bush and its fruit.

Bramble bushes have a distinctive growth form. They send up long, arching canes that do not flower or set fruit until the second year of growth. Many types of brambles bear edible fruit; there are actually hundreds of microspecies. Most species of brambles have recurved thorns that will dig into clothing and, unfortunately, flesh when a person tries to pull away from them. Brambles usually have trifoliate leaves, which means that the leaves are divided, or grouped, into three leaflets. The blackberry produces a juicy purple-black fruit that is loaded with fiber and vitamin C. The fruits of the blackberry are popular for preserves as well as pies.

wild blackberry

The thorny varieties of this plant are sometimes grown for game cover in hedgerows and occasionally for protection. Most species of the blackberry are important for conserving the local native wildlife habitat. The flowers of the blackberry also are useful, as they attract pollinators such as butterflies and bees.

Blackberries were typically not grown as a garden plant because they were so plentiful in the wild. Today there are varieties that are very suitable for a home garden—just be sure to keep them under control, as they will spread and are considered to be aggressive. The blackberry had connections with many different gods, including the Celtic goddess Brigid. Their astrological influence is Venus, and the elemental association is water. Magickally, blackberry fruits, flowers, and leaves are used for healing, money, and protection spells. This is considered a favored faerie plant that helped keep humans out of faerie forts and rafts (where they were never supposed to be).

A Healing Charm with Blackberry

According to old folk magick, the blackberry leaves were a remedy for minor burns but were thought to be their most powerful when accompanied with a healing charm that was repeated three times. Here is a witchy version of the healing charm; hold your hands directly over the burn, and repeat the charm:

> *Three ladies came from the east,*
>
> *One brought fire, two brought frost.*
>
> *Out, fire, and in, frost,*
>
> *In the name of the Maiden, Mother, and Crone.*

Please use your Witch's common sense and have serious burns treated by a medical professional. Use the healing charm in conjunction with good medical care.

Elder or Elderberry (*Sambucus canadensis*)

The elder is technically classified as a shrub, and it is part of the honeysuckle family. This shrub produces thicket-forming root runners with many stems and may grow up to ten feet in height. The flowers bloom May through July and are formed in umbrella-shaped clusters that are described as being delicately scented. The tree produces edible fruit that is often made into jellies or wine. Birds and animals also enjoy the elderberry. The elderberry habitat includes fencerows, ditches, and waste places.

The elder is sacred to many Mother and Crone Goddesses. It was considered to be the ultimate insult to the Goddess to burn the wood of an elder tree. Elder wood was never to be cut from a living tree, nor was it to be burned as firewood, which goes along with the old folk rhyme, "Elder is the Lady's tree; burn it not, or cursed you'll be."

The elder flowers and wood were used in many types of magick, including protection, removing curses, prosperity, and healing; tucking the berries beneath your pillow is thought to help promote a good night's sleep, not to mention giving you a purple pillowcase come morning. Another elder charm included bringing bare (fallen) branches indoors and then hanging them up over doorways to ward your home. According to the language of flowers, the elderberry brings gentleness, sympathy, and passion. The elder's planetary influence is Venus, and the elemental association is water.

elderberry

Elderberry Protective Charm

Gather a bunch of fresh purple elderberries and adorn them with a red satin ribbon. Then hang the little bouquet up in the front window of your home and allow it to dry. This will add another layer of protection to the other shielding and warding spells you already have in place. You may work this spell on a Saturday (Saturn's day) to tap into the closing energies of the week and the banishing influences of the day. Or you could also work on a Friday, a Venus day, to promote love and peace around your home.

As you place the bouquet, repeat this protection charm:

With a red satin ribbon, I hang these berries,

No evil shall enter, no bad luck will tarry.

Elder is the Lady's tree of power,

Protect my home well in every hour.

Close the spell with these lines:

This protective berry spell is spun from the heart,

Worked for the good of all with a Green Witch's art.

Common Gorse (*Ulex europaeus*)

Common names include furse and Irish furze. Gorse is an evergreen spiny shrub and common hedging plant that may grow up to fifteen feet in height. It was often used to enclose and to protect livestock from predators. The branches of this plant end in a spine and are covered with green prickly leaves that range from a half inch to two inches in length. The flowers of the gorse are described as showy. They are yellow pealike flowers, about a half-inch long, and they grow in clumps near the tips of its branches and have a coconut scent. The hard seeds are brown, small, and shiny. They are enclosed in half-inch long, hairy seed pods.

> **Garden Witch Tip:** It is important to note that today, gorse is considered by some to be a noxious weed. Gorse has been identified as a "major weed of agriculture and forestry" in places such as Hawaii and the West Coast of the United States, New Zealand, Spain, Tasmania, and Australia. So before adding this plant to your gardens, check to make sure it is not considered a threat to your area. It is a very aggressive plant, which is a nice way of saying it spreads, or takes over, very quickly.

In the old days, it was said that the spines of the plant were sometimes used to hang the wash out to dry, and the thorns kept the laundry from blowing away! If it was planted around the property, gorse was also thought to keep naughty faeries away from the home. Gorse is in bloom almost year-round in Britain, with the heaviest bloom period being in the spring. Gorse makes an excellent cover for birds. In the language of flowers, gorse stands for "engaging affection." The astrological association for gorse is Mars. Its elemental correspondence is fire. Magickal uses include protection and prosperity. The flowers are utilized in money spells to attract gold.

common gorse

Attracting Prosperity with Gorse

For best results, work this spell on a Mar's day, a Tuesday, and work in a waxing moon phase for increase. Place a gold-colored pillar candle in a fireproof holder, then arrange gorse blossoms around its base. (Make sure you keep the plant material away from the flame.) Now, take a few moments and visualize practical ways that you can increase your prosperity. When you feel ready, repeat the charm:

> *By the power of fire, this spell brings transformation,*
>
> *With a little help from gorse and my own inspiration.*
>
> *Now bring money and success, in the best possible way,*
>
> *With just a touch of hedge magick, this will brighten my day.*

Close the spell with these lines:

> *This hedge prosperity spell is spun from the heart,*
>
> *Worked for the good of all with a Green Witch's art.*

Allow the candle to burn out in a safe place. Return the plant material neatly to nature by adding it to your yard waste or compost pile.

Dog Rose (*Rosa canina*)

Sometimes this plant is simply called rosehips. It has several colorful folk names such as rose briar, dogberry, herb patience, sweet briar, and Witches' briar. This wild rose is grown not only for the pretty pink blossoms but for the bright red fruits, the hips, that it produces in autumn. This rose is native to Europe, Northwest Africa, and Western Asia. The dog rose is a deciduous shrub that can range in height from three to twenty feet tall. The rose may climb even higher if it has the support of a nearby tree. The dog rose's stems are covered in small, sharp hooked "spines"—which help the rose to climb, or ramble, up anything in its path. The leaves are oval and pointed, featuring five to seven leaflets.

The flowers have five petals, and their color can range from the palest pink to deep pink and white. After blooming, the flower's center matures into the hip. In the autumn, this plant really shines as the hips turn a beautiful deep red.

This plant was sacred to the Goddess, as the five petals of the flower formed her star. The plant was also protected by the faeries. Fallen wild rose petals may be added to spells and charms to speed up the results. The rose hips were and still are today used in spells and charms to promote love. As with other roses featured in this book, the astrological correspondence is Venus, and the elemental association is water.

Rosehip and Petal Sachet
to Encourage Romance

For this hedge magick, you will need the fresh petals and the hips of the dog rose. For best results, try working this spell on a Friday, the day sacred to Venus, Aphrodite, and Freya, all goddesses of love and romance. Place the petals and the rosehips together into a six-inch square of natural fabric, and pull up the edges of the fabric, creating a small bundle. Then tie the sachet closed with a red ribbon, and knot it three times, saying:

dog rose

By the Maiden, Mother, and the Crone,

Bless this sachet I made on my own.

Now visualize romance coming into your life. Do not focus on a specific someone—that would be considered manipulation. Instead, focus on the idea of romance and love increasing in your life in the best possible way. Let the magick unfold on its own. Now hold the sachet bag in your hands, and enchant and empower the sachet with the following verse:

The rose is a flower of the Goddess divine,

The fruits of the rose are hips, and they are sublime.

Now place them together in a pouch and bind with red ribbon,

The Witch's rose and its fruits allow the romance to begin.

Close the spell with these lines:

This romantic, rosy spell is spun from the heart,

Worked for the good of all with a Green Witch's art.

Tuck the sachet into your pocket or purse, and carry it with you. Get ready to become more aware of new opportunities for romance.

Garden Witch Tip: If you are interested in the specifics of love and romance magick or just want more ideas and tips on this particular spellcasting topic, then please refer to my book *How to Enchant a Man: Spells to Bewitch, Bedazzle & Beguile.*

rosehips

Hawthorn (*Crataegus mollis*)

This tree takes its botanical name, *Crataegus*, from the Greek "flowering thorn." The hawthorn is a member of the rose family. Some of its folk names include May flower, summer haw, hagthorn, bread and cheese tree, and May blossom. The *haw* in hawthorn translates to "hedge," which is how the fruiting tree got its name: it was the "fruit of the hedge." These smaller trees can grow fifteen to twenty feet tall, and their boughs are covered in large, curving thorns. It blooms April through May, and its flowers are similar to apple blossoms. They are white with five petals and have many stamens. The flower of the hawthorn tree is the state flower of Missouri. The fruit is abundant and scarlet colored and about a half inch in diameter. The fruit ripens in the fall, typically August through September, although other varieties of hawthorns may not ripen until October or November.

hawthorn

The hawthorn tree and its foliage were ancient symbols of hope and protection. During medieval times, cuttings were brought into homes to ward off evil spirits. On an interesting note, it is rumored that the ancient Romans placed hawthorn branches in the boudoir to bless the marriage bed. The hawthorn's astrological correspondence is Mars. The elemental association is fire.

A Springtime Hawthorn Marriage Spell

This spell may be worked in any moon phase. Carefully gather a small sprig of blooming hawthorn. Arrange the twig in a vase, and then set it in a place of prominence in the bedroom. Allow the natural energies of protection and hope to fill the room. This hedgerow magick may be enhanced with the following verse:

> *The hawthorn blesses marriages, and hope now fills this room,*
> *Using hedge magick and the power of a branch in bloom.*
> *This romantic hawthorn spell is spun from the heart,*
> *Worked for the good of all with a Green Witch's art.*

Allow the blooming twig to stay in the vase until it begins to fade. When it does, dispose of the twig neatly in a compost pile. Don't forget to wash out the vase before storing it away.

Wild Crab (*Malus ioensis* or *Pyrus ioensis*)

The wild crab is a smaller tree that may occasionally reach up to thirty feet in height. There are over ninety varieties of crab apples. Unlike the modern cultivars, the wild crab apple was originally a thorn-bearing tree, which made it an ideal specimen for the hedgerow. The bloom time for the crab is April through May; the flowers will bloom as the tree leaves begin to open. Flowers are showy and borne in clusters of three to six along the branches of the tree. They are a deep rosy pink or white blossom with five petals each. The fruit of the wild crab is small, green, and applelike. While the fruits are very fragrant,

wild crab

this particular variety of wild crab is unpleasant tasting and not desirable for human consumption. However, those crab apples are a treat for songbirds and other wildlife.

When I was a girl, my parents had a classic crab apple tree in our backyard. Come summertime, it dropped little "apples" all over the yard—which the birds, squirrels, insects, and bees loved. I was tricked into eating a crab apple by my father—once. Talk about nasty! However, my grandmother swore that the fruits could be made into jams. Today, if you scout around, there are recipes all over the Internet on crab apple jelly, and they all call for copious amounts of sugar to sweeten up those bitter fruits.

Some modern guides to making hedgerows call the wild crab "important for numerous species of birds and small mammals." The wild crab apple grows naturally in open woods, fields, hedgerows, pastures, and streamside. Astrological correspondences are the same as for the traditional apple tree: the planetary influence is Venus, and the elemental correspondence is water.

> **Garden Witch Tip:** The wild crab (*Malus ioensis*) is not the blooming crab tree that you typically find today at the nursery or home improvement store's garden center. Most of the blooming crab trees that are available these days have been extensively hybridized for landscaping and the home gardener such as the popular Brandywine variety *Malus* 'Branzam'. These newer varieties of trees bloom very heavily in the spring and come in flower shades of purple-red and pink, and there are also white varieties as well. The "fruit" of the modern crab apple is tiny and almost unnoticeable. Those miniature fruits from the hybridized trees are still attractive to birds, though, so if this is what you already have growing in the yard, no worries. And best of all, you won't go stepping on old, fallen crab apples and having them squish up between your bare toes in the summertime.

The Crab Apple Spell

Is your love a bit crabby at the moment? Want to sweeten them up and restore their good mood? Try working with the foliage and fruit of the crab apple tree. You may work this spell in a waning moon to decrease their sour mood. Or you could work in the waxing moon and increase the love and restore the happiness that you share as a couple. You can also work on a Friday, a Venus day. It's your choice, and you always have options when it comes to spellcasting.

Gather a few leaves from the crab apple and a couple of the small fruits. Place them carefully around a pink spell candle a few inches away from the base of the candleholder in a ring. The pink candle is used in this spell to encourage romance and warm, fuzzy feelings. Please make sure you keep the foliage well away from the flames, and then light the candle and repeat the following charm:

> *With a rosy pink spell candle burning so bright,*
>
> *Your mood will now improve on this enchanted night.*
>
> *Your sour mood is drawn to the sour fruit of the crab apple tree,*
>
> *With harm to none and for the good of all, as I will, so mote it be.*

Allow the spell candle to burn out in a safe place. Neatly return the foliage to nature by adding it to your yard waste or compost pile, and remember to thank the crab apple tree for the use of its fruit and foliage.

A WALKER BETWEEN THE WORLDS

We live between two worlds; we soar in the
atmosphere; we creep upon the soil…
W. WINWOOD READE

A Witch is a person who walks between the physical world and the astral world. To spend all of their time in either world would make them disconnected from the magick or hold them separate from reality. So, in essence, they easily and happily travel back and forth between the two. For example, Witches may spend their mornings contentedly working in the garden, and be at their job in the afternoon and evening, but they may fill the later evening hours with study, meditation, and spellcraft. This ability to successfully work and live in both worlds is the hallmark of any adept Witch.

There is also a school of thought that says a Hedge Witch straddles the two worlds, and in so doing, the Witch becomes a bridge, or link, between them—in other words, they are "riding the hedge." Visualize this as the Hedge Witch connecting the physical world of nature and green magick with the astral planes, or the spirit world. The hedge itself is a metaphor and a division between the physical world and the world of spirit, while the Hedge Witch becomes the divine connection between the two.

Who Are the Hedge Witches?

When a thing ceases to be a subject of controversy,
it ceases to be a subject of interest.
WILLIAM HAZLITT

The term *Hedge Witch* is a controversial one; let's not pretend otherwise. If you do a search on the Internet and look up "Hedge Witch," you'll find a plethora of opinions, ideas, and definitions. At its most basic explanation, a Hedge Witch is often described as a solitary practitioner who works their magick, using herbs and green magick, quietly and in harmony with the land. The current term "Hedge Witch" was coined by the British author Rae Beth. It's somewhat the British equivalent to being a solitary, self-trained practitioner here in the States today.

However, if you ask several Witches what a Hedge Witch is, you'll very likely get completely different answers. As I researched this topic, I found many different characterizations and opinions on this kind of Witch, but what really caught my attention was the popularity of the term. It seems that everywhere I looked, the term Hedge Witch was popping up—on the Internet, in a lovely article in a magickal calendar, and in more and more magickal books.

An acquaintance of mine, who is a rabid reader and science fiction fan, casually informed me that the term Hedge Witch was a popular term in science fiction/ fantasy novels. He then told me the term denoted a magickal practitioner who was not formally trained. They lived on the outskirts of town or on the edge of the woods and practiced their magick alone and spontaneously with whatever supplies they could gather.

Ah-ha! I pounced on that idea. Practicing magick quietly, with only some down-to-earth and simple items supplied by nature … using plants and your instinct, voice, heart, and two hands to create your spirituality … well, hello. I've been writing about that magickal subject for years now. *Hmmm* … I was off and running.

However, calling oneself a Hedge Witch is a title that either makes a person feel right at home or it makes them argue passionately about what they believe the term truly means. If you do a little digging and research the term, you find some very interesting definitions on this brand of witchery from some of the most respected writers on the Craft today.

Wiccan author Raymond Buckland, in his book *The Witch Book,* claims that a Hedge Witch doesn't use complicated rituals and may not always become involved with the religious aspect of Witchcraft.

In *The New Encyclopedia of the Occult,* author John Michael Greer defines a Hedge Witch in this way: "In modern Paganism, a term used by and for solitary Witches whose practices incorporate large amounts of natural magic, herb lore, and similar subjects, and who generally do not claim a connection with any particular tradition."

Other practitioners believe that a Hedge Witch is a Witch who focuses on more shamanic practices. In Raven Grimassi's book *The Encyclopedia of Wicca and Witchcraft,* he defines a Hedge Witch as an eclectic and self-taught solitary practitioner—a person who typically works with a familiar spirit, herbal magick, trance, and shamanic practices such as drumming to create altered states of consciousness. In Grimassi's characterization, a Hedge Witch only uses natural and very simple supplies for their magickal purposes.

So, with all the fuss about politically correct titles, what is a Witch to do? Truthfully, you are going to have to decide for yourself what suits you the best. There are many paths to the

Craft and to understanding the mysteries. A few of these paths fall under the category of green magick and hearth and home magick.

If you take a good look at all of these different accounts of what a Hedge Witch is, you begin to see that while there is a difference of opinion, there are also many points that are agreed upon. A Hedge Witch is an enigma, and sometimes the best way to gain knowledge of a topic is to study the mystery and consider all the possibilities. Then, as you begin to comprehend its complexities, you start to gain wisdom, and you are, in fact, teaching yourself something new. With that in mind, let's take a deeper look at the magick of the Hedge Witch.

HEDGE WITCH MAGICK

Hedge Witch: a solitary Witch, answering to no one,
belonging to no coven; claiming the right to be
what she or he was born to be—magical.

RAE BETH, *THE WICCAN WAY*

Our modern Hedge Witch practice is a holdover from olden times, when to openly practice Witchcraft was a dangerous thing. However, these very down-to-earth practitioners kept a low profile. They went about the business of tending a home and raising a family. Spirituality was earthy, natural, and a part of their everyday life. The use of everyday items as magickal tools was clever and practical. If all of their magickal tools were hidden as mundane, everyday household accruements, they blended in and were safe.

For example, the one good kitchen knife was also the magickal knife. The broom that was used to sweep the floors clean was the ceremonial magickal staff. The cauldron used for cooking stews, soups, and meals was also the magick cauldron for brews and potions. The herbs drying from the beams in the ceiling, the flowers and plants growing in the garden—everything that a Hedge Witch put his or her hands on with intention was magick. Any item in their home or garden could be sacred—and their homes would have been dedicated to the practitioner's personal gods of hearth and home.

It seems to me that the term Hedge Witch is definitely in vogue. Fifteen years ago, these types of magicians would have been referred to as Kitchen Witches, and they do share many things in common. Both the Hedge and Kitchen Witches are hearth and home practitioners. These folks are no-nonsense, practice a green or nature-based spirituality, and, most importantly, they work natural magick in a practical way with the plants, supplies, and tools that they have on hand.

So using a bit of the Hedge Witch's practicality, let's not get into such a lather about what the title means. Instead, let's enjoy what wonderful, down-to-earth magick and natural enchantments the green practice of the Hedge Witch can share with us.

Green spirituality is a foundation of the Craft. Green is the color of nature and the plant kingdom, and it is the color of life. When we are intimately connected with nature, our spirituality blossoms, and we grow. If you want the chance to spread out and stretch your comprehension of the Craft, then take a real look at the natural world. Spend some time in nature. Plant a garden, or grow pots of herbs on your porch. Go camping, go on a boat trip, or take a walk in the park. Get outside! Because that is where you will find the true advanced lessons.

Everyone is always searching for "advanced" topics and "advanced" books. But what they do not realize is that the advanced spiritual lessons are not held within the pages of a book. The book can guide you and point you down the path, or in my case, this Garden Witch's book is waving its imaginary arms at you like crazy and is pointing frantically outside—it's okay, you can take this guide book with you. Just go outside. However, at the end of the day, each Witch must make the journey out into nature on their own.

It is vital for every Witch to walk their spiritual path all by themselves and for themselves. This is why the enchanting topics of the garden, the trees, and the hedgerow are such important ones. So now I have to ask you: what have you learned so far? Do you believe that you are ready to grow and learn a little more? If so, then go ahead and stroll right into the green world, and look around. Dare to add a bit of the traditional magick of the hedgerow to your herbal magick and to your craft.

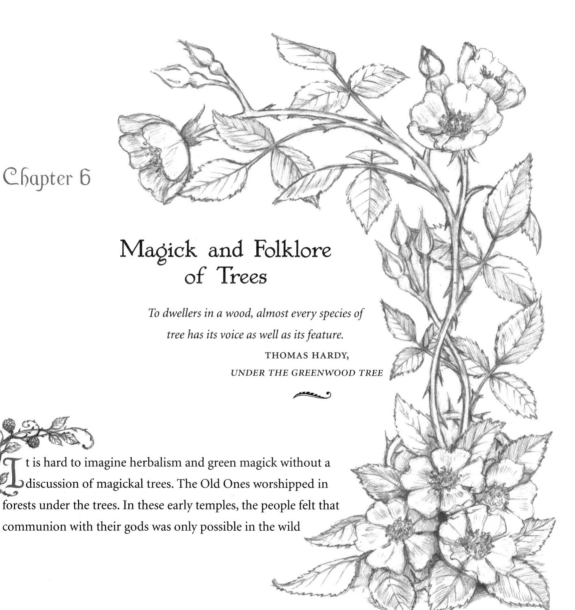

Chapter 6

Magick and Folklore of Trees

*To dwellers in a wood, almost every species of
tree has its voice as well as its feature.*

THOMAS HARDY,
UNDER THE GREENWOOD TREE

It is hard to imagine herbalism and green magick without a discussion of magickal trees. The Old Ones worshipped in forests under the trees. In these early temples, the people felt that communion with their gods was only possible in the wild places in areas away from other people. The land itself held a magickal importance. These natural, sacred spots were called nemetons.

Both the ancient Greeks and the Celts worshiped in sacred groves called *nemetoi*. These spaces were identified as clearings open to the sky and were reserved in the woodland and considered to be magickal places, held in awe by the people. Goddesses such as Nemetona and Arnemetia were the deities of these sacred groves.

The word *nemeton* means a circular clearing in the woods or a mystical, mysterious sanctuary. This was an in-between place; sometimes a spring or stream rolled within or close by the grove. The groves could consist of many types of magickal trees, or perhaps it was a stand of all the same species. Some of the trees in the groves were probably rowan, birch, elm, ash, and oak.

It is believed that these natural groves attracted nature spirits and local land devas to them. You can select your favorite place in nature as your personal nemeton—a secluded spot in a secret area of your garden, beneath a favorite tree, or alongside a natural body of water. Ageless elemental powers reside in the woodlands, and they are hidden in the urban areas as well. While they are tougher to find in the cities and urban areas, their magickal powers are more fierce there. Why? Trees must be tough to survive and to thrive in an urban area. Those who search for these energies will indeed come into contact with them in any place in nature—in the park, under a tree growing along the sidewalk, or in a natural woodland. Remember that when you embrace nature and all of her sacred places, nature then gives you the chance to heal and to reconnect. It makes us feel happier, and our green magick becomes revitalized. Then, finally, our spiritual connection to the Old Ones and to nature is reestablished.

THE GROVES:
CLOSER THAN YOU THINK

The groves were God's first temples.

WILLIAM CULLEN BRYANT

What exactly do I mean by a sacred grove? The Latin word for *sacred* gives us the word *sanctuary*—a word describing not only a sacred site but also a place of shelter and protection. A grove is defined as a small wood or a lush green niche found within a woodland or a great forest. A grove may be discovered alongside natural bodies of water, at the borders of creeks and streams. A grove may even be created within your own backyard—a personal sanctuary of sorts. This can be anywhere you like, tucked under older trees and between tall shrubs or sheltered within a modern hedgerow. By allowing a little corner of your property to grow somewhat wild, you can create a secret, sacred garden for yourself and the animals and birds. In other words, a sacred grove.

Now, some folks are happy enough just standing back and looking at the trees in the yard, the park, or the forest. They might breathe deeply and look around in awe at the natural beauty that surrounds them and sit for a while to read or meditate or eat their lunch. Later, when they leave, they usually feel lighter and happier. Other people may find peace and contentment strolling along a shady, secluded, leafy garden path. They might be inspired or relaxed by the natural loveliness that they encounter, but other than enjoying the scenery, what do you suppose they really learn?

Many of the great naturalists of our time—Henry David Thoreau, Ralph Waldo Emerson, John Muir, and even Theodore Roosevelt—believed that the forests and woodlands were sacred places that beneficially influenced the spirit. Why do you suppose that herbs, flowers, and trees have such a soothing, uplifting, and cheerful influence on us? Maybe it is because they so completely change the natural ambiance that surrounds them. Take an hour out of your hectic life and blow off some steam by strolling around the local park. Toss a blanket on the grass in the backyard and watch the sunlight filter down through the leaves. Try walking among the local trees and quietly talking to them, and see what lessons they may have for you. I imagine that you too will feel lighter and happier if you reconnect to nature. Do you suppose it is possible that plants and nature could be spiritual and magickal filters? You bet they are.

The average person usually lacks the desire to look closer at the secret places of nature where the far greater mysteries lie. As green magick practitioners and Witches, we more than anyone will need to look a bit deeper at nature, listen a little harder to the flora and fauna, and pay attention to all of our senses while we are outdoors. For those practitioners who want to explore their green spirituality further and who want to expand their magickal abilities to the advanced or to an adept level, they can begin this process by acknowledging the very spiritual side of the natural world. Look to the trees.

TREE WISDOM

I went to the woods because I wished to live deliberately, to front only the
essential facts of life, and see if I could learn what it had to teach…
HENRY DAVID THOREAU

A tree can, in fact, be a tangible manifestation for the old Craft adage, "As above, so below." The tree may be considered a sort of magickal bridge between heaven and earth, as it is rooted to the earth but reaches for the sky. Throughout history, trees have been considered sacred and honored because they were the tallest and most lasting of all living organisms. Trees have embellished and blessed homes and gardens with their beauty, structure, and shelter. Trees have provided us with bark and foliage that yield various dyes to add color to cloth and produce flavoring for food or herbal medicines for the sick. Trees interact dynamically with the environment, as they produce oxygen for the planet and provide both food and shelter for wildlife as well as humans.

In the woods and forests, a naturally occurring circle of trees was considered a primitive and sacred grove. Stands of elms and oaks and junipers were protected and cherished. These natural groves were sacred and holy places where people could gather and pay homage to the old gods of forest and stream. Indeed, even the trees' leaves and blooming branches were and are used to celebrate the holidays, observe the changing seasons, and decorate religious altars.

The old folk healers, the herbalists, and the wise women and men were the first to discover and utilize the potent magick of the trees. Deep in the forests and alongside springs and streams, they gathered their barks, berries, herbs, and plants and worked their wonders.

Some herbal trees and plants were encouraged to grow on the healer's property. These early gardens contained plants for medicine and plants for magick. The common folk did not dare to disturb these gardens, for only the wise ones knew for certain which plants brought comfort and healing and which plants could bring about suffering and death.

Tree magick is a sensory type of enchantment that is available to you all year long. See the pristine blooms of the rowan and hawthorn declare joy and wonder as the earth renews herself each spring. Listen for the wisdom in the quiet rustle of ash leaves on a warm summer evening. During the fall months, you can catch a glimpse of a tree's humor as acorns drop down upon you, full and ripe, from the branches of old sentinel oaks brushed with a brilliant fall color. During the winter, it is the trees who remind us that life does indeed go on, for the holly, pine, and spruce are still luxuriously green and fragrant.

The old wise ones are whispering to us even now. Are you listening? It only takes an open mind and an accepting heart to hear them. As we delve deeper into the folklore, myth, and magick of the natural world, the greatest tools that a Witch can possess is an open heart and an open mind. The imagination can be a wonderful gift from the mind, and your instincts are an endowment from the old gods to your heart.

Take a walk in the park or the woods. Get to know the trees growing close to your home. While you are taking note of the various species of trees, be sure to look up at those beautiful leaves, gaze at the landscape around you, and cast all of your senses outward. Green magick and witchery surrounds you at all times, and its natural energies are present each and every day of the year. And here is a prime example of that year-long wonder: the trees and plants of the Celtic year.

THE CALENDAR OF CELTIC TREES

Of all the trees that grow so fair,
Old England to adorn,
Greater are none beneath the sun,
Than oak, and ash, and thorn.

RUDYARD KIPLING

The following herbal trees and plants marked out the thirteen months, or moons, of the old Celtic year. A few of these magickal trees were also featured in our hedgerow chapter as well. A few of the "trees" of the year are not trees at all—such as the ivy, the vine, and the reed.

Each of the following trees or plants is listed along with its approximate calendar dates. The tree's botanical name, folklore, deity associations, and magickal information will follow. At the end of the information is the Celtic name for the featured plant. There are magickal information and ideas for each plant, so you can try your hand at conjuring up some green magick of your very own design. See how much of this green, leafy magick you can add into your life and your craft.

Birch (*Betula* spp.)
December 24–January 20

The birch tree symbolizes the rebirth of the sun at the winter solstice. The beautiful white bark of the birch makes it a very popular wood for Yule logs. This tree symbolizes new beginnings. The goddess Arianrhod was petitioned for her aid in childbirth and initiations by way of the birch tree. In Norse mythology, Thor, Frigga, and Freya were all linked to the birch tree as well.

In olden times, hanging birch branches inside of your home was thought to protect you from infertility, the evil eye, and lightning. The silver birch, a popular wood for a woman's ceremonial broomstick, is sometimes called the "lady of the woods." This is a feminine tree and one of enchantments. The elementary association for the birch tree is water, and the planetary ruler is Venus. In some traditions, the birch is linked with a Maiden Goddess such as Eostre. This Anglo-Saxon goddess was celebrated as the birch leaves grew from her time of the Spring Equinox until Beltane.

The birch is associated with faerie magick and Beltane, for the trees were popularly used as Maypoles. In addition, the birch has been linked with the sabbats of Samhain and Lughnasadh, the final and the first harvest festivals, respectively. In some northern countries, the leafing out of the birch tree signals the start of the agricultural year, but in truth, the magickal birch is venerated practically year-round. The Irish name for the birch is Beith.

birch

Rowan (*Sorbus aucuparia*)

January 21–February 17

The rowan is also known as mountain ash and is a sacred tree for all earth religions. Some old folk names for the rowan are quickbeam and quicken. A rowan growing near a stone circle was believed to be especially protective and powerful. Rowan tree day is celebrated on May 3. The Celtic goddess Brigid was associated with the rowan tree, which makes sense, as the sabbat Imbolc/Candlemas (also known as Brigid's Day) is celebrated during this Celtic month on February 2. Brigid, a triple goddess of fire, smithcraft, and poetry, is still a wildly popular goddess with modern Witches.

All parts of the rowan are utilized in magick: the leaves, blooms, twigs, and berries. The berries are especially sought after by song-birds. In the garden, the rowan, or mountain ash, is a small tree that has four-season interest, from the springtime blooms to the lush green summer foliage. In the fall, it shows off golden scarlet leaves and finally produces red berries for the birds in the winter.

The rowan has the planetary association of the sun and the elementary correspondence of fire. As a tree of old magick, and considering its protective qualities, the fire association seems appropriate. Groves of rowans were preserved and protected as visionary sanctuaries. The rowan/mountain ash is a Druid's tree and one of the holy trees of the ancient Celtic forests. It is rumored that the faeries may adopt a solitary rowan tree, taking it over as

rowan

a home and a sort of magickal safe house. Any earth magick can be enhanced by working beneath a rowan tree or by fashioning a wand out of a fallen branch. Other associated sabbats include Lughnasadh, Beltane, and Midsummer. The Irish name for the rowan is Luis.

Ash (*Fraxinus excelsior*)
February 18–March 17

The ash is part of the faerie trinity of trees (the oak, ash, and thorn). The ash is rumored to be a tree of enchantment and is a very suitable wood for a wand or staff, as it is a strong, supple wood. In Norse mythology, the ash plays a significant role. The sacred ash tree Yggdrasil was the divine frame that supported the entire world. It was a tree of life and also a popular tree with the faeries. It is thought that if you make a heartfelt request for healing and protection and tie a strand of your own hair onto the branch of an ash tree, the faeries will grant your request. This tree is associated with Woden, Thor, Neptune/Poseidon, and the Greek goddess Nemesis, who was thought to carry an ash branch as a symbol of divine justice.

The ash is associated with the element of water, and its planetary ruler is the sun. Carrying ash twigs fashioned together in a solar cross was thought to protect you from accidents on the water. (If you own a boat, perhaps you could tuck the amulet somewhere inside of the boat.) The element of water relates to emotions and psychic gifts. If you place an ash leaf beneath your pillow, it is said to encourage psychic abilities and cause prophetic dreams.

ash

The leaves of the ash tree may be used as an offering while you cast a circle. As you call each quarter, scatter a handful of ash leaves to the winds. By doing this, you tap into the vast elemental powers of the trees and the earth. Wands made from ash wood are used for healing, prosperity, and protection. Displaying a staff made out of ash at the entrance of your home, perhaps hung over the inside front door, wards the home from negativity and theft.

Also, placing an ash leaf at each of the four corners of your home was thought to help protect your home from unwanted astral visitors and manipulative magick. It also denotes a magickal safe house. Its Irish name is Nuin.

Alder (*Alnus glutinosa*)
March 18–April 14

The alder tree is reported to be popular with the undines and water spirits. A tree native to Europe, the alder is an unusual tree in that it is the only broadleaf tree that bears cones. The alder is often linked to the willow, as they are both water-loving trees and were thought to bless pools and springs by growing nearby. The alder is associated with beginnings, birth, and healing. It has links to mystical white faerie horses and to the unicorn. An alder was also a way to gain access to the faerie lands.

An old alder spell was to place a leaf in each shoe when traveling. This was thought to cause the faeries to bless you while on your journey. Try casting alder leaves at each quarter of your circle on the eve of the Spring Equinox, or the festival of Ostara, if you care to try to communicate with the faeries. Please remember to thank the nature spirits when you have finished your ritual, and leave

alder

them a small token such as a crystal point or a small, plain cake (in other words, a cookie). In the Italian tradition, the alder is associated with spring fire festivals.

Alder's further correlations with the element of fire may seem contrary, and they are a little intense. In old Ireland, it was believed that if you purposely cut down an alder, it would cause your house to burn down. The alder has links to the god Bran, a beloved Pagan god whose totem animal was the raven. The raven is a bird of wisdom whose appearance often signifies change.

The alder is ruled by the planet Venus. It is also associated with the autumnal equinox and the sabbat of Samhain. The element of water is associated with the western direction as well as the season of autumn, as the west is the direction of the setting sun, the waning year, and the direction of the Summerland. The Irish name for the alder tree is Fearn.

Willow (*Salix* spp.)
April 15–May 12

A willow is a tree of the element of water and is ruled by the moon. It is incorporated into lunar magick, prophecy, healing, and women's mysteries. The wood of the willow makes a powerful healing wand for a woman. There are many goddesses associated with the willow tree such as Hecate, Lilith, Persephone, Morgana, and Cerridwen. The sorceress Circe was thought to have cared for a cemetery planted with the willow and dedicated to Hecate. Hecate, the only Titan who kept her powers after Zeus took over, was a willow and dark moon goddess. This three-faced goddess guarded the crossroads, and it was believed that when dogs howled at night, they were answering Hecate's call. Hecate is a powerful deity to call upon, for she rules the earth, the sky, and the sea—all three magickal realms. The willow tree, Hecate's tree, has been a popular tree for magick and enchantments for centuries.

The strongest times of the year for working willow tree magick would be at the full moons and the sabbats of Beltane and Samhain, those two nights when the veil between the physical world and the spirit world is the thinnest. Working with willow leaves or burning them on a bonfire at Samhain was thought to call spirits forth. While this is an intriguing notion, be sure that you are working within a cast circle and that you actually know how to send a spirit back to the other side before you try this. (If you're not sure, then leave this type of magick alone.) Remember who is associated with the willow, after all; if you work with Hecate carelessly, you'll get more than your fingers slapped. Consider yourself warned.

On a lighter note, it was thought that if you gently tap your knuckles on the trunk of the tree three times, it would ward off bad luck: "Knock on wood." The faeries are also linked to this tree, and you should feel their presence if you meditate under a willow tree on Beltane eve. An old charm is to stand under a willow's weeping branches and gaze up at the full moon. Make an unselfish wish, and then gently tie a loose knot in the supple branch of the willow tree. Breathe upon it, and blow a kiss to the moon. Your request is sure to be granted. Its Irish name is Saille.

willow

Hawthorn (*Crataegus* spp.)

May 13–June 9

The hawthorn is the second part of the faerie trinity of trees. The hawthorn represents the element of fire and is ruled by the planet Mars. This tree stands for magickal secrets, fertility, and eternal life. The hawthorn also made an appearance in our hedgerow chapter. This tree in its many varieties is a wild and bewitching tree. Some folk names include whitethorn and may. An amulet to protect against fire can be made from the twigs of a hawthorn tree; bind the twigs together with red thread into the shape of a pentagram, then hang up the star in the kitchen with a white ribbon. This will protect against household fires. An early hawthorn goddess was Olwen. Wherever this goddess walked, white flowers would spring up beneath her feet. Because of this, she was called Olwen of the white track, or path.

It was thought that if you gathered together hawthorn blooms and sat quietly and serenely beneath the tree on any of the following evenings—Beltane Eve, summer solstice, or Samhain—your patience would be rewarded by a visit from the nature spirits and the faeries. The blooms from the hawthorn were fashioned into garlands and swags for celebrations as well as bridal bouquets. Try floating a few hawthorn blossoms on the water, and make a request to the Lord and Lady for fertility and prosperity. The Irish name for the hawthorn is Huathe.

hawthorn

Oak (*Quercus* spp.)

June 10–July 7

The oak is the final companion in the faerie trinity of trees, and as you would expect, the oak is compatible with faerie and nature spirit magick. The elemental correspondences for this tree are earth and fire. A sentinel oak is often used as a marker to denote a magickal place. It is a protective and wise tree and one well worth growing on your property. The oak tree has an ancient and knowing spirit. The rustling of oak leaves is thought to be the whispers of the old gods. Meditate on that sound; what do you think they are trying to teach you? As acorns drop down in September, what little nuggets of wisdom do you think may be falling into your life?

There are many different species of the oak; however, the magickal associations are typically the same. The oak is associated with sky gods and, of course, the Oak King and the Holly King. Many goddesses of fire and fertility have ties to the magickal oak such as the Celtic triple goddess Brigid. The oak is the favored sacred tree in the Druidic tradition. In this magickal tradition, the gods were usually celebrated at the solstices and the equinoxes, and the goddesses were celebrated at the cross-quarter days of Imbolc, Beltane, Lughnasadh, and Samhain.

The oak is associated with the element of fire and the sun. Magickally, the oak and the acorn are worked into charms for fertility and prosperity. The acorn may also be a natural symbol for the God. Work with the oak's leaves in your spells and charms to encourage valor, truth, and strength. The Irish name for the oak is Duir.

oak

Holly (*Ilex* spp.)
July 8–August 4

Both the oak and the holly are symbolized by the summer and winter solstices. The holly is a symbol of the life force. It is a lucky tree to grow at home in your garden, as it is believed to protect the home and its occupants from lightning, negativity, and bad luck. A popular plant with the winter nature spirits, this shrub (or standard tree, depending on the variety) is one to consider adding to your gardens. The male holly was thought to be auspicious for men, while the female holly was a good-luck charm for women.

How do you tell a male from a female holly? Well, the female holly produces plenty of berries, and the male holly produces small, pale green flowers (for pollination) and only a few berries. Also, if you have a female holly in your yard but there is no male to pollinate it, it will not produce any berries. You will need at least one male to fertilize all your female holly plants. Also, look at the names of the shrubs at the nursery such as 'China Girl' or 'China Boy'.

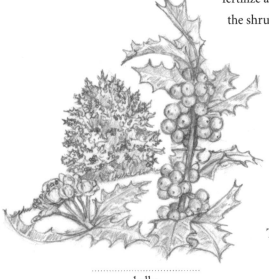

Some of the older varieties of the holly feature smooth leaves that are variegated, smooth, and lobed (female) or that are solid colors with prickles (male). The elemental correspondence for the holly is fire, and its planetary influence is Mars. Magickally, the holly is used for protection from angry spirits. The holly features prominently in winter solstice celebrations and is used to decorate Yule logs, wreaths, and midwinter altars. The Irish name for the holly is Tinne.

holly

Hazel (*Corylus avellana*)

August 5–September 1

The hazel is associated with the Celtic star goddess Arianrhod. Arianrhod was thought to have blessed the hazel tree with wisdom, knowledge, beauty, and fertility. Hazel is also a popular choice for hedgerow planting, and it is a tree of wishes, magick, and Witchcraft. Hazel is a popular wood for divining rods. White hazel wands were thought to have been carried by the Druids as a symbol of their authority. Planting a trio of hazel trees on your property was rumored to encourage the faeries to live there. In this miniature grove, all earth magick was thought to be doubly blessed.

Weather omens were sought by looking at the shells of the hazelnut. If the shells were thin, then a mild winter was predicted. If the shells were thick, then a long, cold winter with many storms was expected. The elemental correspondences for the hazel tree are both air and fire, and its planetary association is Mercury. The nuts, which become ripe in the fall months, are worked into charms for fertility, knowledge, and divination. Try painting a rune for inspiration on a hazelnut, and carry that with you as an amulet or charm.

If you'd like to protect your home from fire and misfortune, then bundle together a small bunch of hazel twigs on the spring equinox, the sabbat of Ostara. Tie these little twigs together with a white satin ribbon and bless these in the name of Arianrhod. Hang them near your home's fireplace to ward off chimney fires and accidents in the home.

hazel

Sabbat associations for the hazel tree are Ostara, Beltane, and Mabon. Weaving sprigs of hazel into a chaplet for your hair and wearing this on Beltane eve was thought to grant you good luck for a year and possibly the power of invisibility. Hazel branches cut on Midsummer's eve are often used for divining rods. The Irish name for the hazel is Coll.

Vine (*Vitis vinifera*)
September 2–September 29

vine

The grapevine symbolizes emotions, sensuality, the harvest, and prosperity. Prophecy, truth, and intuition are also associated with the vine. Although there are many varieties of vines, the usual reference in sacred or magickal art and symbolism is the grapevine. Grapes were cultivated by the Egyptians some 6,000 years ago and were most likely introduced into Britain by the Romans. This fruit-bearing plant has the magickal associations of the moon and the element of water. The grapevine also corresponds to the sabbat Mabon, the autumnal equinox.

The wine god Bacchus/Dionysus is traditionally entwined into the grapevine mythology, as well as a few harvest goddesses such as Ceres/Demeter. In some magickal traditions, the elm tree and the grapevine are looked upon as magickal partners, as elm trees were often planted in the vineyards to help provide shade and to shield the grapes.

The grapevine wreath is a standard base for many decorative wreaths today. Try using a little magickal creativity and work in the ancient symbolism of the harvest. You could add silk grape leaves and artificial grapes and embellish your prosperity wreath with deep purple ribbons. If you want something less harvest-oriented, you could cover the grapevine wreath with an assortment of magickal herbs, rosehips, or even dried chili peppers. Either way, it would create a great-smelling, practical magick wreath to hang up in the kitchen. In the Druid's alphabet, the letter for the vine is M; the Irish name is Muinn.

Ivy (*Hedera helix*)
September 30–October 27

The evergreen ivy is a symbol of the faerie. Ivy represents visions, inner knowledge, and the enigmatic and mystical. The ivy vine may be worked into spells and charms to call in the faeries and for magickal protection, bindings, and to ward off psychic attack.

Wherever ivy grows or is strewn, it guards against negativity and adversity. There is an old charm that tells a young woman to gather a leaf from the ivy vine and hold it close to her heart to divine who her future husband will be. Here is a more modern spin on that old herbal charm: gather the ivy leaf on the evening of a waxing crescent moon. Tie a small piece of white ribbon in a bow around the ivy stem as you imagine the personality qualities that would make for a good partner (remember not to focus on a specific individual). Face west, and watch the moon for a few moments as it sets. Then repeat this charm three times:

ivy

Ivy leaf, ivy leaf, I love you
Pray show me now a love so true
The first young man who speaks to me
My future husband he shall be.

Keep the leaf with you until the moon waxes to full, then keep the ribbon as a token of the spell, and return the leaf to nature. The variegated ivy actually symbolizes fidelity, which helps explain its popularity in bridal bouquets.

According to flower folklore, the solid green-colored ivy denotes friendship and constancy. It was also rumored that ivy was used to decorate fertility wands—so if you're looking to conceive, you may want to take that into consideration.

The magickal associations for the vine are the planet Saturn and the element of water. Finally, along with holly, these two magickal plants are traditional herbal symbols for the God and Goddess, with the holly representing the male aspect and the ivy representing the female aspect. The ivy plays a prominent role at Yuletide, as the ivy is classically linked with the holly; think of the line from that Old English carol, "The Holly and the Ivy." The Irish name for the ivy is Gort.

Reed (*Phragmites communis*)
October 28–November 24

Yes, you are correct: the reed is not a tree. However, the reed was an important product for ancient people. Reeds were used for thatching, woven into mats, crafted into pipes, and burned for fuel. During hard times or famine, the reed's roots and shoots could be eaten.

While this may sound incredibly unappetizing to a modern person, if your family was starving, you foraged and gathered whatever you could.

The magickal associations of the reed are action, strength, and power. Its planetary association is the sun, and since the reed grows along wet banks and in marshes, its elemental association is water.

There is the story of Pan, who pursued a nymph named Syrinx who was so anxious to get away from him that she turned herself into a reed. Hiding among the other reeds on the riverbank, she was hidden. Since Pan was unable to figure out which reed was his beloved, he cut several reeds and fashioned them into a musical pipe—the panpipe that he carried with him always.

According to old flower folklore, the reed symbolized music and complaisance. It also carries the message "You have bewitched me with your song." (Well, I guess we can stop wondering how the reed earned its magickal association.) The deities associated with the reed are Pan, Taliesin, Osiris, Isis, and Horus. At this dark time of Samhain, the reed represents the mysteries of mortality and is also a symbol of royalty. The royal connection comes about from an ancient tradition that tells how a sacred king often held a scepter crafted out of reeds. When the king died, the scepter of reeds was broken. The Irish name for the reed is Ngetal.

reed

Elder (*Sambucus canadensis*)
November 25–December 23

An extremely old and powerful magickal tree, elder is a member of the honeysuckle family. This popular hedgerow tree also made an appearance in our last chapter and has the astrological correspondence of Venus and the elemental association of water. The elderberry, as it is also called, is sacred to many goddesses, many of whom are aspects of the Crone. Leave this tree to grow happily in nature, for it is believed to be a benevolent tree that is zealously guarded by the faeries and the Goddess.

If you plant an elderberry tree in the yard, you will invite the elves, nature spirits, and the faeries into your life. However, give the tree its own wild little corner of your property if you want the tree to flourish. This is a faerie tree, and they like their space. The elderberry tree is rightly thought to have a strong feminine spirit, which may explain its strong connection to

elder

Witchcraft. Folktales warn never to burn the wood of the elder tree—"Burn it not or cursed you'll be"—or to even bring elder flowers into the house. According to German folklore, bringing a leafy elder branch into your house was thought to invite ghosts. Conversely, in Scotland, the elder branches were hung over doors and windows inside the home to keep evil spirits away.

The creamy white flowers of the elderberry tree have been used in bridal bouquets for centuries. These flat heads of star-shaped flowers are arranged in clusters of blooms. They have a pleasant musky scent, and in the language of flowers, they signify both kindness and compassion. During the summer months while the tree is in bloom, it is thought that if you gently gather elderberry blossoms and breathe in the scent on Midsummer's Eve, then you will be visited by or receive a vision of the faeries. If you should discover this tree while on a ramble, or nature walk, then be kind to the tree, and greet it with respect and affection. The Irish name for the elder tree is Ruis.

Mystical, Magickal Trees

I am a willow of the wilderness,
loving the wind that bent me. All my hurts
my garden spade can heal. A woodland walk,
a quest of river-grapes, a mocking thrush,
a wild-rose, or rock-loving columbine,
salve my worst wounds.

RALPH WALDO EMERSON

With the elder, we finish our Celtic calendar of trees. The elder has an extensive magickal history, so it was featured in the previous hedgerow chapter as well. Overall, the elder tree is a symbol of both endings and beginnings, so it's very appropriate to close up both this tree year calendar and the chapter with this tree.

The elder reminds us that the magick of trees continues throughout all of the four bewitching seasons. It's simply up to us to absorb the green wisdom inherent in all of nature and then to discover and work wisely with these natural enchantments ourselves.

In the spring, you can tap into all that burgeoning energy and expansion. Use this season and your tree magick as an opportunity for new growth. What wonderful things could you bring to blossom? During the summer, you can revel in the lush foliage and the abundant and thriving fertility energy that is found all around us, for as nature flourishes, sets its fruits, and grows strong and true, so, too, will you.

As the autumn rolls in and the leaves begin to lose their green mask of chlorophyll, the hidden colors of the reds, browns, oranges, and yellows begin to show in the leaves. During nature's big, colorful autumn show, you have the opportunity to work tree magick with the energies of change, bounty, and the harvest. Reap what you have sown, and be thankful for all your blessings.

Finally, when winter holds the land, look to the evergreens—pine, cedar, spruce, and the holly—for proof that life does indeed go on. Even while nature is resting, it is also gaining strength for the next season. Use the winter months and the quiet and strong magick of the evergreens to gain a deeper understanding of nature and the power of all of her cycles and seasons.

The trees can truly teach us about the cycles of the earth; they have much wisdom to share. It's up to us as green magickal practitioners to stop, to look, and to carefully listen. Most importantly, we have to be receptive and allow ourselves to learn.

TREE SPIRITS

That thou, light winged Dryad of the trees,
In some melodious plot
Of beechen green, and shadows numberless,
Singest of summer in full-throated ease.

JOHN KEATS

If you'd like to take your study of trees and green magick a bit further, you can learn to work with the spirits of the trees, the dryads. To begin, you need an open heart and a questing mind. Then take a walk, and find yourself a nice, healthy, established tree. You are going to want to choose a tree that has some character and some age.

Walk up to the tree and get a feel for its energy and its presence. Then splay your fingers wide, and lay both hands gently upon the trunk of the tree. Close your eyes, and let your mind open to the sensations of the tree. Now, you may "see" images or you may simply feel emotions. If you sense a sort of heartbeat within the tree, don't be alarmed. That is simply the sap, or life's blood, of the tree rushing throughout and circulating through all the branches and leaves.

You should be aware that the tree is not a shell holding the dryad within. The tree and the tree's spirit—its dryad—grow together. There is a symbiotic relationship between a dryad and its tree. While the tree is young, the tree spirit is thought to flit about and move around the tree and to visit (for lack of a better term) its neighbors in the wood or garden. But as the tree grows and ages, the dryad develops as well. Once the tree reaches maturity, it raises its vibrations, and the dryad is thought to move deeper within the spirit of the tree, becoming stronger and more substantial and eventually merging with the tree so that they are one.

This is the presence, or personality, that you can sense when you bond with an older tree. For the most part, dryads are quiet, shy, and kind. They may not be very trusting of you the first time you try to connect with them, so be patient. Now, just so we are clear, I am not telling you to expect the dryad to come popping out of the tree and shake your hand. I am telling you that in time and once you build a relationship with a tree, the spirit within may send you visions, messages, and if they *really* like you, they can boost your green magick as well.

How will you know when that has happened? You'll feel it in your heart center. You might get a little flip of the stomach or a pleasant tug at your heart. This will be followed by a nice little warm rush of sensation and a feeling of contentment. That's how you will know. This type of green magick is intensely personal, so different Witches may experience a variety of sensations. You will have to carefully take notes and keep track of your experiences. Then, over time, you can see how the relationship between you and the tree spirit develops.

If, for some reason, you believe that you have encountered a cranky tree spirit—and yes, I have heard of folks who are terrified when they think they have angered a tree somehow—then casually back away from the tree, whisper a wish for the tree to grow strong and true, and leave the tree alone. I would suspect that this is your fear playing out more than a tree's supposed bad attitude, though it could be an angry land deva who is upset that the area was disturbed.

For example, if an old, wooded area was stripped bare to make room for a new subdivision, then you bet you are going to experience some angry earth spirit energy. But the sturdy old pine, elm, oak, willow, ash, magnolia, or maple tree growing in your backyard or neighborhood park shouldn't be a problem. If you think you have encountered an angry tree or land spirit, do not panic. Just be calm, center yourself, look around, and try to befriend a different species of tree. The tree spirits won't mind.

Trees do mediate between the astral realm, or heaven, and the physical realm, the earth. And some would say that these spirit-bearing trees actually work as go-betweens for the gods and humanity. The oldest trees watch over the wise ones and the people who value nature as a sacred place. There are plenty of "green-souled" folks out there who are not magickal practitioners such as the naturalists, conservationists, gardeners, and activists who work to protect our environment and our natural resources. We are all connected to each other in many ways, both magickally and spiritually. As a wise man once said, what we do to the earth, we do to ourselves. Consider that while you are working to deepen your connection to the green world.

LESSONS FROM THE TREES

Nature is, after all, the only book
that offers important content on every page.
JOHANN WOLFGANG VON GOETHE

For now, I want you to go find a tree, any tree, and go sit under it for a while. Open your heart and open your mind, and see what nature has to teach you. If the dryads come out and play, then sit back, let your mind wander, and see what images and emotions you pick up from the tree spirits. I bet you'll be surprised at what mysteries they can teach you.

When you are finished, be sure and thank the dryads for their presence. Leave a small gift at the base of the tree—a tumbled stone, a seashell, a bit of birdseed for the local birds and squirrels, or even a strand of your hair. Or, if you are in a public park, then take a moment to pick up any trash that may be laying around. Leave the area looking better than when you found it; that would really make both the land spirits and the dryads happy. Plus, it's a great way for you to help the environment. Imagine what would happen if every person stopped and picked up trash when they found it. Think of the difference it would make.

In our next chapter, we will be taking a look at the dark side of herbs. There is a very good reason that herbal lore has been so enduring; you can thank the gothic herbs and poisonous plants of old for that. So let's take a look together at these gothic herbs and botanicals, for these forbidden plants offer yet another opportunity to expand our knowledge of green magick, witchery, and herbalism.

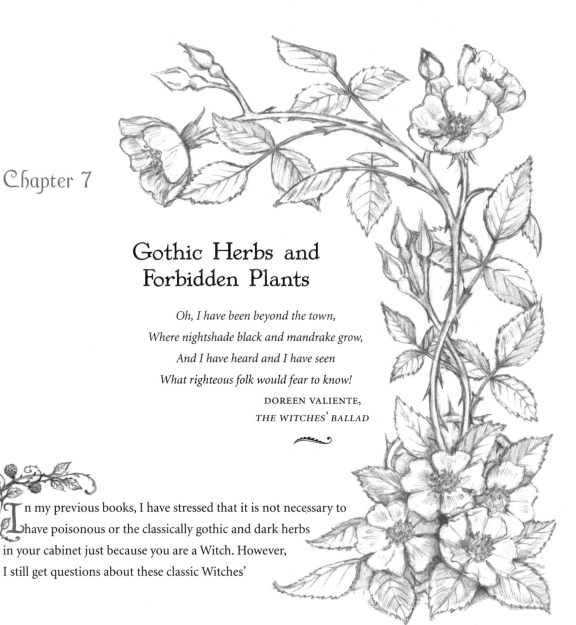

Chapter 7

Gothic Herbs and Forbidden Plants

Oh, I have been beyond the town,
Where nightshade black and mandrake grow,
And I have heard and I have seen
What righteous folk would fear to know!

DOREEN VALIENTE,
THE WITCHES' BALLAD

In my previous books, I have stressed that it is not necessary to
have poisonous or the classically gothic and dark herbs
in your cabinet just because you are a Witch. However,
I still get questions about these classic Witches'

herbs on a regular basis. So I decided it was past time to take a good look at these plants and to share some information. I suppose you could say that we are now exploring the "darker green" magick.

Please remember that the herbs featured in this chapter are classified as baneful herbs—which means *herbs that can cause death*. They are toxic and should not be used—or, in my opinion, even handled—by a novice or a dabbler. The herbs listed in this chapter are for informational purposes only. Plus, please keep in mind if you go to the local metaphysical shop or garden center looking for these plants, whether in the fresh or dried form, you will raise a lot of eyebrows and probably have people treat you very suspiciously.

Once, when my mother came over for a visit, she was in the kitchen with me, helping me with dinner. As I directed her to where the serving bowls were so she could help dish up the food, she opened the wrong cabinet and came nose to nose with my magickal herbs, all of which were in various funky-shaped bottles of pretty colored glass. Each of the bottles was neatly labeled. There were jars of dried lavender, yarrow, rose petals, monarda, mint, thyme, rosemary, sage, and way in the back, a prized bottle of mistletoe.

She stopped and looked over at me, aghast. "Is this your spice rack?"

With a quick glance, I answered, "No, those are the flowers and herbs I gathered and then dried from the garden."

I watched her squint her eyes and lean in further to read the labels. Unconcerned, I went about my business, only to find her sputtering in disbelief at the jars a few moments later. She looked like she was about to have an aneurysm.

I saw her reach up with shaking hands and pull down a large bottle of dried lavender. She waved it toward me and with a red face demanded, "What is 'eye of newt,' young lady?"

What? I grabbed the bottle and looked at it. Apparently my husband, Ken, had decided to play a practical joke. He had relabeled all of my jars with titles like dragon's wing, toe of frog, and, yes, eye of newt. Oh, for Goddess's sake.

Once I stopped laughing, I explained this to my mother, who did not see the humor in the situation, that this was my husband's idea of a joke. I peeled off the taped-on labels and showed her the real label underneath.

"Mother, it's lavender. Smell it for yourself!" I invited. For some reason, she refused, and to this day, she will not open a kitchen cabinet door in my home.

In the past when I have done research on herbs, I often contacted a non-emergency poison control hotline. Yes, the non-emergency line—I did not want to tie up the phone lines in case there was an emergency situation and someone else was desperately trying to get through to the hotline. To say that they treated me suspiciously when I first began calling them a few years ago would be an understatement. I half expected the police to come knocking on my door, wanting to know why I was so interested in poisonous plants. But once I explained why I was gathering the information, the poison control folks enjoyed hearing from me. It got to be that they knew me by the sound of my voice.

All I would have to say was hello, and the response would be, "Hey, Ellen! What book are you working on now?"

So if I am so cautious about these types of botanicals, then why am I writing about them now? Am I contradicting my earlier books? No, I am not. What I am doing is diving into a topic that often gets ignored, hushed up, or makes many folks very nervous—or it makes them laugh at how overly dramatic some magickal folks can be.

What do I mean by that? Well, I have a story for you.

The Garden Witch and the
Case of the Gothic Herbs

If there were no mystery left to explore,
life would get rather dull, wouldn't it?

SIDNEY BUCHMAN

Back in 1999, I was working a seasonal job at a local nursery. That summer had been tough. We had endured a record-breaking high-temperature summer, and the job was miserable. The only air conditioning was in the owner's office—a place where the employees were not allowed. The owner himself was usually off betting at the racetrack in the afternoon, so all the employees just drank lots of water and worked carefully and slowly in the heat to avoid heat exhaustion. Plus, we stayed in the shade whenever possible. I was the only female employee at the nursery that year—all the other women had quit after a week or so because of the working conditions and the fact that they had to lift, haul, and carry just like all of the guys.

So there I was one miserably hot afternoon, in the shade, drinking a bottle of sports drink with the other employees. That day it was myself and a pair of brothers, one who was in his late twenties, fresh out of a military special forces unit and learning to readjust to civilian life, and his younger brother, who was in his early twenties and fresh off his latest brush with the law. To say that they were colorful characters would be an understatement. These brothers were built and attractive, however, and that spring and summer, the nursery had lots of women customers who would stroll through just hoping that the brothers were there.

Hard to blame them, really—they were a couple of good-looking, rough-around-the-edges bad boys. At least when I worked with those two, I was never bored, though I frequently had to referee. I will admit that I often felt like Wendy with the Lost Boys, and I was crazy about them. We all got along well because I worked as hard as they did. I was married with kids and had no designs on them personally, and I didn't put up with any crap. Over the course of the summer, we had become casual work friends—and yes, they both knew about my psychic abilities and the Witchcraft.

The psychic abilities had saved their bacon a few times, like when the usually absent owner would decide to drop by and check on the nursery. Or in the days before caller ID, I always knew who was on the phone and what the problem was before they would call. At first, they assumed I was just spooky, then after a while they figured it out and thought it was pretty interesting.

So there we were one day as the brothers exchanged their typical insults back and forth. A thunderstorm was predicted that afternoon, so the humidity was high, and it was cloudy and overcast. Business had been very slow that week because of the extreme August heat, and as the three of us stood in the shade, trying to catch a breeze, a long black car with tinted windows pulled into the nursery parking lot.

Like in a scene from a cheesy B movie, as the driver's door opened up, a clap of thunder rolled through, and the driver climbed out of the car. The driver of the car was a young man dressed in solid black. His hair was long and obviously dyed black; his jeans, shirt, sunglasses, and long leather coat were also all black. Think of *The Matrix*, only this guy wasn't nearly as trim or attractive as Keanu Reeves. Remember that it was 100 degrees outside that day, and with the high humidity, it was stifling. To say this guy looked ridiculous in the long black coat was an understatement.

Both of the brothers looked at me and in unison said, "This one's yours, Ellen."

My response to the two of them was rude, short, and inelegant.

As the customer in question skulked closer, I could see that he was covered in spiked metal jewelry and his fingernails were also black. Heaving a sigh, I approached him, put on my sunniest smile, and asked if I could help him find anything. He looked me over, pulled down his dark sunglasses, and dismissed me as a mundane and as a peon.

"Hello…" he began in what I am sure he thought was a mysterious and sinister tone. "I am looking for a certain type of botanical. For a—" (dramatic pause here) "certain type of recipe."

Trying not to giggle, I stood there and radiated my "hi-I'm-a-friendly-middle-age-suburban-mom-nursery-employee" vibe. I smiled and cheerfully asked him what type of herb he was looking for as I steered him over to our display of culinary herbs.

"Well…" he dragged the word out and looked carefully around, then lowered his voice even more. "Are you familiar with the Latin names of plants? There are seven plants I am looking for, and I wouldn't want to confuse you—" (again with the dramatic pause) "or to scare you."

I cocked my head to the side and sent him a sweet smile. Still keeping my Midwestern mom vibe going, I told him, "Try me."

Pulling a list out of his pocket, he read them off to me. "I need aconite, belladonna, cannabis, hellebore, mandrake, nightshade, and wolf's bane."

"That's actually five herbs," I responded, impressed that the boy even knew how to alphabetize.

"No, I listed seven herbs," he argued back. "I know what I am talking about, and I'll prove it." Affronted, he frowned at me and then played what I am sure he thought was his trump card. He pulled out a big pentagram from under his shirt and dangled it in front of my eyes.

I smiled even bigger then. Did this guy need a smackdown or what? "Listen, slick," I told him in my best mom's voice. "Wolf's bane and aconite are the same thing. *Aconite* is the botanical term, or Latin name, of that particular plant."

His jaw dropped open.

I continued on mercilessly. "Mandrake isn't a plant carried in nursery stock here in the Midwest, or in most of the United States, for that matter. Mandrake, or *Mandragora*, is native to Europe. Also, nightshade is belladonna. The botanical term for nightshade is, in fact, *Atropa belladonna*."

He began to stammer.

Feeling positively evil, I continued. "Now, hellebore is also called the Christmas rose, so you may find that as a houseplant at a local florist just before Christmas. Oh, and by the way," I took a deep breath and continued my lecture, "we don't sell cannabis, you moron, as marijuana is illegal to grow or to possess."

He turned beet red.

I then added the finishing touch to my lecture by looping my finger under the collar of my nursery polo shirt and pulling out my own silver pentagram. I let it dangle from my finger in his face. "Surprise!" I sang. Then I put away my pentagram and told him quietly, "Next time, save the I'm-so-scary-with-my-deep-voice-and-dressed-all-in-black crap for the tourists."

"Oh, man, I am so sorry," he apologized. "I wanted the herbs for magick, you know?"

I asked him for his name and patted his shoulder in sympathy. Then I asked him for his list of herbs. I pulled a pen out of my pocket, and on the back side of his list, I made him a reading list of good books on herbs and magick, many of which could be borrowed from the local library. He listened attentively, and then I took him through the herbs that we had left and explained some of the basic magickal uses of herbs like basil, rosemary, and mint.

After that, I took him on a tour of the perennials and trees and pointed out all the plants that were also herbs and what their magickal uses were. As we toured around the nursery, he took off the trench coat and started to smile and talk in a more normal tone of voice.

"Wow, so you really know your stuff, huh?" he said, impressed. "I would have never thought that you were a Witch," he confided.

"Oh, yeah? Why's that?" I asked him, even though I knew what his answer would be.

"Well, you look so …" He trailed off, stumped for the correct word.

"Normal," I finished for him.

"Yeah, I mean, you look like a regular mom. No offense," he smiled.

"Well, I am a mom, so no offense taken."

As I rang up his purchases and helped him load all the herbs he had bought in his car, he looked at me and said, "You know, you should write a book on herbs and gardens. There are a lot of people out there who really need good magickal information." He smiled at me and promised to read the books I had suggested.

I waved as he pulled out of the parking lot, and the two brothers walked up behind me. The oldest brother dropped his hands on my shoulders. "Are you okay?"

I looked over my shoulder at him. "Why wouldn't I be?"

"I watched in case there was trouble," he said.

Now there was a sobering thought, the special forces guy ready for trouble. "I'm fine. Don't worry." I patted his hand and moved away.

"You know," the oldest brother looked me over speculatively, "I knew you knew a lot about plants, but I had no idea you had all that kind of information running around in your head. Are all Witches like that?"

I only smiled.

"Remind me not to piss you off or ask you to make me a salad," the younger brother teased.

The interesting part of this story is that I had just been contracted to write a *2001 Magical Almanac* article on a Witch's garden, and I had been putting together ideas for a book on practical garden magick and herbalism. That autumn, I began my Master Gardener training program and took the next few years working at different nurseries in the summer to get more hands-on landscaping and plant experience. I submitted the manuscript for my first book, *Garden Witchery*, a few years later.

So fast forward to the present day some nine years and ten books later, and we find the Garden Witch writing on the topic of baneful herbs. Right on cue, my black cat has jumped onto the writing desk and has begun to purr. She just leaned in and gave me a kitty kiss on the nose, which is unusual for this cat. The only time she is affectionate is if you open up canned cat food or let her outside to romp in the catnip. Hmmm, I suppose she approves.

Read the following botanical information very carefully. You will see that according to old plant lore, many of these baneful herbs have common names and titles that are the same. There are a few mandrakes; likewise, there is a nightshade that is known as belladonna and a nightshade that is not, which was new information to me. I suppose you *can* teach an old Garden Witch a new trick. Also, I guess this means that that kid could have had six herbs on his list after all.

The folk names, or common names, are there for the information, not for plant identification. Always use botanical names, which are listed in italics, for proper plant identification. Please use your common sense if you decide to work with these botanicals. Be smart and safe and keep these herbs well out of reach from children. Also, you should never use cooking utensils, pots, bowls, or dishes to work with or to store these herbs—they should have their own dedicated equipment. Should you decide to store any of these botanicals, clearly label these herbs as toxic and list the botanical name as well as the common name.

Always wash your hands carefully after handling any of these botanicals. Finally, there is no room for mistakes with any of these baneful herbs. For no reason whatsoever should any of these be taken internally. The consequences are deadly.

Thirteen Gothic Herbs of Lore and Legend

Double, double, toil and trouble
Fire burn, and cauldron bubble.

SHAKESPEARE, *MACBETH*

Aconite (*Aconite napellus*)
Also known as monkshood and wolfsbane; some other folk names include blue rocket, friar's cap, and Venus's chariot. As stated earlier, many classically gothic poisonous plants have the same common names; this is why botanical names are crucial for identification.

Among the deadliest of plants, aconite is a hardy perennial that is a native of Europe and Asia, and it thrives in shady areas. Aconite produces tall stems of up to five feet in height and bears beautiful, purple-helmeted flowers in the early summer. The herb has delphinium-looking foliage. This plant is inexorably linked with Witchcraft, magick, and poison gardens. The tales of the dangers of aconite are prevalent in old herbals.

In the language of flowers, monkshood has the definition of deceit and warns that a deadly foe is near. (I think that deadly foe may be the plant itself.) Magickally, this herb will grant invisibility and protection from werewolves and vampires. This plant is sacred to Hecate; it is also supposed to cure lycanthropy. Astrological associations for this feminine herb are the planet Saturn and the element of water.

To give you an idea of just how deadly this herb is, in the dark times, aconite was an arrowtip poison used to kill wolves. It was also a "death drink" given to condemned prisoners.

> **Warning:** This plant is subject to legal restrictions in some countries. Do not take internally or wipe any part of the plant on the skin. The plant will cause skin irritation, and even skin-to-plant contact can be dangerous. Always handle with gloves. All parts of this plant are exceptionally toxic.

aconite

Black Hellebore (*Helleborus niger*)

Also known as the Christmas rose, snow rose, or winter rose. This is a traditional cottage garden plant that blooms from late autumn to early spring. This winter-blooming plant often blossoms in the snow. This baneful herb grows up to fifteen inches tall and is part of the buttercup family (*Ranunculaceae*). It has evergreen compound leaves of seven or more leaflets, and it bears white flowers that age to pink. There are large-flowered cultivars available, as are pink-flowered and double-flowered varieties. Hellebore has become a popular early spring garden perennial these days. I saw it for sale everywhere in one-gallon containers this past April.

For practical magick use, I would grow this plant in the garden and enjoy the pretty flowers in late winter. Magickally, hellebore was thought to cure madness. Interestingly enough, in the language of flowers, it signifies a scandal. It is a feminine plant, sacred to Hecate and ruled by the planet Saturn. Its elemental association is water.

Warning: This plant is an abortifacient; it is toxic and should not be ingested.

black hellebore

Black Nightshade (*Solanum nigrum*)

Also known as garden nightshade, black nightshade's folk names include hound's berry, small fruited nightshade, and poison berry. This plant is often called garden nightshade as it was often found growing wild, or volunteering, in the garden. A native plant of southern Europe, this variety of nightshade is an annual. The black nightshade has been introduced to the Americas and grows one to two feet in height. The plant has irregular toothed, oval, or heart-shaped and pointed leaves that are arranged on hairy stalks.

The black nightshade bears white flowers from midsummer to early fall that are arranged in clusters. The white flowers have five petals each and yellow anthers. The berries follow the flowers, and they begin as green and then ripen to a shiny black in the fall. All parts of this plant are considered toxic, the berries most of all. This plant is poisonous to both humans and animals. However, because the plant tastes bitter to animals, they typically will leave it alone.

Further along in this list, you will see a second variety of nightshade: the deadly nightshade *Atropa belladonna*, which is simply known as belladonna. The differences between these two types of nightshade are many, most notably in the flowers. The black nightshade (*Solanum nigrum*) has white flowers arranged in clusters. This plant has smaller berries, borne again in clusters, and is a shorter annual plant reaching only one to two feet in height, while deadly nightshade (*Atropa belladonna*) has purple, trumpet-shaped flowers borne singularly. The

black nightshade

deadly nightshade is a herbaceous perennial and can grow up to five feet in height. The berries of deadly nightshade are described as large and looking like black cherries.

In the language of flowers, black nightshade warns of false and dark thoughts. Magickal uses are protection and defense magick. This plant is also sacred to Hecate. Black nightshade is associated with the planet Saturn and is linked to the element of water.

> **Warning:** All parts of this plant are toxic. Use extreme caution handling this plant. Do not ingest.

Common Foxglove (*Digitalis purpurea*)

Folk names include fairy's gloves, folks' gloves, fairy weed, bloody man's fingers, Witches' gloves, and Witches' thimbles. A classic faerie plant that is popular in gardening and landscaping, many people have no idea that it is a toxic plant. This is another plant that you may want to avoid if you have small children. Digitalis is used as a drug for heart failure. The foxglove leaves contain glycosides, which are used as a heart stimulant. The foxglove is classified as a biennial and can grow up to three feet in height. There are also a few other varieties of perennial foxglove. The foxglove blooms in the late spring–early summer from the bottom of the flower stalk up toward the top. There are white- and purple-blooming varieties of common foxglove.

In the language of flowers, foxglove warns of insincerity and fickleness, and cautions that "your love is as changeable as the breeze." Magickally, foxglove may be used for faerie spells, deflecting negative magick, and defense. If you grow it in your magickal gardens, it will protect your home and property. It also encourages the faeries to live in your magickal gardens. This feminine herb is ruled by the planet Venus and claims the elemental association of water.

Warning: This plant is toxic and should not be ingested.

Garden Witch Tip: There are dozens of varieties of foxgloves available to purchase at nurseries and garden centers these days. As a matter of fact, I have four different varieties of foxglove in my perennial garden right now: the classic *Digitalis purpurea*, plus a soft yellow perennial variety that is called *Digitalis grandiflora*—its common name is simply yellow foxglove. I also added a variety called 'Foxy' that I am crazy about. At the moment, it is over three feet in height and is blooming in purple, white, and pink. I found another new foxglove variety this year that is called 'Camelot'. I bought the lavender assortment, and I can't wait to see how it turns out.

Remember, if you want to have foxglove blossoms every year, when you first purchase your foxglove plants, buy two plants—one that has a bloom stalk and one that does not—and plant them side by side. Foxgloves are biennials, which means that they bloom one year and are vegetative, or dormant (without flowers), the next. This way, you will have a foxglove plant in bloom each year.

common foxglove

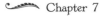

Datura (*Datura stramonium*)

Folk names include Jimson weed, thorn apple, devil's apple, and angels' trumpet. This annual plant may grow up to two feet in height. It has large leaves with incised edges; the leaves have a musky scent, and the large, trumpet-shaped flowers also have a peculiar odor. The flowers may be white, yellow, or purple and bloom from midsummer through autumn. The plant then produces a green, spiky seed pod.

I wrote about datura in my first book, *Garden Witchery*. I had bought the plant by accident from a plant vendor at a flea market. He referred to it as a moonflower bush. After I planted it in my gardens and it bloomed, I began to realize it was an altogether different sort of plant. Since my children were small at the time, once I identified it as a highly toxic plant, I did remove it from my magickal gardens. On an interesting note, it was years before anything else would grow in that spot.

Magickally, the plant is used to break hexes and manipulative spells, or any spell that has been cast against you. To do this, you need to sprinkle the petals of the flowers around the outside of your home. If you are considering trying this, I would recommend wearing latex gloves that you could dispose of immediately. (If you have sensitive skin, this plant may cause contact dermatitis just by brushing against the leaves or flowers—I wasn't kidding about those gloves!) Also, I would not have this plant around children or nibbling pets. The consequences could be tragic.

datura

162

This baneful herb is considered to have feminine energies. Its astrological influence is Saturn, although some sources say Jupiter, and the elemental association is water.

> **Warning:** This plant is restricted in some countries. The datura, or thorn apple, is exceptionally poisonous; some herbal reference guides bluntly say that it causes insanity and death.

Deadly Nightshade/Belladonna
(*Atropa belladonna*)

Also known as nightshade. Folk names include bane wort, fair lady, and Witch's berry. It is also fascinating to note that this particular plant was referred to as "the mandrake of Hecate." Both *Mandragora*, the classic mandrake, and *Atropa belladonna* come from the night-shade family (*Solanaceae*), which they share with other plants such as potatoes, tomatoes, eggplants, tobacco, and chili peppers. The nightshade is a native plant to the Mediterranean and Eurasia. It is also sacred to the triple goddess Hecate.

This herbaceous perennial has red stem sap and solitary trumpet-shaped purple flowers that blossom from mid-summer through autumn. The flowers are followed by shiny black berries. (The berries are the most virulent part of the plant.) This perennial is described as short-lived and may reach heights of up to five feet. In the past, an extract of the belladonna plant was used to dilate the eyes; this was thought to make a woman look more beautiful. This practice is not recommended today.

deadly nightshade

The botanical name for this plant, *Atropa belladonna*, may be linked to one of the three goddesses of Fate, also called the Norns. One goddess wove the strand of each person's life, another sister measured it, and the third cut the strand when the mortal's life was to be ended. Atropos is the name of the goddess that snips the thread of life. How very appropriate.

In the language of flowers, deadly nightshade whispers of fascination and Witchcraft. Magickal associations are varied; this plant was once used in charms to encourage visions (because of its hallucinogenic properties, I'm sure). It will also protect against evil and manipulative magick. *Atropa belladonna* is also thought to have the ability to make you forget your old flame. Classified as a feminine plant, its astrological influence is Saturn. The elemental association is water. Belladonna is thought to be at its most powerful at Beltane.

> **Warning:** Subject to legal restrictions in many countries. All parts of this plant are extremely poisonous and should be handled with extreme caution. Do not take internally.

fly agaric

Fly Agaric (*Amanita muscaria*)

Common names include agaric, Deadly Amanita, death cap, redcap mushroom, and raven's bread. Technically, this is not a botanical; it is a fungus. This storybook-looking toadstool comes into fruiting in the autumn. It can grow up to ten inches in height and is described as having a "fruit body," with a stem ringed with remnants of a veil and a bright red cap dotted with white warts. This fungi's bright red color boldly declares its lethal nature. The cap is large (four to six inches) and spreads out quite horizontally. This mushroom's habitat is birch, pine, spruce, and cedar forests in Europe and North America. It grows in poor soils in marshes and along roadsides. The quintessential toadstool, it is one of the most recognizable of the gothic plants today.

Though it is considered highly poisonous, *Amanita muscaria* is believed to be the world's oldest hallucinogen. It was used by Siberian and Lapland shamans in vision quests and in healing rituals, which gave them a sense of flying. This mushroom is reported to be a popular food for reindeer. Interestingly, the shamans in Lapland ate it for enlightenment—which may explain where the legends of the flying reindeer and Santa all dressed in red and white came from! In Europe, these mushrooms were thought to be symbols of good luck at the winter holidays and New Year's Day. This red and white mushroom also became a popular motif in early twentieth-century European postcard art.

Magickally, the fly agaric is associated with the Norse god Odin, who was a shamanic god of knowledge. According to old folklore, these fungi bring good fortune and luck to you, and they also open a doorway to the world of the fae, elves, and other earth elementals. The astrological association is Mercury. The elemental correspondence is air.

> **Warning:** While researching this fungi, I discovered a lot of conflicting information about its legality. In some countries, it is considered illegal to grow, sell,

or to possess the fly agaric mushroom. Other places warn that it is a "Class A drug"—meaning possession could get you a fine and up to seven years in jail. Finally, this toadstool, while gorgeous, is considered intensely poisonous. Should you stumble across some growing wild in the woods, leave them be. Just as in the Wildflowers and Witchery chapter, I suggest that you leave these toadstools alone and work your spontaneous magick for good luck right there while leaving the plant untouched.

Hemlock (*Conium maculatum*)

Folk names include warlock's weed, winter fern, water hemlock, poison hemlock, spotted hemlock, spotted cowbane, and water parsley. This is a biennial plant native to Europe, but it now also grows widely throughout America. It flourishes in waste areas and damp habitats.

According to herbal history, death by hemlock poisoning was the official method of execution in ancient Athens. Hemlock contains the extremely toxic alkaloid coniine in all of its parts, but most particularly in the seeds. Socrates was a famous victim of this toxic plant.

The plant is often mistaken for fennel (*Foeniculum vulgare*). However, the fennel plant has foliage that is described as airy and feathery. I think fennel foliage looks like the delicate asparagus fern, and to help you with further identification, the fennel flowers are aromatic and yellow.

Another hemlock look-alike is the wild carrot, also known as Queen Anne's lace (*Daucus carota*). The flowers of Queen Anne's lace typically have a central floret that is purple. Another noted feature of this

hemlock

wildflower are the hairy stems, and you'll also notice that as the flowers of Queen Anne's lace wither, they contract into bowl-like shapes into which the seeds fall.

Hemlock is also distinguished from similar-looking plants by its foul smell and the markings on its stem. Hemlock's stems are smooth and green and have purple spots, or red and purple streaks, on their lower half. A way to determine whether a plant is poison hemlock is to crush some leaves and smell the result. The fennel smells like anise or licorice, while the smell of poison hemlock is often described as rank, "mouselike," or musty.

Hemlock has fernlike leaves and may grow up to six feet in height. The plant blooms from May through September. It bears white, compound umbel-type flowers that look remarkably similar to Queen Anne's lace. (Hence the careful description of the flowers and the markings on the hemlock stems.) Remember, there will be no central purple floret on hemlock flowers.

Magickal uses are purification, and it was believed to squash your libido. This is another herb that is sacred to the goddess Hecate. Hemlock has feminine energies. Its astrological association is Saturn, and its elemental association is water.

> **Warning:** A baneful herb, hemlock causes death by respiratory paralysis. Do not ingest. It also causes skin irritation on contact.

Mandrake (*Mandragora officinarum*)

Folk names include devil's apple, herb of Circe, ladykins, mannikin, and womandrake. This baneful herb is sacred to Aphrodite and is a native plant of Europe. It has long, oval-shaped leaves that are pointed at the tips. The leaves are described as "malodorous," meaning they stink. The plant does bloom—a pale violet-colored flower in the spring that then matures to round, yellow, pineapple-scented fruits. These toxic fruits were called the golden apples of Aphrodite.

Mandragora can grow up to twelve inches in height and has a long, parsnip-looking root that often resembles a human shape. According to plant folklore, the mandrake screams when it is pulled from the earth—and for best results, you were supposed to pull out the plant by circling it with silver and then in one swift pull remove the entire plant, with the root intact.

The root of the mandrake is what is typically used in magick. Mandrake root is one of the world's oldest narcotics. It is a hallucinogen, and this is one of the herbs often worked into "flying ointments." This herb is classified as a masculine herb, and it has the reputation of being a Witch's hexing herb. For magickal operations, the mandrake is employed as an amulet. The root of the mandrake was often used as a poppet to represent a person. Just possessing a mandrake root and carrying it as a charm was thought to protect the bearer from possession and to bring good health. The root was sometimes displayed upon the mantle of the fireplace to bring success, wealth, and joy to the entire home.

In the language of flowers, mandrake signifies rarity. The astrological correspondence for *Mandragora* is Mercury, and the elemental association is fire.

Warning: This plant is legally restricted in some countries. All parts of the mandrake are extremely toxic and should be handled with caution. Do not ingest.

mandrake

Rue (*Ruta graveolens*)

Folk names include herb of grace, mother of the herbs, Ruta, Witch bane, and garden rue. The rue is an evergreen shrub that can grow from two to three feet in height. It bears small, bright, buttonlike yellow flowers in the summer. The leaves are smooth, deeply divided, and have a greenish blue color. The scent of the rue is described as bracing, and the leaves of this plant are covered in oil glands.

I grow rue in my sunny perennial gardens. It makes a lovely specimen shrub. I clip it into a neatly shaped shrub every summer after it has finished blooming. I wear gardening gloves to do this because the oil from the leaves gives me a bit of a mild rash. Discarded rue foliage is also supposed to help your compost pile break down faster. I toss a few stems into my compost heap every year.

In magick, rue is often used for hex breaking and for warding off the evil eye. Rue is also a classic herb for protection magick and to increase your psychic powers; also, some old love spells call for rue. You can easily tuck a few rue leaves or flowers into a protective sachet. The scent of the plant is strong, so I would not recommend wearing the charm bag; instead, place it inside a purse, briefcase, or drawer. Just be sure to keep it out of the reach of children. Also, to be on the safe side, women who are pregnant should avoid contact with rue.

In the language of flowers, rue signifies grace, clear vision, virtue, atonement, and fresh starts. Rue is a popular herb with Italian traditional Witches, the Strega. Rue foliage is a common theme in magickal silver jewelry called the cimaruta as well. The plant is

rue

sacred to Diana and Aradia. This masculine herb is ruled by the sun, and its elemental correspondence is fire.

Warning: Rue is a toxic plant. Brushing against the foliage may cause contact dermatitis. Do not take internally. It is also an abortifacient.

Wild Poppy (*Papaver rhoeas*)

Folk names include corn poppy, corn rose, field poppy, scarlet poppy, and red poppy. The red wild poppy is an annual that grows to about twelve inches in height. It has long, narrow leaves and a black, hairy stalk. The scarlet-colored flowers bear four petals and have a black center; it blooms in the late spring. The nectar from the field poppy intoxicates bees. These enchanting flowers make an excellent substitute in a Witch's garden for the opium poppy (*Papaver somniferum*), which is banned worldwide, as it is illegal to grow or to possess.

In the language of flowers, the wild poppy has many definitions. An orange poppy symbolizes vanity, while a red poppy stands for comfort. A white poppy whispers of a forgetful and restful sleep and that "I need time to consider your proposal." The Oriental poppy demands silence, while a scarlet-colored wild poppy shouts of decadence.

The poppy is also a symbol of remembrance for those who have fallen in battle. The poppy is also associated with fertility. There are also rumors that the field poppy seeds were once worked into antidotes to unethical love potions.

wild poppy

Magickal uses include love, good luck, prosperity, and sleep—remember the scene from the *Wizard of Oz* movie when Dorothy and her companions fall asleep while running through a field of red poppies? Since the earliest of times, the red poppy has been a symbol of agricultural fecundity. The poppy is sacred to the agricultural goddesses Demeter and Ceres, and it was also grown in the garden of Hecate. It is also a symbol of the messenger god Hermes. Ruled by the moon, the poppy—no matter what its color—is associated with the element of water.

Warning: The foliage of *Papaver rhoeas* is mildly toxic.

Wormwood (*Artemisa absinthium*)

Folk names include absinthe, green ginger, and old woman. A perennial plant that is native to Eurasia and North Africa, it has silvery green foliage, grows to about three feet in height, and can be grown into a hedge. The leaves and the flower heads are a pale green color; as the flowers mature, they change to a golden brown. Wormwood blooms in midsummer.

Wormwood is the bitter herb used to flavor vermouth and the liqueur absinthe. The scent of wormwood is thought to increase psychic abilities. This herb is also dried and worked into sachets to repel moths and fleas. Legend states that if you burn the plant at a graveyard, it will summon the spirit of the departed. If wormwood is carried in a sachet or charm bag,

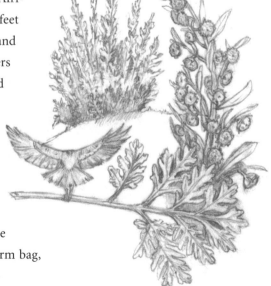

wormwood

it protects against bewitchment. This baneful herb was also worked into enchantments for love. It is sacred to Artemis, Pan, and Diana.

In the language of flowers, wormwood symbolizes a sad parting of friends. This is classified as a masculine plant. Its astrological influences are the planet Mars and the element of fire.

Warning: This plant is considered to be toxic and should not be ingested.

Yew (*Taxus baccata*)

The English yew was considered protective if grown in the garden, yard, or churchyard. Yew is a slow-growing and long-lived evergreen that can grow from fifty to eighty feet in height. The tree has a rounded crown and rusty brown, scaly bark. The "leaves" are deep green, flattened needles alternately arranged on the stems. This is a dioecious tree, meaning there are male and female plants. The male yew has flowers that are small, round cones. They release their pollen in the early spring. The female yew has a flower that is described as a small green bud, which is then followed by the red, fleshy fruit.

This tree was sacred to the Druids and is rumored to have been used in their ceremonies. In the old days, wood from the yew was often made into longbows and dagger hilts, as the wood was both flexible and close-grained. Today, this is a popular tree in landscaping and garden design. The yew grows wild in Europe, North America, and Asia. Yew is considered a "tree of death," as its poisonous properties are so well known. Conversely, it is also known as a symbol of immortality and life after death, which explains its popularity in church graveyards.

yew

In the language of flowers, yew symbolizes both sorrow and perseverance. The yew is the tree of Hecate, goddess of Witchcraft. Few plants will grow under the branches of the yew. To grow such an enchanted tree in your garden is a sign of commitment to the old religion, for it symbolizes magickal protection, defense, and comfort gained from the wisdom of the Witch. Yew is ruled by the planet Saturn, and its elemental correspondence is water.

> **Warning:** Yew is toxic to both animals and people; do not ingest. The needlelike leaves are toxic. The red berries the female yew produces and the seeds inside the fruit are even more lethal.

MACABRE NAMES, MAGICKAL PLANTS

What's in a name? That which we call a rose
By any other name would smell as sweet.

SHAKESPEARE, *ROMEO AND JULIET*

In the old days, magickal spells listed wild ingredients with macabre, bloodcurdling names. My theory is that this was done for a couple of reasons. First, should someone discover the ingredients for a Witch's spell, they would have no idea what the real herbal components were. Second, as very few people could read or write, giving the plants outrageous names helped folks to remember their spell ingredients.

I honestly could not write on gothic herbs and forbidden plants without including this list; it was simply too entertaining to pass up. Here is a list of these dramatically named herbal spell components and the actual plant they describe, then the botanical name for proper plant identification. Once again, these plants are listed for informational purposes only. Some of these plants you will recognize as common garden plants, like the snapdragon, pansy, willow, chamomile, and holly. Meanwhile, other plants in this list are classified as toxic, even though they may be popular landscape specimens, and the poisonous plants are denoted with an asterisk.

It's up to you to use your own good sense and to handle all botanicals correctly and carefully. After all, even the innocent-looking azalea shrub and the morning glory vine are both poisonous—but I trust that you won't go and munch on those either.

ADDER'S TONGUE: plantain (*Plantago major*)

BAT WINGS: holly leaf* (*Ilex* spp.)

BAT'S WOOL: moss

BIRD'S EYE: pansy (*Viola tricolor*)

BLOODY FINGERS: foxglove* (*Digitalis purpurea*)

CALF'S SNOUT: snapdragon (*Antirrhinum majus*)

CORPSE CANDLES: mullein (*Verbascum thaspus*)

DRAGON'S SCALE: bistort leaves (*Polygonum bistorta*)

DRUID FOOT: common club moss (*Lycopodium clavatum*)

EYES: English lawn daisy (*Bellis perennis*)

FIVE FINGERS: cinquefoil (*Potentilla* spp.)

GAGROOT: lobelia* (*Lobelia* spp.)

GHOST FLOWER: datura* (*Datura stramonium*)

GHOST HERB: St. John's wort (*Hypericum perforatum*)

GRAVEYARD DUST: mullein (*Verbascum thaspus*)

GROUND APPLE: chamomile (*Anthemis nobilis*)

GROUND BREAD: cyclamen* (*Cyclamen* spp.)

HAG'S TAPERS: mullein (*Verbascum thaspus*)

HEAVEN'S KEY: primrose (*Primula veris*)

JOVE'S NUTS: oak (*Quercus* spp.)

KNIT BONE: comfrey (*Symphytun officinale*)

LION'S FOOT: lady's mantle (*Alchemilla vulgaris*)

LION'S TOOTH: dandelion (*Taraxacun officinale*)

NOSEBLEED: yarrow (*Achillea millefolium*)

OLD LADY: elder tree (*Sambucus canadensis*)

OLD MAN: mugwort* (*Artemisia*)

PISS-A-BED: dandelion (*Taraxacun officinale*)

QUICKBANE: rowan tree, aka the mountain ash
    (*Sorbus acuparia*)

SCAFFOLD FLOWER: carnation (*Dianthus*)

SKULL: skullcap* (*Scutellaria incana*)

SNAKE WEED: bistort (*Polygonum bistorta*)

SORCERER'S VIOLET: periwinkle* (*Vinca minor*)

STINGING NETTLE: nettle (*Urtica dioica*)

STINKWEED: garlic (*Allium sativum*)

oak

THORN: hawthorn tree (*Crataegus mollis*)

TREE OF ENCHANTMENT: willow (*Salix* spp.)

TREE OF EVIL: English walnut tree (*Juglans regia*)

TREE OF LOVE: apple tree (*Pyrus Malus*)

WINTER BLOOM: Witch hazel (*Hamamelis virginiana*)

WITCHES' BANE: rowan (*Sorbus acuparia*)

WITCH'S ELM: European white elm (*Ulmus laevis*)

WITCH'S EGG: Fly agaric mushroom * (*Amanita muscaria*)

WOUND WORT: yarrow (*Achillea* spp.)

YELLOW HENBANE: Flowering tobacco * (*Nicotiana*)

HECATE AND HERBALISM

O night, faithful friend of mysteries;
and you golden stars and moon,
who follow the fiery star of day;
and you Hecate, goddess with the threefold head,
you know my designs and come to strengthen
my spells and magic arts…
OVID, *PRAYER OF MEDEA TO HECATE*

As I am sure you have noticed, many of the featured herbs in this chapter are sacred to the triple goddess Hecate—especially the yew tree. The yew symbolizes wisdom, death, and rebirth, just as Hecate does herself. Hecate, or Hekate, was the only Titan to retain her powers when the twelve Olympians took over. According to legend, Zeus respected Hecate so much that he gave her dominion over parts of the heavens, the earth, and the sea. Not only was Hecate a triple goddess, she could appear as a beautiful maiden, a seductive and mature woman, or as an old woman.

Often described as "tenderhearted and loving," there is much more to her than many people realize. She was also known as the queen of sorcery, queen of ghosts, and of course as the patroness of Witches and magicians. Hecate is a multifaceted deity. She is the guardian of the crossroads, a light-bringer, a midwife, and the goddess of death. It is important to realize that Hecate does not bring death—it is she who is waiting for you when you cross over to lead you on to the afterlife.

In ancient times, the first herbalists were Witches, or wise women. Hecate has always been connected to Witchcraft, fertility, and agriculture, just as the two other goddesses she is often associated with—Persephone and Demeter—are connected. In this trinity, Persephone is the Maiden, Demeter is the Mother, and Hecate is the Crone.

Hecate as a goddess of fertility, death, and rebirth makes sense to me, for as a seed falls to the ground from a declining plant, that seed goes through its dark days and germinates in the black soil. Then, after a time, it begins to grow toward the light, so from the dark earth springs life. As any gardener or Witch knows, death is not the end. It is only part of the cycle.

Over the years, when I have taught classes to the public, I find people have very strong reactions to Hecate. They either adore her or she scares the hell out of them. For myself, I have found that as I grow older, the more Hecate appeals to me. I have always been comfortable with her, but as my children have grown into adults and are leaving the nest to go off to college, Hecate calls to me even more. And I know many other Witches who feel the same way.

Medea, a famous sorceress from ancient times, was a priestess of Hecate. Medea prayed to Hecate for knowledge and skill when it came to handling her herbs and poisons for her Witchcraft. It is part of her prayer that is the quote at the beginning of this section. In the *Orphic Song of the Argonauts*, a garden of Hecate is described, along with her sacred plants, some medicinal and others not.

A few more herbs that are sacred to Hecate and that were grown in her garden are dandelions, date palm, garlic, germander, lavender, mallow, mint, mugwort, myrrh, pea, pennyroyal, peony, pomegranate, saffron, sarsaparilla, and thyme. These additional trees fall under her patronage as well: black poplar, cedar, cypress, hazel, juniper, silver poplar, and willow.

I have to say, by the time I finished writing this chapter, I felt like I should be sitting in my office, twiddling my fingers and saying, "Mwha-ha-ha." Maybe that's because I find it very interesting that the classic Witch's garden of plants was thought to be filled with the most potent of poisons. Or perhaps some clever Witches got the rumor going to keep people out of their gardens.

In some books, Witches are still portrayed as being absolutely wicked, and their gardens are described as places that the rest of humanity recoils from. There are some gothically creepy descriptions of Witch's gardens as dark, foreboding grounds filled with the most evil of plants. I imagine the person who wrote such ominous prose decided that we were all out there skulking about—under the cover of darkness, no less—gathering our plants and plotting something sinister while we threw our heads back and cackled at the waning moon.

Oh, please. Now I will admit to feeling rather sinister from time to time, but that's usually just my PMS talking. But to say that a plant is "wicked" is ridiculous. In nature, nothing is "good" or "evil." Nature is a neutral energy, just like magick. And both nature and magick are a force and a power that is to be respected and revered. It's how this force is used that is the deciding factor as to whether the magick is beneficial or detrimental.

In closing, here is a prayer to Hecate. May she grant you the perception and the wisdom to use all of your herbal magick skills wisely.

A Prayer to Hecate

Hecate Phosphorous, the light bringer, shed your illumination down on me,

Hecate Trivia, triple faced, protect me whether I am in air, on land, or at sea.

Hecate Nykterian, lady of the night, guide my hand and heart,

Teach me to use your sacred plants wisely and grow in my Witch's art.

willow

Chapter 8

Herbs and Plants
of the Sabbats

Herbs, like everything in the universe,
have an aura, an invisible charge of energy
that radiates from within and without.

LAURIE CABOT,
CELEBRATE THE EARTH

At the different sabbats during the Witch's year, there are certain botanicals that align with the energies of the season. In this chapter, we will take a look at some of the herbs, plants, and flowers that are associated with each sabbat and their magick and folklore. Included in this category will be their magickal and planetary associations, florigraphy information, and an accompanying spell or flower fascination for each sabbat.

Remember that for a plant to be classified as an herb, some part of the plant—such as the flower, fruit, seed, leaf, bark, or even the wood—must be used for scent, food, flavorings, dye, or medicine. This is the classic definition of the word *herb*.

Admittedly, some of this botanical information may surprise you. For example, in the Yule section, I did not want to rehash information that was previously given in chapter five, like how holly and ivy, while being two of the featured trees from the Celtic year, also play a significant role in Yuletide festivities—which I am sure you are already aware of. So in order to present some fresh information, the focus here will be on other plants that are available to you at this time of year in nature or herbs and botanicals that you can easily procure.

Magick happens during all of the seasons. Take a new look at these herbs of the sabbats, and let this information inspire you to create even more herbal spells of your own design.

SAMHAIN
Halloween

O hushed October morning mild,
Begin the hours of this day slow.
Make the day seem to us less brief.
ROBERT FROST

Rosemary (*Rosemarinus officianalis*)

The herb rosemary symbolizes remembrance. I think this herb is highly appropriate at Samhain, as we remember our loved ones and the women and men who died for our religious freedom. If rosemary is burned during a ritual, it has a powerful cleansing effect. Sprigs of rosemary may be worn or braided into your hair to boost personal protection. It may also be used as a more affordable substitute for frankincense. This is a must-have herb for any sunny herb garden. The very fragrance of rosemary smells like Witchcraft to me.

A tea made from rosemary is thought to boost your psychic powers and to open up the third eye. In the art of florigraphy (also known as the language of flowers), the rosemary says, "Your presence revives me!" It also symbolizes fidelity, devotion, and good luck in the new year.

Magickal associations of rosemary include protection, love, sleep, boosting psychic power, exorcism, and healing. Rosemary is classified as a masculine herb. The astrological correspondence for rosemary is the sun, and the element is fire.

Lesser Periwinkle (*Vinca minor*)

This popular evergreen can be found in most garden centers across the country. This popular nursery plant can grow up to twelve inches in height, and it widely spreads out to form a dense mat of groundcover for shady areas in the garden. The folk names of this plant are many, but my favorite has to be the sorcerer's violet. Periwinkle blooms twice a year: once heavily in the spring and then again lightly in the autumn. The flowers are purple and have five petals with a white star in the center—which is how the plant got its folk name, after all; the five-pointed magician's star was right there for everyone to see.

Please do not confuse the annual sun-loving flower vinca for the periwinkle. I get letters from gardening Witches about this question every year. The botanical name of this enchanting herb is *Vinca minor*, and it is often how this magickal plant is identified and sold. You will find it in the shady groundcover section at the nursery.

Old plant lore claims that this herb should only be gathered on the night of the new crescent and the night before the full moon, for gathering an herb during the waxing moon would only increase its protective powers. This herb has ties to Samhain, as legend has it the periwinkle was commonly grown across graves in France, which means it was often gathered by magickal practitioners at the local cemeteries (and probably under the cover of darkness so folks would be able to gather the herb discreetly for their various magickal workings).

Magickal associations include protection, love, prosperity, banishing, and bindings, and as you would imagine, the herb neatly wards off the evil eye. The periwinkle is considered to be a feminine plant. Its astrological influence is Venus, and the elemental correspondence is water.

Pumpkin (*Cucurbita*)

The vining annual plant is native to the Americas. It bears fruit in late autumn. The plant creates large, broad leaves and shoots out with trailing vines that blossom. Technically, the male flowers are in leaf axils, while the female, fruit-bearing flowers are born along the vine. At the base of the blossom, a tiny pumpkin will grow.

The pumpkin is indeed considered to be an herb because parts of the plant (the fruit and the seeds) are edible. Pumpkins replaced the traditional turnip in Samhain festivities, as they are much easier to carve into lanterns for frightening away those roaming spirits. If created with intention, a carved jack-o'-lantern is indeed a powerful and protective tool.

The magickal associations of the plant are protection, harvest, abundance, and lunar magick. The pumpkin is considered a feminine plant. Its astrological correspondence is the moon, and the elemental association is water.

Recently, I was in Salem, Massachusetts, during late October for an author event. It was wild—think Mardi Gras with a witchy theme. To my amusement, I noticed people buying pumpkin seeds by the bagful in various magickal shops. When I asked one store's proprietor, who happened to be Laurie Cabot, what was up with the pumpkin seeds, she responded that if a Witch carried pumpkin seeds in their pockets, they would be invisible.

With a clever smile, she basically explained to me that when she carried the pumpkin seeds in her pocket, she could then go about her business and walk home to her apartment without being bothered or even noticed by others. The enchanted pumpkin seeds cast a glamour of sorts on the carrier, enabling them to blend in and not draw attention to themselves. Brilliant! When you think about it, this would come in damn handy during all the tourism and Witch-wannabe craziness that hits Salem in October. That information has been tickling my imagination ever since, so here is a pumpkin seed spell inspired by my trip to Salem.

Salem Pumpkin Seed Glamour

For best results, perform this glamour during a waning moon. As the moon becomes smaller, so too will your chances of being noticed. If you like, you can place the enchanted seeds inside of a sachet bag or tie them inside of a three-inch square of plain black fabric (a very appropriate color for Samhain), and then tie it up with a satin ribbon. I would recommend using a grey-colored ribbon, both to represent the glamour and that you are working to blend in and go unnoticed.

Hold up the seeds in your hands, and visualize them glowing with a bit of your own personal power. Now, see in your mind's eye what it is you want these pumpkin seeds to do, which is to make your actions go unnoticed and to allow you to blend in to your environment. Now, repeat the following spell verse three times:

The pumpkin is the fruit of the Lady Moon,

Now enchant these seeds and grant this Witch a boon.

My movements go unnoticed and I pass easily by,

Be it bright sunshine or midnight's mysterious sky.

A trick from a clever Salem Witch, I'll seem invisible to all.

With a bit of glamour in my pocket and the magick of the fall,

By all the magick of three times three,

As I will it, then so must it be.

When you have finished the spell, slip a few of the seeds into your charm bag and tie it closed, or simply tuck a few seeds into your pocket or purse. Now, just go about your witchy business, confident in your spellwork.

Yule
Winter Solstice

I have forgotten much, but still remember
The poinsettia's red, blood-red in warm December.

CLAUDE MCKAY

Poinsettia (*Euphorbia pulcherrima*)

A very popular tropical plant for the winter holidays, some folk names for the poinsettia include "most beautiful spurge" and "flower of the holy night." The poinsettia has some very interesting Pagan lore. The poinsettia symbolized purity for the Aztecs and was known as Cuetlaxochitle. The plant was used both medicinally and to produce a reddish dye. Tradition has it that the Aztec king Montezuma enjoyed the poinsettia so much that he would bring the plants into his home. According to the Mayan folklore of South America, the poinsettia is considered to be a sort of divine life form.

As you would expect, the poinsettia is a native plant of Mexico and Central America, where the plant may grow as tall as a tree. The flower part of the plant is the small, golden-colored buds in the center of the colored leaves. These golden buds are correctly called cyathia. The red "flower petals" of the plant are actually not the flowers at all—those are, in fact, colored bracts, or leaves.

While the poinsettia, a member of the *Euphorbia* (spurge) family, is not edible, it is not as toxic as you may have heard. Spurges in general tend to be harshly laxative; while the poinsettia may make you ill, it is typically not deadly—an upset stomach is more likely. The sap of the plant may cause contact dermatitis (skin irritation), and allergic reactions to the plant, such as sneezing, are not unusual. To avoid problems, I would simply keep this plant well out of reach of nibbling pets and small children.

The poinsettia plant is a fairly new addition to winter holiday customs here in the United States. It was brought to the United States in the early 1800s by Joel Robert Poinsett, the first ambassador to Mexico. The story goes that while living in Mexico, he was so impressed by the showy plant that he brought cuttings back to his home in South Carolina, where it then thrived in his greenhouse, as poinsettias will not survive in temperatures below 50 degrees Fahrenheit. The flowers did so well that Mr. Poinsett gave the tropical plants away as gifts to his friends.

Today, hybridizers have gone crazy with the traditional red poinsettia, and now you can find these plants in shades of red, pink, white, and yellow. Also, speckled varieties in a mixture of colors are common. One of my favorite things to do on a gloomy day in early December is to visit a local greenhouse and see all the thousands of poinsettias in all their various colors all lined up on tables and waiting to be purchased.

There are no "traditional" magickal associations of this tropical plant, so I'd say it's about time to assign it some. Due to the plant's tropical nature and ties to the Aztecs and Mayans, the astrological association of the sun would be very complementary. The element of fire also fits nicely, since this plant is originally a flame red color and demands warm temperatures.

Mistletoe (*Viscum album*)

Mistletoe is commonly found growing as a parasitic plant; however, it can be a semi-parasite (the correct botanical term for this is a hemi-parasite). As a parasitic plant, it grows on the branches or trunk of a tree and actually sends out roots that penetrate into the tree and take up nutrients. However, mistletoe is also capable of growing all on its own; like other plants, it can manufacture its own food by photosynthesis.

Folk names include the golden bough and the kissing bunch; the Druids called it all-heal. Mistletoe grows on deciduous trees such as apple, ash, hawthorn, birch, and occasionally on oak trees. The plant forms pendent bushes that are two to five feet in diameter. It has been found growing on almost any deciduous tree, preferring those with soft bark. Finding mistletoe growing on an oak is rare, which is why the Celts and Druids prized it so. Mistletoe is still used today for powerful protection magick and fertility magick, as the white berries were thought to resemble drops of semen.

There are two types of mistletoe. The mistletoe that is commonly used as a winter holiday decoration is typically *Phoradendron flavescens*. This is a native species to North America and grows as a parasite on trees from New Jersey to Florida. The other type of mistletoe, *Viscum album*, is of European origin. The European mistletoe is a green shrub with small yellow flowers and white sticky berries that are considered the most poisonous. Both varieties of the plant are toxic and have twigs that fork around a central flower cluster, which produces white berries. Folk names for this plant include the golden bough, birdlime, Witches' broom, and holy wood, while the Celts called it "a different twig."

According to Druidic customs, the plant was to be harvested at Midsummer with a golden sickle and was never allowed to touch the ground.

The practice of kissing under the mistletoe comes from old Pagan fertility rites or some say from the legend of Balder. Balder was the best loved of all the Norse gods and the son of the Mother Goddess Frigga. She loved her son so much that she wanted to make sure no harm could ever possibly befall him. So she went through the world, gathering promises from everything that sprang from the four elements—earth, air, fire, and water—that they would never harm her son, but she overlooked the mistletoe. Enter into this story Loki, the trickster god, who discovered her oversight. He made an arrow from the mistletoe and then took the arrow to Balder's brother Hoder, who was blind. Guiding Hoder's aim, Loki directed the arrow at Balder's heart, and he fell dead.

In the account of the story with a happy ending, Balder is restored to life, and Frigga's tears became the mistletoe's white berries. The goddess was so grateful that her son was restored that she reversed the reputation of the offending plant, making it a symbol of love and promising to bestow a kiss upon anyone who passes under it.

In the language of flowers, mistletoe conveys the flowing message, "I give you as many kisses as there are stars in the sky." This magickal plant is considered masculine. Its magickal associations are protection, love, fertility, hex breaking, and the removal of entities and evil spirits. Its astrological correspondence is the sun, and the elemental association is air.

Pine (*Pinus* spp.)

The noble pine tree is a gorgeous evergreen tree classified as a coniferous tree. There are over one hundred varieties of the pine. Pines grow all over the globe, in many shapes and sizes. Some varieties of this tree may reach heights up to 135 feet. A few varieties you may be familiar with are the slash pine (*Pinus elliottii*), the Eastern white pine (*Pinus strobus*), and the Scots pine (*Pinus sylvestris*), which is the national tree of Scotland.

The fruit of the pine tree, the cone, is a fertility symbol and is often used to tip magickal wands. The pine was the sacred tree of the goddess Astarte and also of the gods Pan, Dionysus, and Sylvanus, who often accompanied each other (all three were gods of the woods, forests, and fields). Pine boughs, trees for decorating, and other items made from the pine, such as wreaths, are a classic plant to add to your Yuletide festivities and decorations.

Bringing fresh greens in the house at midwinter was thought to ensure health and good luck for the entire year. Rumor has it that it also gave the winter faeries a place to hide, as they came inside with the greenery, giving the faeries a holiday of sorts as they enjoyed the warmth, activity, and mood of the home during the Yuletide festivities.

In the language of flowers, the pine tree symbolizes friendship, loyalty, endurance, and long life. The astrological correspondence for the pine tree is Mars, and the elemental association is air. The tree is considered to be masculine, and the magickal uses for pine are many, including protection, prosperity, and healing. Also, it is said that burning pine needles will return any manipulative spells straight back to the sender.

Return to Sender: Pine Needle Spell

This spell can be cast at any time, day of the week, or moon phase. What matters most is your intention. If your intention is to end the manipulation of another by magick, then put on your game face, take a deep breath, and get down to business.

This spell requires an old cauldron or fireproof dish, matches, and a small handful of dry pine needles. You will also need a small container full of water when the spell is finished. It is best to work this spell outside and with safety in mind. Set the cauldron in a clear, safe area—on top of a table or in the middle of a concrete, brick, or stone patio. Make absolutely sure that the cauldron or burning dish is resting on a fireproof area.

Next, arrange the needles inside of the cauldron and strike the match, setting the needles to light. In this case, we want the smell of sulfur to sting the air. Visualize that the smell of sulfur will follow the troublemaker around for a time. Sound nasty? Well, breaking a spell that was cast on you is not for the faint of heart. Self-defense is your duty; this is a serious spell and not one to be done casually.

As the pine needles start to burn, repeat the spell for as long as there is a flame. If you have to relight the needles to burn them all away, then do so.

These fragrant pine needles, so green and so lush,

Return all spells cast on me back in a rush.

As the pine burns, all ties to me fade away,

Now I am uncrossed, free and clear, come what may.

As the smoke billows up, return the spell back to sender,

May this teach them a lesson they will always remember!

After the needles are completely burned away, keep an eye on them for at least fifteen minutes. While you are doing so, contemplate why the person who cast on you would have been foolish enough to do so. What have you learned from this? After the fifteen minutes has passed, take the water and pour it on top of the ashes. Then say the following to close up the spell:

By fire this spell was cast,

By water it is finished.

As I will it, so must it be.

Remember to be smart and safe and use your common sense. Never leave the small fire unattended, and keep extra water nearby in case of an emergency.

Imbolc
Candlemas

Why, what's the matter,

That you have such a February face,

So full of frost, of storm and cloudiness?

SHAKESPEARE, *MUCH ADO ABOUT NOTHING*

Common Crocus (*Crocus*)

Do not confuse the early spring-blooming garden variety crocus with saffron crocus. The everyday variety (*Crocus*) comes in over eighty species, and the predominant colors of the blossoms are white, purple, and yellow. Found in rock gardens and flower beds, these cheerful and hardy blooming bulbs come in all sorts of combinations and colors, even stripes, and yes, they have been known to bloom cheerfully away in the snow and ice.

In the language of flowers, the common crocus symbolizes that you shall remain young at heart, no matter what your age. The magickal associations are freshness, love, and romance. The astrological association for the feminine common garden crocus is the planet Venus, and the elemental correspondence is water.

> **Garden Witch Tip:** The common crocus is not meant to be consumed. However, in the interest of lending some clarity to these two bewitching plants, here is the information on the saffron crocus as well.

Saffron Crocus (*Crocus sativus*)

Unlike their common garden-blooming cousins, the saffron crocus does, in fact, bloom in the autumn, and the flowers are a soft lilac-pink color. The stigmas of the saffron crocus are a highly prized culinary spice. Why? Because they are expensive and costly to gather. It takes over 1,700 flowers to produce one ounce of saffron. Saffron is also used as a dye and in cosmetics. Magickally, saffron was considered to be an aphrodisiac and was used to promote love and lust as well as to strengthen psychic abilities.

The definition in the language of flowers is different than that of the common crocus. Here, the masculine energies of the saffron crocus warn you of excess and not to overdo it, which is probably a nod to the cost of obtaining this magickal herb. The planetary correspondence for saffron is the sun; its elemental association is fire.

Common Snowdrop (*Galanthus nivalis*)

The botanical name for this flower translates to "milk-white flower." Folk names include Fair-Maids-of-February, winter bell, Candlemas bells, and the milk flower; it was known to all the old-time botanists as a bulbous violet. This plant begins flowering in late January or early February in the northern temperate zone. The white flower has six petals, the outer three segments being larger and more curvy than the inner petals. The plant grows four to six inches tall. There are about twelve species of *Galanthus* and many variations of the spring-blooming, bulbous herb.

In the language of flowers, this plant means hope, renewal, and also consolation. The snowdrop is a divine flower; it brings the hope and promise of spring during the darkest and coldest winter days. As I researched this flower, I discovered that this is the flower of the archangel of Saturn, Cassiel, who is also known as the angel of temperance, creativity, and good fortune. He is associated with the following attributes: acceptance, wisdom, good luck, creativity, and optimism. This archangel inspires us to expand our minds, be creative, and think on a higher level. Cassiel, as the angel of good fortune, will help you to create your own luck, so you can have the strength and the conviction to work hard and then to reap the rewards of all that effort.

The astrological correspondence for the snowdrop is Saturn. A good elemental association for this flower would be the element of earth.

An Angelic Herbal Enchantment for Motivation

I designed this spell for myself when I was under the deadline gun to finish this very book. It was early December, and the completed manuscript was due in mid-February. My nerves were shot, as I was constantly interrupted by phone calls, errands, my kids coming home from college, decorating for Yule, and my other family commitments, not to mention trying to find time to shop for Yule presents.

As I researched the snowdrop plant, I stumbled across the information on the archangel Cassiel and his links to it, and I felt my stomach flip over. I got that psychic tingle that lets me know when I am on to something good. In the past, I had worked magick with angels, but it wasn't something I did on a regular basis.

Regardless, I knew there was a reason I had found all the information and how suitable and appropriate it seemed for my needs. It felt like the universe was giving me a psychic nudge. After all, I had been asking the God and Goddess for help to get this project finished on time, and right there, falling neatly into my lap, was this fabulous information. So, with the holidays fast approaching and the deadline getting closer every day, I decided to give this a try. It worked so well for me that I decided to share it with you. Oh, and if you are wondering—yes, Witches can work with angels. Try it out for yourself and see how you do.

Since this archangel is aligned with Saturn, work this spell on a Saturn's day—Saturday. If possible, work with the snowdrop plant; a blossom or two in a little vase would be lovely. If you cannot procure the fresh blossoms, then I would light a snow-white candle instead. Votive, pillar, jar, or taper candle—it's your choice. (Being a practical Witch, I found a picture of the blooming snowdrop plant on the web, printed it out, and glued it onto a seven-day jar candle.)

Once you have the flowers arranged and/or the candle burning, repeat the following spell verse:

I call upon Cassiel; the snowdrop is your sacred flower,

Help me finish my project in a timely manner and hour.

Even as the snowdrop blooms in the darkest and coldest of days,

Help me to remain strong, focused, and motivated, come what may.

May Cassiel, the archangel of creativity,

Assist me now, and as I will it, so must it be!

Allow the candle to burn out in a safe place on its own.

OSTARA
Spring Equinox

Spring, the sweet spring, is the year's pleasant king;
Then blooms each thing, then maids dance in a ring,

THOMAS NASHE

Violet (*Viola odorata*)

Folk names for this fragrant herb include blue violet and sweet violet. The heart-shaped leaf of the violet is an amulet that protects from all evil. Wearing a chaplet of violets is an old way to cure a headache. Violets were often utilized with rose petals and lavender in love-drawing sachets and as a main spell component for romance magick. As these little beauties are a sacred plant of the goddess of love, Venus, she is sure to lend you a hand with your herb magick when the spell ingredients feature the violet.

In the language of flowers, the violet symbolizes modesty and sweetness, while a rarer white violet declares innocence and honesty. Magickal uses are protection, love, and lust. Also, the violet is a classic plant that is used to protect a person from being faerie led or tricked. Its protective qualities make it an ideal plant for working faerie magick. Try gathering the violets into a little posy and tucking it into a small glass or vase. This is thought to appease the nature spirits and the faeries.

On an interesting note, the violet is also the sacred flower of the archangel Sachiel. Sachiel is the archangel of Jupiter. His day is Thursday. Sachiel's energy brings riches and a sense of charity. All financial situations, politics, and material wealth are under his influence, which

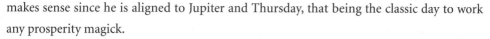

makes sense since he is aligned to Jupiter and Thursday, that being the classic day to work any prosperity magick.

So here is another bit of information for you to file away. Yes, the traditional magickal correspondences for the violet are Venus and love. However, the violet is a powerful little flower with many uses and associations such as the following little morsel of flower lore. According to tradition, all "blue" flowers are sacred to Aphrodite and Venus. Adding this spring flower to any spell or ritual while invoking the goddesses of love will gather their attention and grant their favors. The classic astrological influence of the violet is the planet Venus, and the elemental correspondence is water.

Dandelion (*Taraxacum officinale*)

Easily identified by its bright yellow flowers, dandelions may be considered weeds by many a homeowner, but in the old days, dandelion greens offered a much-needed edible source and a spring tonic. The flowers can be made into wine, and the leaves—which have lots of vitamin A and C—may even be tossed into a salad. A few of the folk names for dandelion are blowball, lion's tooth, and wild endive. The root of the dandelion will yield a magenta dye.

In the language of flowers, the dandelion is called an oracle of love. It also reminds you that wishes do come true. The magickal properties of this herb include divination, increasing psychic abilities, and granting wishes. Old flower folklore suggests plucking a dandelion's seed head on the night of a full moon, then requesting the aid of the four winds. Make a wish, and blow away the seeds.

This masculine plant is sacred to Hecate. Its astrological influences are Jupiter, and the elemental correspondence is air.

Red Clover (*Trifolium pratense*)

This variety of clover and the following one are common plants that have some similar properties as well as their own unique messages and magick. Clover is a perfect plant to celebrate the spring, green magick, and new beginnings. Tucking the four-leaf clover in your wallet will encourage an increase in your cash. Traditionally, placing a four-leaf clover in your shoe is thought to ensure good luck and ease on your travels; it will also allow you to see the faeries. To do that, you are supposed to stand still for three hours. (Good luck.) All varieties of clover are sacred to the faeries. Wear a crown of clover blossoms and sit out in the garden this spring, and see what they show and teach you. You remember how to make those, don't you? Just about every kid has made clover flower necklaces and crowns at some time. Seems to me a little foolishness this spring will do you wonders. Besides, the faeries will get a good chuckle at you sitting there trying to make it perfect. Don't obsess over it being gorgeous; instead, just relax and enjoy yourself. The clover is a perfect plant to incorporate into your springtime magick.

In the language of flowers, the four-leaf clover announces that "you are mine" and that "you are lucky." The three-leaf clover is a symbol for the power of three. Those three leaves are also a sacred symbol of the Celtic triple goddess Brigid. While the red clover's flower is typically a reddish color, there are some varieties of red clover that produce pink flowers. These pink-blooming clovers warn you, "Do not trifle with my affections," while the red clover requests entreaty and asks that you "remain faithful even though we are apart."

Magickally, the masculine red clover may be utilized in prosperity spells and is used to promote love and a dose of healthy lust. Carrying red clover blossoms on your person was thought to attract a new lover. It also helped you heal after a breakup or a love gone sour. The astrological association for the red clover is the planet Mercury, and the elemental association is air.

White Clover (*Trifolium repens*)

The white clover is a plant that is grown either as a hay crop or as a method of putting nutrients back in the soil as a type of green fertilizer. White clover has pale blossoms, which state in the language of flowers that "I will be faithful."

Clover foliage is also used to predict the weather. If you find clover with their green leaves closed up tight, that is thought to be a sign of a coming rainstorm. Magickal uses besides the obvious four-leaf good-luck clover are varied and interesting. Scattering the blossoms of the white clover at the four main corners of your home will ward off ghosts and entities. Also, the white clover, with its pale crescent marks on the leaves, is thought to counteract a hex or manipulative magick. The astrological powers are the same as the red clover: the planetary influence is Mercury, and the elemental association is air.

A Silly Springtime Clover Spell for Prosperity

Head out to the yard or park this spring, and gather up a handful of blooming clover. Any moon phase or day of the week will work out fine, just pick out a pretty spring day that you can enjoy. To begin, tie the stems from the clover into a chaplet or necklace, and then sit on the grass like a kid. Take off your shoes and socks, and dig your toes into that new green grass. Feel the gentle spring breeze; now, ask the faeries to bless you with prosperity and generosity this spring. Sure, the following verse is tongue-in-cheek—it's supposed to be silly and make you smile. Repeat the following verse three times:

Here I sit in my crown of clover,
Spring faeries, come and look me over!
If you bless me with good luck and prosperity this year,
I vow to be generous and help others far and near.

Enjoy the pretty spring weather and stay on the grass for a while. When you are ready to go, wear your flower chains home and allow them to dry out. Save them, and use them in other spells and charms.

To hold up your part of the vow to the fae, donate to a charity. How about the American Cancer Society, the Humane Society, or a local animal shelter? They can always use a donation or a volunteer. I have a friend that knits little blankets for a cat shelter and another who knits blankets for babies in the ICU. You could adopt a shelter animal, take good care of it, and give it a loving home. Help out a kid, and purchase something from their fundraiser for their school or sports team. Come on, there are plenty of opportunities out there for a little kindness. Give something back, and the faeries will reward your kindness.

BELTANE
May 1

The fairy queen
Bids you increase that loving humour more.
THOMAS CAMPION

Meadowsweet (*Filipendula ulmaria*)

Folk names for this lovely perennial herb include queen of the meadow, lady of the meadow, trumpet weed, and little queen. This blooming herb is almond-scented with creamy white flowers. This was a popular flower in bridal bouquets, which helped earn the flower another one of its folk names, bridal wort. This was a classic strewing herb in medieval times, for not only were the flowers fragrant, but the foliage had a clean hay scent as well. Meadowsweet was also popular for use in the creation of perfumes, as the oil from the flower buds is sweetly scented. It is also a classic dyeing herb; the flower tops yield a yellow-green dye, the leaves and stems a blue tint, and the roots yield a black dye.

This was a sacred herb in Druidic tradition, and it formed a sort of magickal trio of herbs with vervain and mint. Meadowsweet is popular to work into faerie magick, as the fae value strongly scented flowers and herbs. In magick, the meadowsweet flower is worked into spells, arranged into tussie-mussies, and tucked into sweetly fragranced charm bags and sachets to encourage love and good cheer. Meadowsweet promotes peace and contentment, and it also aids in divination. This herb has the planetary correspondence of Jupiter and the elemental association of air.

Male Fern (*Dryopteris filix-mas*)

There are many varieties of ferns from all over the world; however, I want to focus on a common fern that is considered an herb: the male fern. This species of fern is found growing in shady, damp woodlands and hedges in North America and Eurasia. This is a gorgeous specimen of deciduous fern, and it is described as having elegantly divided green fronds that will unroll from the crown of the rhizome. Actually, the young curled fronds of the male fern can be boiled and used as a vegetable. You will see these referred to occasionally as fiddle-heads.

Magickal uses of the male fern include invisibility, faerie magick, protection, healing, lust, and also for encouraging good luck. According to old herb lore, dried fern, when burned indoors in the fireplace or woodstove, will drive away negative spirits and entities, while if the dried fern fronds are burned outdoors, the smoke is thought to encourage rain. The seeds that appear on the underside of the fern fronds are said to grant invisibility. The fern's root, or rhizome, was a popular ingredient in old love spells.

In the language of flowers, the fern symbolizes fascination and a tempestuous passion. The masculine energies of the fern have the planetary correspondence of Mercury and the elemental association of air.

English Daisy (*Bellis perennis*)

This perennial daisy is also known as the lawn daisy. This dainty flower is a native of Europe and Western Asia. It grows up to six inches in height, and the flowers are tiny with white ray florets surrounded by yellow discs. This plant attracts pollinators such as bees and butterflies. It is described as being short-lived and is a classic symbol of innocence, youth, and spring.

Magickally, this flower induces loving feelings and fascination. Also, it is a classic herb to use in children's magick; in fact, one of its folk names is bairn wort, which translates to "babies' herb." In floral vocabularies, the English daisy symbolizes a newborn baby and happiness. The astrological association for the English daisy is Venus, and the elemental correspondence is water.

American Oxeye Daisy (*Chrysanthemum leucanthemum*)

This perennial daisy is much larger in stature than its tiny cousin. The sun-loving oxeye daisy grows up to three feet in height and is a popular flower for gardening and floral arrangements. This particular daisy is sacred to Artemis, Maiden Goddess of the hunt and of the waxing moon. One of the folk names for this flower is rather illuminating: moon daisy. This plant has feminine energies and is considered to be a woman's herb. White daisies are a classic Beltane flower, and legend has it that the daisy, in all its shapes and sizes, is a faerie plant.

In the language of flowers, the oxeye daisy symbolizes purity, simplicity, and patience, and is used to signify affection. It may also be used in divination. The classic "he loves me, he loves me not" charm is typically worked with a daisy. Magickally, the oxeye daisy is worked into faerie magick, love and romance spells, and spells for children and happiness. The magickal correspondences for the oxeye daisy are the planet Venus and the element of water.

A Goddess Blessing for Children

Here is a good spell to work with your children. For best results, work the spell during a waxing moon. As the moon grows fuller, so will the Lady's blessing increase upon your child. If you'd like to work the spell as soon as possible, you can always work on a Monday, no matter what the lunar phase, for Mondays are sacred to the moon and all of her magick.

Gather a few daisies. These may be picked from your own garden or purchased from the local florist—whichever is the easiest and most practical way for you to procure the flowers. Now gather the flowers together, trim the stems to a workable length, and bind them together loosely with a white ribbon. Tuck the flower stems into a sturdy little vase or cup filled with water, and set them in a prominent spot in the child's room.

Bless the flowers by holding the child's hands above the flowers and repeating the charm three times. Note that this is worded either for an older child to work the spell all by themselves or for an adult to work the spell for a young child.

> *By the light of the Lady's waxing crescent moon,*
>
> *Artemis, hear my call, and grant me now/this child a boon.*
>
> *Please bless and protect me/them through all of my/their days,*
>
> *May I/they come to know your magick in wonderful ways.*
>
> *By the fascination of flowers and the charm of daisies,*
>
> *May my request be granted with the power of three times three.*

Allow the daisies to remain in their vase until the flowers begin to fade. Once they do, remove the ribbon, and then return the flowers to nature neatly by adding them to your compost pile or putting the faded flowers with your other yard waste. Save the ribbon as a token of the Goddess's favor and affection.

MIDSUMMER
Summer Solstice

Merry Margaret,
As midsummer flower,
Gentle as falcon
Or hawk of the tower.

JOHN SKELTON

Vervain (*Verbena officinalis*)

Vervain is a plant with power and magickal versatility; some folk names include enchanter's plant and holy wort. Vervain is a hardy perennial plant with small, pale pink- and lilac-colored flowers that bloom midsummer. It is the herb most often used to "make spells go," as vervain gives magick a little extra kick and punch and speeds up the outcome of your spellwork. It will nicely complement any type of spellwork—love, protection, vision questing, purification, prosperity, turning your rival into your ally, bestowing peace, healing, and granting a good night's sleep.

In the language of flowers, this feminine herb speaks of granting good luck and making wishes come true—perhaps because of this, vervain is considered to be an excellent herb for a bride to carry in her bouquet. In the older language of flowers, the definition of the blooming vervain is just one word: Witchcraft.

Other quick herb magick tips include tucking a sprig of vervain into your wallet; it's thought to help you hold on to your cash. If you grow vervain in your Witch's garden, it will bring prosperity to your whole house. Lastly, if the blossoms are hung in the bedroom, they promote conjugal bliss and pleasant dreams. The planetary correspondence is Venus. The elemental association is Earth.

A Vervain Charm for Prosperity

A good time to work this spell would be during a waxing moon. As the moon grows fuller, so will your cash increase. If you do not have the option of waiting for the waxing moon, then work your prosperity spells on a Thursday. Thursday is associated with the planet Jupiter and the magickal influences of prosperity, financial gain, and health.

To begin, take a fresh sprig of vervain (you could use dried if that's all you can find), and hold the herb in your hands. Close your eyes, and visualize that the herb is surrounded with a bright green light. It pulses with positive energy, and your hands will probably start to feel warmer. Clearly see that this herbal charm will bring prosperity and cash in the best possible way, straight into your hands. Then tuck the herb in your purse or wallet, and repeat the following charm three times:

As I tuck a sprig of vervain into my purse or pocket,

Money will always be found, so they say, right in my wallet.

I empower this herb of Venus to grant me prosperity,

Bound by the element of earth and the power of three time three.

Cinquefoil (*Potentilia reptans*)

This herb is also called five-finger grass, as the shape of the leaves look like little hands. Wearing a sprig of cinquefoil is very protective and will bestow articulacy upon the wearer. Magickally, cinquefoil increases cash, strengthens the bond between mother and child, and it can also cleanse you of any negativity. But what this herb is most famous for is that it can break any spells cast on or against you, whether you feel this is a serious problem from an unethical caster, an overzealous lover who is dabbling, or someone who is trying to persuade you to be their friend. In this last scenario, you would feel tugged or pulled toward another person that you previously disliked or were very distrustful of. Now you notice these new feelings out of the blue, and when such a switch is out of character for you, there might be manipulative magick afoot. If you begin to suspect that someone else's magick is at work and it is influencing your actions, then this is the masculine herb to work with for both speedy and excellent results.

According to some floral languages, cinquefoil symbolizes a loving relationship between mother and daughter, which is interesting, as traditional magickal correspondences list this as an herb aligned with masculine energies. Its astrological correspondence is Jupiter, and the elemental association is fire.

St. John's Wort (*Hypericum perforatum*)

Folk names for this herb include "the leaf of the blessed" and Tipton's weed. This perennial herb has woody stems and grows up to three feet in height. The five-petaled, golden yellow flowers bloom midsummer and yield yellow and red dyes. Some sources claim that the plant is toxic and may harm livestock if eaten in large doses, while other herbal reference guides warn that it may cause contact dermatitis (skin rash). This perennial is aggressive and can take over a garden in a few years, so plant it in a spot where it can go crazy or be prepared to keep it under control by thinning it out every other year.

If St. John's wort is gathered on the day of the summer solstice, it is thought to be doubly powerful, granting the powers of invincibility and making you seem irresistible to others. Flower folklore also states that it will help improve your mood and ward off depression. If the stems of this herb are bundled together with a red string or ribbon and hung inside the home, it is thought to protect your home from lightning and from negative entities or ghosts.

Another simple herbal spell calls for the blossoms and leaves of the herb to be placed under your pillow before you turn in for the night. If you do, it is thought to grant visions of your future spouse.

The folklore about this plant is fascinating. The plant's botanical name, *Hypericum*, is derived from a Greek term meaning "over an apparition," which links into the belief that the herb was so intolerable to evil spirits that a mere hint of the fragrance of the plant would cause them to fly away. This also explains the custom of bundling the herb with a red ribbon and then hanging it up in your home on Midsummer's day.

In the language of flowers, this magickal herb declares that you are a prophet, and it also symbolizes protection and superstition. A masculine herb that has long been associated with Midsummer as it blossoms right at that time, St. John's wort has myriad other magickal uses too. This herb may be worked into spells for faerie magick, protection from malevolent faeries, healing, protection, potency, love, joy, and divination. Its astrological association is the sun, and the elemental correspondence is fire.

LUGHNASADH
August 1

If August passes flowerless,
and the frosts come,
will I have learned to rejoice enough
in the sober wonder
of green healthy leaves?

DENISE LEVERTOV

⌁

Sunflower (*Helianthus annus*)

The sunflower is indeed classified as an herb, as the seeds are edible. This fast-growing and stately flower comes in myriad varieties, colors, and heights these days. The stems are typically thick, tall, and hairy. The sunflower produces heart-shaped leaves, and typically its blooming time is late summer. The sunflower is easy to start from seeds and is a very popular garden plant for sunny gardens—especially children's magickal gardens. The sunflower is a plant of the Americas and was utilized in Aztec rituals and perhaps worn by priestesses to denote their rank. Also, the sunflower is thought to be a favored plant by the garden faeries.

According to flower folklore, sleeping with a sunflower beneath your pillow will tell you the truth in any matter. In florigraphy, the sunflower symbolizes haughtiness and ostentation. Other definitions declare that this bright solar flower says you have lofty but pure goals.

Magickally, the sunflower is used to symbolize fame, riches, and royalty. Growing the tall flowers in your sunny gardens is thought to bring success and good fortune to the gardener of the home. As you would expect, the masculine energies of sunflowers carry the planetary association of the sun, for the head of the flower turns toward the sun and follows it during the day. Its elemental correspondence is fire.

Hollyhock (*Althea rosea*)

What is an old-fashioned Witch's garden without the stately hollyhock? There are over sixty varieties of these plants, which are classified as biennials. If you are unfamiliar with the term, a biennial is a plant that grows vegetatively the first year and then is fruiting or dormant the second year. Hollyhocks thrive in full sun and are drought-resistant plants. They can grow up to six feet in height and come in single- and double-blooming varieties. They come in a rainbow of colors: white, red, burgundy, dark purple, yellow, and many shades of pink, from the palest blush to a deep rose. I love these old-fashioned flowers and have yellow hollyhocks planted next to my arbor.

The flowers of the hollyhock are at their peak in July and August, thus making it a perfect flower for Lughnasadh. In the language of flowers, the hollyhock symbolizes fertility and abundance. It also says that "You have inspired me to achieve great things." A white blooming hollyhock indicates female ambition.

Magickally, hollyhock flowers will attract prosperity, success, and wealth. These are a favorite faerie plant, and if you plant hollyhocks by the entrance of your garden, the plant's lucky energies will bless your home with prosperity all year long. The faeries are thought to favor white and pink hollyhocks most of all; supposedly they like to use the hollyhock petals for dresses. The hollyhock's astrological influence is the planet Venus, and it is considered to be a feminine plant. The suggested elemental correspondence is water.

Calendula (*Calendula officinalis*)

Folk names for calendula include pot marigold, summer's bride, and marygold. This tender perennial can grow up to twenty-eight inches in height and is not to be confused with the French marigold. The calendula bears tall, orange-yellow flowers that resemble daisies, and their leaves are paddle shaped. The petals of the pot marigold may be tucked into a charm bag and taken into court to help grant a favorable outcome of the proceedings. Sprinkling the golden calendula petals under the bed will make your dreams come true.

Magickally, the flowers themselves promote cheer and good health. They were also popular as bridal flowers and are often worked into love-promoting sachets and romantic charm bags. In florigraphy, the calendula blossoms symbolize affection, constancy, and an enduring love. The pot marigold is considered to be an herb with masculine energies. Its planetary association is the sun, and its elemental correspondence is fire.

French Marigold (*Tagetes patula*)

This little pungent sun-loving annual is a popular bedding plant, and when you say marigold, typically this is the variety of plant everyone pictures. What makes the French marigold so strongly scented? The fernlike leaves are dotted with scent glands. Marigolds come in a variety of colors: gold, orange, and yellow and red combinations. They are typically found ready to plant in six-pack cells at the nursery and garden center.

French marigolds are popular companion-planting specimens. I always plant marigolds with my tomatoes, as they strengthen the tomato plant and actually ward off some pests that tomatoes are prone to. The marigold will also protect other plants from rose, tulip, and potato nematodes. All the flowers of the *Tagetes* species will yield a yellow dye, and the flowers are often added to potpourri mixes for their sharp scent and bright colors.

A common magickal use for the French marigold is to string together heads of the golden flower and to create a garland out of them. Then the garland is hung across the doorway to repel evil and stop it from entering the house. Oddly enough, in the language of flowers, the French marigold warns of jealousy.

This marigold is also wildly popular in the Hispanic Festival of the Dead celebration and is used as decorations on November 1. The petals are scattered on gravesites, and the marigolds are strung together into garlands that adorn the graves of the beloved dead. The planetary association for the French marigold is the sun, and the elemental correspondence is fire.

A Marigold Protection Charm

For this herbal charm, you will need thirty-six inches of strong, white cotton thread, a medium-sized sewing needle, and about twelve to eighteen marigold blossoms. I would work this spell on a bright sunny day. If you'd like to add some energies for specific days of the week, consider a Sunday for success, a Tuesday to incorporate Mar's warrior energy, or choose a Saturday to add the banishing energies of Saturn.

To begin, thread the needle and tie a large knot at the end of the thread. Set this aside for the moment. Now, from your garden, gather a dozen or so French marigold blossoms. Remember that the scent of these flowers is strong, so if you find it displeasing, wear garden gloves as you gather the blossoms. Once you have the flower heads gathered, pick up your needle and thread, and string the flowers one by one onto the thread. I find it best to go through the green, fleshy part of the flower underneath the petals.

Thread them together carefully; if you get too rough with the flowers, they will shatter or break apart. Once the flowers are all strung, slide them to the center of the thread, and remove the needle and put it away. Now, tie a knot on the other end and fasten the marigold garland above the outside of your front door. Arrange the flowers again as you like. You can space them out or keep them in the center.

Once they are set up to your liking, hold your hands up to the garland and enchant it with a bit of your own personal power. Visualize that the marigold garland is growing brightly and will deflect and neutralize any negativity. See in your mind's eye that the flowers act like a barrier and no evil or bad luck will be able to enter your home. Now open your eyes, and repeat the following charm three times:

With this garland of French marigolds,

All around my home protection grows.

On a bright summer day, I spin this spell,

Bringing harm to none, may it turn out well.

Allow the garland to stay in place as long as you wish. Once the flowers dry out, you may save the garland and use it in other protection spells, or if you feel that the magick in the flowers is spent, return the flowers to nature by adding them to your compost pile or into your yard waste.

MABON
Autumn Equinox

Autumn resumes the land, ruffles the woods
with smoky wings, entangles them.

GEOFFREY HILL

Maple Tree (*Acer* spp.)

What is autumn without the maples turning red, orange, and yellow across North America? The maple tree can reach heights of up to 115 feet. The maple tree is also an herbal tree, as the sap of the sugar maple (*Acer saccharum*) is boiled down into maple syrup. In fact, it is the syrup that "flavors" the magickal associations of this gorgeous herbal tree; magickal uses include prosperity, sweetening up someone, children's magick, and love spells.

In the language of flowers, the maple leaf symbolizes elegance and beauty, while other floral languages say it signifies reserve and shyness. Astrological associations for all species of this masculine tree are Jupiter, and the tree has the elemental association of air.

A Harvest Maple Leaf Spell for Abundance

For best results, work this spell on a Thursday (Jupiter's day) during a waxing moon. You will need one orange candle, a candleholder, matches, maple leaves, and a safe, flat surface to set the spell up on.

Gather together a handful of pretty maple leaves that have started to change over to their autumn colors. Arrange these around the base of the orange candle in its holder. (We are using the color orange in this herbal candle spell to symbolize success and the season of harvest.) Please be sure to keep the foliage well away from the candle flame. Once the candle is burning away, repeat the following spell verse three times:

> *I call upon the power of Jupiter—aid me, please,*
>
> *Bring abundance into my life by the power of three.*
>
> *I am open to new opportunities and success,*
>
> *As this maple leaf spell spins out, may I be truly blessed.*
>
> *By the power of the harvest and of the herbal trees,*
>
> *In the best possible way, abundance will come to me!*

Allow the candle to burn out in a safe place. Once it does, gather up the maple leaves and any leftover candle wax, and tuck them into a small envelope. Seal up the envelope, and carry it with you to keep those prosperous and abundant vibes going strong.

Solomon's Seal (*Polygonatum officinale*)

Folk names include lady's seal and St. Mary's seal. This shady perennial belongs to the same family as lily of the valley. It is readily available as a nursery plant and grows from eighteen inches to two feet in height. It bears white, tubular flowers that dangle from the stems in clusters. While the plant is considered toxic, so long as you do not have toddlers running amok who may want to nibble on the leaves, you should be fine. Consider adding this enchanting plant to your shady sorceress gardens this year.

Magickal uses include exorcism and protection. Some texts suggest sprinkling the plant in the corners of the house to drive away entities and all negativity. Since this herb is toxic, though, I would suggest instead that you place some of the foliage and the flowers into sachet bags and then tuck those up and out of reach of pets or small children. Classically, however, it is the root that is often used in magickal procedures.

This enchanting herb is considered to be feminine. The astrological correspondence is Saturn, and the elemental association is water.

Woodbine (*Lonicera caprifolium*)

Woodbine is known today as honeysuckle. This shrub and vine blooms in the summer, and then it continues to bloom sporadically throughout the early fall. It adapts easily to sun or shade and is worth growing in your magickal gardens.

There are over 300 varieties of honeysuckle worldwide; they thrive from Asia to America. Most of these plants are deciduous; however, a few such as the Japanese honeysuckle

(*Lonicera japonica*) do stay evergreen. The blossoms are sweetly scented and trumpet-shaped and come in myriad colors, depending on the variety of the honeysuckle. It also produces clusters or single red to black poisonous berries in the fall. Berry color and arrangement will vary widely according to the subspecies of the honeysuckle, but all of the berries are considered toxic.

Woodbine is also associated with the Ogham, which is a magickal alphabet and divinatory tool all in one. The lesson of the woodbine is to embrace the sweetness of life. According to flower folklore, the honeysuckle, or woodbine, promotes prosperity and good fortune. When the flowers are brought into the house, they bring money-drawing energies into your home. In the language of flowers, the honeysuckle/woodbine symbolizes a person who is generous with their affections and a devoted friend. Other florigraphy charts list the plant as suggesting the bonds of love and fraternal joy. In a more old-fashioned definition, the plant is said to mean "a plighted troth."

As you would expect, honeysuckle attracts bees, hummingbirds, butterflies, and the fae into your garden; most sweet and strongly scented old plants will. If, however, a honeysuckle vine or shrub is growing outside of your business or home, then the prosperous vibrations from the plant will bring wealth straight to your door.

Magickally, honeysuckle foliage and flowers are often incorporated into money spells and worked with a complementary green-colored candle. The astrological correspondence for this masculine herb is the planet Jupiter, and the elemental association is earth, both of which link neatly with prosperity magick.

A Song of the Seasons

I have found all things thus far, persons and inanimate matter,
elements and seasons, strangely adapted to my resources.

HENRY DAVID THOREAU

Magickal herbalism and green witchery are enchantments suited to all four of the bewitching seasons. The trick here, my witchy friends, is to open your eyes and take a careful look around you at the natural resources that are available to you all year long. For those of you who have read my books before, you know that this is a common theme of mine; it is an important one. Green magick happens all year long, not just on soft summer evenings when you've been puttering in the garden.

Look within yourself, and then look carefully at the natural world around you. Magick is everywhere. It has always been up to you as to how to proceed and what to do with the opportunities that surround you.

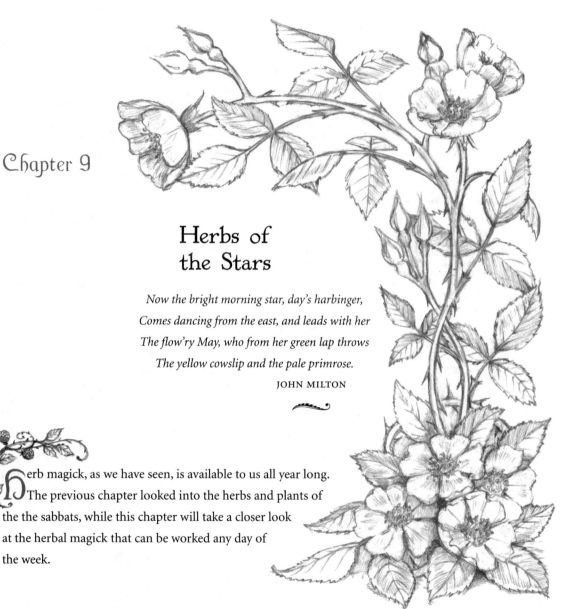

Chapter 9

Herbs of the Stars

Now the bright morning star, day's harbinger,
Comes dancing from the east, and leads with her
The flow'ry May, who from her green lap throws
The yellow cowslip and the pale primrose.

JOHN MILTON

Herb magick, as we have seen, is available to us all year long. The previous chapter looked into the herbs and plants of the the sabbats, while this chapter will take a closer look at the herbal magick that can be worked any day of the week.

Now, there are the basic correspondences of the specific planets, moon, sun, and the four natural elements, which I am sure you have noted as you have read along in this herbal so far. However, there are even more enchanting herbal associations to consider, such as the individual signs of the zodiac and the days of the week, and I was charmed to discover that even the archangels of the planets have their own sacred herbs and plants.

You will notice that the first catalog goes in order of the days of the week. I have done this to help simplify the information and to help you quickly pick out the botanicals that are harmonious to each day's magickal theme. You will see a neat list of correspondences for each day, plus a quick catalog of herbs and plants that are linked with the day. This daily list is by no means all-inclusive; instead, it focuses on the botanicals featured within this book and plants or essential oils that you should be easily able to procure. This leaves it open for you to add whichever coordinating herb from the day's list you would like to choose for that day's spell.

At the end of each section, you'll also find an herbal spell for the featured day of the week that works neatly with that day's specific planetary energy. Feel free to personalize these herbal spells with your chosen botanicals that complement that particular day. Look over the day's list and add a corresponding crystal or dress that day's colored candle with a harmonious essential oil. Have fun, be creative, and make these herbal spells personal and uniquely your own.

Remember that herb magick is considered to be a major magick, meaning it takes a grasp of several different types of magick, such as astrological timing and color magick, to work it successfully. By experimenting and adding a few of the accompanying stones, oils, colors, and candles to your spellwork, this will increase the potency of your spell, giving you better and stronger results.

THE CLASSIC SEVEN PLANETARY ASSOCIATIONS

Out of the window,
I saw how the planets gathered
Like the leaves themselves
Turning in the wind.

WALLACE STEVENS

The Sun

MAGICKAL USES: success, wealth, the God, fame, riches, achieving personal goals

SIGIL: ☉

ASSOCIATED DAY OF THE WEEK: Sunday

DEITIES: Helios, Brigit

COLORS: gold, yellow

METAL: gold

STONES: topaz, diamond

ESSENTIAL OILS: bergamot, cinnamon, frankincense, orange, rosemary, saffron

HERBS, TREES, AND PLANTS: agave, angelica, ash tree, bay, calendula, carnation, cedar, chamomile, cinnamon, cockscomb, French marigold, hazel tree, heliotrope, juniper, mistletoe, oak tree, orange, peony, poinsettia, reed, rosemary, rowan tree, rue, saffron crocus, St. John's wort, sunflower, tickseed coreopsis, witch hazel

Herbal Spell for Sunday

By Sunday's bright glow of magick and success,

May my herbal spells now quickly manifest.

Herbs of the golden sun, add your energy to mine,

Bring this positive change and happiness for all time.

The Moon

MAGICKAL USES: women's mysteries, illusions, dreams, psychic abilities, fertility, the Goddess

SIGIL: ☽

ASSOCIATED DAY OF THE WEEK: Monday

DEITIES: Selene, Artemis, Diana, Thoth

COLORS: white, silver, palest blue

METAL: silver

STONES: moonstone, pearl

ESSENTIAL OILS: jasmine, lemon, sandalwood, stephanotis (Madagascar jasmine)

HERBS, TREES, AND PLANTS: aloe, desert four o'clock, eucalyptus, gardenia, grape, grapevine, honesty, jasmine, lemon, mallow, moonflower, nicotiana, poppy, portulaca, pumpkin, sandalwood, willow tree, wintergreen

Herbal Spell for Monday

May Monday's mysterious energy hearken unto me,
My herbal spells will bring the Lady's power and prophecy.
Herbs of the silver moon, add your energy to mine,
Bring this positive change and happiness for all time.

The Planet Mars

SIGIL: ♂

MAGICKAL USES: passion, aggression, warrior attitude, bravery

ASSOCIATED DAY OF THE WEEK: Tuesday

DEITIES: Mares, Ares, Lilith

COLORS: scarlet, red, black, orange

METAL: iron

STONES: bloodstone, garnet, ruby

ESSENTIAL OILS: black pepper, ginger, pine

HERBS, TREES, AND PLANTS: allspice, basil, chili, cactus, coriander, garlic, ginger, gorse, hawthorn tree, holly, lupin, mustard, nettle, onion, pepper, pine tree, prairie anemone, prickly pear, snapdragon, sweet woodruff, thistle, wormwood, yucca

Herbal Spell for Tuesday

Tuesdays bring drive for passion and success,

May my herbal spells now quickly manifest.

Herbs of the warrior, add your energy to mine,

Bring a positive change and add courage with this rhyme.

The Planet Mercury

MAGICKAL USES: communication, speed, creativity, writing, intelligence, cunning

SIGIL: ☿

ASSOCIATED DAY OF THE WEEK: Wednesday

DEITIES: Mercury, Hermes, Iris, Odin, Athena

COLORS: purple, orange

METAL: quicksilver

STONES: opal, agate, aventurine

ESSENTIAL OILS: bergamot, mint, lavender, lemon verbena, lily of the valley, sweet pea

HERBS, TREES, AND PLANTS: almond, aspen tree, bergamot, clover, dill, fennel, fern, fly agaric, horehound, Jacob's ladder, lavender, lily of the valley, mace, mandrake, marjoram, mint, parsley, pomegranate, red clover, white clover

Herbal Spell for Wednesday

By Wednesday's speedy energy, I work this herbal charm,

Increase my communication skills and bring no one harm.

Herbs of the fleet-footed God, add your energy to mine,

Bless me with creativity and cunning for all time.

The Planet Jupiter

MAGICKAL USES: prosperity, abundance, leadership, good health, healing

SIGIL: ♃

DAY OF THE WEEK: Thursday

DEITIES: Thor, Juno, Jupiter, Zeus

COLORS: royal blue, green, purple

METAL: tin

STONES: sapphire, amethyst, turquoise

ESSENTIAL OILS: clove, honeysuckle, meadowsweet, nutmeg, sage

HERBS, TREES, AND PLANTS: anise, borage, butterfly weed, chestnut, cinquefoil, clove, dandelion, honeysuckle (woodbine), hyssop, linden tree, maple tree, meadowsweet, nutmeg, oak tree, sarsaparilla, sage

Herbal Spell for Thursday

By Thursday's energies of prosperity and health,

In the best possible way, may this spell bring me wealth.

Herbs of Jupiter, add your abundant energies to mine,

Bring to me a positive change that will last come rain or shine.

The Planet Venus

MAGICKAL USES: love, romance, sexuality, fertility, friendship, beauty magick

SIGIL: ♀

DAY OF THE WEEK: Friday

DEITIES: Venus, Aphrodite, Eros, Freya, Frigga

COLORS: aqua, pink

METAL: copper

STONES: rose quartz, coral, emerald

ESSENTIAL OILS: apple, chamomile, freesia, gardenia, geranium, lilac, rose, thyme, vanilla

HERBS, TREES, AND PLANTS: alder tree, American oxeye daisy, apple tree, aster, birch tree, blackberry, catnip, cherry, columbine, common garden crocus, dog rose, elderberry, elder tree, English daisy, feverfew, foxglove, geranium, goldenrod, hollyhock, Indian paintbrush, iris, lady's mantle, liatris/gayfeather, lilac, magnolia, mugwort, orchid, pea, periwinkle, plum tree, prairie rose, primrose, raspberry, rose, sage brush, spiderwort, strawberry, tansy, thyme, valerian, vanilla, vervain, violet, wild crab, vanilla, yarrow

Herbal Spell for Friday

By Friday's power of love and sexuality,
May my herbal spells bring joy to my loved ones and me.
Herbs of Venus, add your romantic powers to my charm,
Bring beauty and pleasure without causing anyone harm.

The Planet Saturn

MAGICKAL USES: banish negativity, break manipulative spells, remove obstacles, protection

SIGIL: ♄

ASSOCIATED DAY OF THE WEEK: Saturday

DEITIES: Saturn, Hecate

COLORS: black, deep purple

METAL: lead

STONES: obsidian, Apache tear, hematite, jet

ESSENTIAL OILS: cypress, myrrh, patchouli

HERBS, TREES, AND PLANTS: alder buckthorn, *Atropa belladonna*, black hellebore, black/garden nightshade, blackthorn tree, comfrey, cypress tree, deadly nightshade, elm tree, hedge bindweed, hellebore, hemlock, ivy, lobelia, mimosa, morning glory, mullein, pansy, poplar tree, quince, skullcap, snowdrop, Solomon's seal, yellow lady's slipper, yew tree

Herbal Spell for Saturday

By Saturday's energy, I banish my troubles away,
This herbal spell will bring security for many a day.
Herbs of Saturn, add your strong energy to mine,
I am protected, safe, and secure for all time.

With Saturday and Saturn, we close up the traditional seven and the classic daily magickal correspondences. If you really want to get a feel for the daily planetary energies and how each one differs from the other, I have a witchy homework assignment for you. Pick a day to start, then gather your herbal supplies and work the featured daily herbal spell. For the next week, I want you to work each day's specific herbal spell. (There is one for every day of the week, so you can start any time you wish.)

Take the time to tune in and to get a feel for each day's specific planetary energy and magickal theme; you'll be glad that you did. Besides that, once you have worked your way through an entire week, think of all the positive changes you'll have brewing, not to mention all of the hands-on experience you'll be gaining. For with experience, we gain knowledge, and in time, knowledge becomes wisdom.

Magickal Associations of Uranus, Neptune, and Pluto

We all come from our own little planets.
That's why we're all different. That's what makes life interesting.
ROBERT E. SHERWOOD

To the ancients, the known planets at the time were the sun, the moon, Mars, Mercury, Jupiter, Venus, and Saturn. Interestingly, ancient people believed that the planets all revolved around the earth. In the simplest of terms, the seven "planets," or luminaries, and their movements all represented the will of the gods and their direct power over human affairs.

As I researched further into which plants, herbs, flowers, and trees were associated with the different planets, I found myself hip-deep in astrology, which I admit is a topic that I do not fully comprehend—it's too damn much like math! (Yes, I've tried taking classes. I have even had friends send me simple astrology books.) But I doggedly persevered.

However, while I was bravely investigating the planetary herbs, I found myself pulled off my comfortable herbal path by some new, fascinating planetary information that I honestly can say I did not know about our solar system. Hmmm... I firmly believe that nothing happens without a reason, so I used this as an opportunity to expand my horizons a bit—to boldly go where no Garden Witch has gone before (well, at least not this particular gardening Witch)!

Now, as practical Witches, it is safe to assume that most of us work with the daily energies of the seven days of the week and their classic planetary associations most of the time. They are familiar to us, and some Witches can rattle off the daily basic correspondence charts in the blink of an eye. I wonder how many of you did your week-long herbal assignment? If you did, then you are one of those folks who knows their daily correspondences cold. Congratulations!

But what about the other three planets in our solar system? Seems to me they deserve a little attention and herbal magick, too. The last three of our planets—Uranus, Neptune, and Pluto—do not have as much historical information in regards to herbal correspondences. Why? The simple answer is that these last three planets were not discovered until more modern times. Therefore, there is not as much folklore and legend built up around them and their use in contemporary magick.

I honestly found this information about these last three planets to be fascinating and valuable from a practical magick standpoint, because don't we all enjoy learning something new, no matter how long we have been practicing our craft?

The Planet Uranus

Uranus was discovered in 1781 and was named after the Greek god of the sky. This brilliant blue planet is the third largest planet in our solar system and is seventh from the sun. Uranus is classified as a "gas planet" and has a tilted axis. There are eleven known rings around Uranus, very faint, and the brightest is known as the epsilon ring. Astronomers have recently discovered that the planet Uranus has a bright blue outer ring—only the second found in the solar system. (The other planet that sports a bright blue outer ring is Saturn.) Like the blue ring of Saturn, this newly discovered ring probably owes its existence to an accompanying small moon; in Uranus's case, this moon is named Mab. To date, Uranus has at least twenty-seven known moons. The two largest moons of Uranus are named Titania and Oberon, and they were discovered in 1787.

The magickal correspondences for Uranus are as follows:

MAGICKAL USES: change, unexpected situations, originality, genius, invention

SIGIL: ♅

COMPLEMENTARY DAY OF THE WEEK: Wednesday (as Mercury resonates with Uranus)

DEITY ASSOCIATION: Uranus, the Greek god of the sky

COLOR: bright blue

METAL: titanium

STONE: quartz crystal

ESSENTIAL OILS: clove, ambergris

HERBS AND PLANTS RULED BY URANUS INCLUDE: Clove, mistletoe, foxglove, rosemary, and valerian. To add a bit more of Uranus's blue magick into your life, you could work flower fascinations easily with this planetary influence by adding true blue flowers from your garden; for example, the blue blossoms of the 'Nikko Blue' hydrangea. Try the old-fashioned love in a mist (*Nigella damascena*); this dainty annual has fabulous blue, feathery blossoms. The gorgeous and stately delphinium comes in many shades of blue, from deep to pastel. The unusual Himalayan poppy is a true blue. Oh, and don't forget the annual blue lobelia and the friendly faced pansies in pale sky blue. In addition, we have the grape hyacinth, campanula, and the bluebell. Also, you may want to consider working with garden perennials that have bluish-colored foliage, such as hostas and ornamental grasses. Here are a few varieties of bewitchingly blue hostas to try: 'Elegans', 'Blue Moon', 'Love Pat', and 'Halcyon'. For ornamental grasses, consider 'Blue Fescue' and 'Blue Lymegrass'.

Herbal Spell for Uranus

By Uranus's power, I bring positive change into my life,

This herbal spell invokes genius and does protect me from all strife.

Herbs of this blue, ringed planet, add your energy to mine,

Situations that come my way will always work out fine.

The Planet Neptune

Neptune was discovered in 1846. Another gas giant, Neptune is the eighth planet from the sun and the fourth largest by diameter. (Neptune is smaller in diameter but larger in mass than the planet Uranus.) Neptune is bluish green in color and, like Jupiter, has a "great dark spot." This spot has been baffling science for years, as it constantly changes its shape and appearance. From time to time, the spot is not seen at all. Just to keep things interesting, Neptune also has four faint rings. Neptune has thirteen known moons, including Triton. Triton is curious, as this moon travels retrograde, or backward, in its orbit around Neptune.

The magickal associations for Neptune are as follows:

MAGICKAL USES: inspiration, dreams, compassion, clairvoyance, magick, spirituality

SIGIL: ♆

COMPLEMENTARY DAY OF THE WEEK: Friday (as Venus resonates with Neptune)

DEITIES: Poseidon and Neptune, the Greco-Roman gods of the sea

COLOR: bluish green

METALS: shell, iron, bronze

STONES: abalone, coral

ESSENTIAL OILS: lily, violet

HERBS AND PLANTS RULED BY NEPTUNE INCLUDE: All underwater and sea plants, such as kelp, sea grass, seaweed, and water lilies; also water and pond or bog plants that grow along the banks half in and half out of the water such as pitcher plants, reeds, rushes, and some varieties of iris and the lily.

Herbal Spell for Neptune

By Neptune's energy, I call magick and witchery,

This herbal spell will now enhance my spirituality.

Add your power now to mine, plants of the water and the sea,

Bless me with inspiration true; as I will, so mote it be.

The "Dwarf Planet" Pluto

Pluto was originally discovered in 1930, and for seventy-five years was known as the ninth planet in our solar system. Then, in the year 2006, Pluto was demoted to the rank of a "dwarf planet," and the debate continues on what its planetary status should be. Pluto does have a large moon called Charon. Charon is unusual as it is the largest moon in regard to its primary planet in our solar system, which was once thought a distinction held only by the earth's moon). I also find it interesting that some folks prefer to think of Pluto/Charon as a double planet instead of a planet and a moon. Charon is named after a noble centaur of mythology, Chiron. Just to keep us on our toes, in 2005, two more Pluto moons were discovered with the Hubble telescope. These tiny moons are named Nix and Hydra.

The magickal associations for Pluto are as follows:

MAGICKAL USES: transformation, renewal, breaking up blocks, removing obstacles

SIGIL: ♇

COMPLEMENTARY DAY OF THE WEEK: Tuesday (as Mars resonates with Pluto)

DEITIES: Hades and Pluto, the Greco-Roman gods of the underworld

COLOR: black

METAL: pyrite

STONES: black opal, jet

ESSENTIAL OILS: pine, cypress

HERBS AND PLANTS RULED BY PLUTO INCLUDE: Cypress, mandrake, mushrooms, pine, poppies, and wormwood. Also consider garden plants that have black blossoms. Look for these varieties for adding a touch of witchery and Pluto's energies: Columbine variety 'Black Barlow'. With pansies, try 'Black Prince' or 'Black Magic' varieties. For black hollyhocks, which have been around since the 1600s, look for *Alcea rosea nigra*, sometimes referred to as 'Nigra', also 'Black Beauty' and 'Night Watchman'. If you enjoy daylilies, then try the plants 'Midnight Oil' and 'Starling'. For tulips, plant 'Queen of the Night'. A gorgeous black iris to grow is called 'Before the Storm'. Look for black or chocolate cosmos and roses in the deepest reds that look black. A few suggested dark roses are 'Black Magic', 'Baccara', and 'Black Beauty'.

Herbal Spell for Pluto

By Pluto's energy, I call for transformation today,
This herbal spell will remove any obstacles, come what may.
Herbs of Pluto, bring renewal and rebirth to this time and place,
Your power resonates with mine from the deepest reaches of space.

I hope you will find this "new" planetary-herbal information to be useful. I personally had a blast trying it out and researching the magickal correspondences. Next up is a look at the ten planetary angels and the herbal magick that is associated with them.

The Planetary Archangels

It is not known precisely where angels dwell—
whether in the air, the void, or the planets.

VOLTAIRE

Well, here we go. You may be wondering why in the world I decided to tackle the topic of angels in this herbal. (No, I have not gone all fluffy, white light, and hot tubs on you, so relax.) The answer is simple: I found this information valuable from a magickal standpoint. Many other magickal systems work with the angels, such as Qabalah and ceremonial magick. I will also say from my own personal experience that angel magick is potent and powerful material. Over the years, I have discovered that angel magick can take you for quite a ride if you do not approach it in the correct manner. By "correct manner," I mean reverently, carefully, and with the knowledge that the angels are not the ethereal, romantic beings that popular culture imagines them to be.

Many folks who love the idea of magick but who are nervous about leaving Christianity behind think angel magick is just the ticket. They dive in, set up altars, display romantic angelic pictures all over the house, and start working angel magick with abandon. Then, after a time, much to their surprise, their world implodes.

I have seen it happen dozens of times over the years. Picture a tear-streaked face coming to your door and someone begging to know what went wrong. Why, it's angel magick … that can't be bad, right? They are angels, after all—aren't they all sweet and pretty and good? Why all the chaos and painful change? I once had someone tearfully demand to know why this had happened to her. After all, angel magick should be safer than Witchcraft.

Once I stopped laughing at her snobbishness, I tried to explain it to her. Angels are an incredible energy source. They honestly do not care if you are Pagan, Christian, Buddhist, or whatever other denomination you care to name. They don't care what your underlying goals or motivations are. If you call on them properly, they will answer.

In this silly woman's case, she had a teenage child who was always in trouble with the law. The boy dropped out of school, started stealing cars, was on probation, got mixed up with drugs, and was basically ruining his parent's social lives. (Sad to say, if she would have spent half of her time focused on her children instead of herself, her family life would have been much happier.) However, she decided it was time to work magick with the angels. Why, it was just the thing for her. After all, she informed me, she was into metaphysics, she collected angel statues, and she was a good Christian, so obviously this was the thing for her to do. It was like fate, she announced as she waved her newly purchased book on angels and magick.

I did try to warn her, but she wouldn't listen. Her reasoning for ignoring me was that as I am a Witch, what would I possibly know about angels? So, she speed-read the book, set up her altar, and starting working her mojo with the archangels; she asked them to stop her son from breaking any more laws and to stay out of trouble for at least six months.

What do you suppose happened? You guessed it. The kid got arrested on a felony offense, got locked up in juvie, and this time when he went in front of a judge, the judge was not amused, nor was he impressed by the parents' social standings. He sentenced the boy to six months of living in a home for troubled boys. The court took custody of the boy and shipped him several hours away from his family—basically a step above prison, but not by much. And his mother was devastated. What would people say? What would people think? And my personal favorite—how could this have happened to her?

Yeah, she gets my vote as "Mother of the Year," too.

Bottom line, she asked and they delivered. Angels are an energy source, and they are not there for you to go yanking on their astral chain (or wings, as the case may be) anytime you get bored. No, indeed. Think of the Lesser Banishing Ritual of the Pentagram, or the LBR as it's often called. When working the LBR, you are invoking four archangels at every direction to protect and guard you. The LBR is a powerful protective ritual, and it is typically approached with reverence and used only as needed, not for every hangnail life throws at you.

Please keep all of this in mind as you work with the planetary angels and their associated flowers. Angel magick is fascinating and powerful. However, respect, knowledge, and care are your keywords (and actions) here.

Flowers and Herbs
of the Planetary Archangels

What angel wakes me from my flow'ry bed?
SHAKESPEARE, *MIDSUMMER NIGHT'S DREAM*

In angelology, there are many different versions of archangels that are associated with the planets of our solar system. Various magick systems assign an archangel to correspond with one of the traditional seven luminaries in the sky—those that, in turn, correspond to each day of the calendar week. There are also archangels assigned to the rest of the planets in our solar system as well.

Researching which angel went with which planet took weeks. In the end, I went with the most common planetary associations and decided to let folks decide for themselves. So, by all means, if you have different magickal correspondences for the planetary angels and it works for you, then stick with that. Follow your instincts and intuition, and see where your Witch's heart leads you. Remember to work this type of magick carefully and be very specific in what you ask for. Angels don't choose favorites; they are a force of nature, and they are neutral. Use your common sense and your intelligence, and you'll be fine.

The following ten planetary archangels and their coordinating magickal information are listed this time in order of how they are arranged in our solar system, beginning with the sun.

MICHAEL, ARCHANGEL OF THE SUN: His flower is the marigold, his day is Sunday. You can call on him for strength, divine protection, truth, and illumination.

RAPHAEL, ARCHANGEL OF MERCURY: His flower is the iris, his day is Wednesday. Raphael can be called on for healing, power, information, purification, and determination.

ANIEL/ANAEL, ARCHANGEL OF VENUS: Her flower is the wild rose, her day is Friday. Call on her for love, sympathy, consideration, peace, beauty, and wisdom.

GABRIEL, ARCHANGEL OF THE MOON: Her flower is honesty, her day is Monday. Call on Gabriel to help make your dreams come true. She can help bring new projects and ideas to fruition. Gabriel is the angel of magick, clairvoyance, and visions, and she also assists with issues of fertility, birth, and children, and for the courage to overcome your darkest fears.

SAMAEL, ARCHANGEL OF MARS: His flower is the woodbine (honeysuckle), his day is Tuesday. Call on him for courage, bravery, and self-empowerment. He can help you right wrongs, increase your strength of will, and give your personal energy a boost.

SACHIEL, ARCHANGEL OF JUPITER: His flower is the violet, his day is Thursday. Call on him in matters of justice, the law, understanding, wealth, victory, keeping a sense of humor, and for kindness.

CASSIEL, ARCHANGEL OF SATURN: His flower is the snowdrop, his tree is the cypress. His day is Saturday. Also known as the angel of temperance, he brings creativity, confidence, and good luck. (Recall the flower fascination for creativity worked with Cassiel from chapter 8.)

AURIEL/URIEL, ARCHANGEL OF URANUS: Her flowers are the gentian and the torch lily, which is commonly known as the perennial named red hot poker. Call on Uriel when you feel stressed and out of sorts and are in need of peace and tranquility. Her complementary day is Wednesday.

RAZIEL, ARCHANGEL OF NEPTUNE: His flower is the poppy. This angel rules over the seas, enchantment, intuition, visions, precognitive dreams, and miracles. Raziel is also the keeper of the mysteries of all magick and esoteric knowledge. His complementary day is Friday.

AZRAEL, ARCHANGEL OF PLUTO: His herb is basil and the blossoms of the green bean. The time to contact this angel is at midnight. He can help you remove blocks to your spiritual growth. He can also assist you in discovering what is hidden and in looking beneath the surface to see the truth. His complementary day is Tuesday.

FLOWERS, HERBS, AND TREES
OF THE ZODIAC

See how nature—trees, flowers, grass—
grows in silence; see the stars,
the moon and the sun,
how they move in silence....
MOTHER TERESA

As I worked my way through this topic, I began to notice there were two schools of thought on the flowers of the zodiac. One presented flowers, herbs, and trees that coordinated with the ruling planet's energies, and others disregarded it all together. My old *Culpepper's Herbal* sometimes clashed with the astrological associations of *Cunningham's Encyclopedia of Magical Herbs*, and I began to feel the grey hairs popping right out of my head—not to mention all the other reference books piled upon my desk and a nearby card table that did not agree with each other's correspondences either.

This is what happens when a Witch doesn't like astrology and turns up her nose at it. Eventually it bites you in the behind. In my quest for a deeper look into magickal herbalism, I received a bit of a life lesson, and if you listen closely, you'll hear the gods chuckling at me right about now. Even in the green world of herbs and botanicals, the plants have energies and magickal powers that are ruled by the planets. Talk about your Witchery 101 refresher. Everything in nature and magick is interconnected.

Now, in popular culture, there are floral associations for the zodiac—and I have to say that they usually have absolutely nothing to do with the ruling planet of their particular

239

astrological sign. How these plants came to be associated with them is anyone's guess. I knew I was in trouble when even the local florists had lists of which flowers and trees were "best suited" to your astrological sign.

Imagine the look on the florists' faces when I began frowning over their lists and muttering to myself, "Ah, hello, the rose is a flower of Venus, not the sun or Leo …" I received some pretty strange reactions, let me tell you. What can I say? People are weird.

So in order to keep things less confusing, I stuck with the herbal associations that link back into the ruling planet or planets of the astrological sign. This struck me as truer, and at the end of the day, it's where your heart leads you that matters the most. My heart insisted on staying with the traditional astrological associations. Oh my Goddess, you realize what this means, don't you? I've gone astrological!

THE PLANTS OF THE ZODIAC SIGNS

Nature speaks in symbols and signs.

JOHN GREENLEAF WHITTIER

CAPRICORN (DECEMBER 22 TO JANUARY 19; RULED BY SATURN): cypress, hemlock, holly, nightshade, pine tree, rue, snowdrop, Solomon's seal, spruce, yew

AQUARIUS (JANUARY 20 TO FEBRUARY 18; RULED BY SATURN AND URANUS): blackthorn, foxglove, mullein, pine tree, red hot poker, snowdrop, valerian (*note:* Uranus resonates with Mars, so some of these Aquarian plants are also Mars' herbs)

PISCES (FEBRUARY 19 TO MARCH 20; RULED BY NEPTUNE AND JUPITER): anise, catnip, clove, eucalyptus, gardenia, honeysuckle, jasmine, lemon, nutmeg, sage, sandalwood, sea plants (*note:* Neptune resonates with Venus, so a few of these Piscean plants are also Venus's herbs)

ARIES (MARCH 21 TO APRIL 19; RULED BY MARS): allspice, cactus, carrot, chili powder, fennel, frankincense, garlic, ginger, gorse, holly, hops, pepper, peppermint, pine, snapdragon, thistle, woodruff, wormwood, yucca

TAURUS (APRIL 20 TO MAY 20; RULED BY VENUS): apple, birch, cardamom, catnip, cherry, daisy, honeysuckle, lilac, magnolia, myrtle, orchid, rose, sycamore, thyme, vanilla, violet, walnut, yarrow, ylang-ylang

GEMINI (MAY 21 TO JUNE 20; RULED BY MERCURY): almond, bergamot, caraway, clover, dill, elecampane, fennel, horehound, lavender, lemongrass, lily of the valley, mace, mandrake, marjoram, mint, parsley, pecan, pomegranate

CANCER (JUNE 21 TO JULY 22; RULED BY THE MOON): eucalyptus, gardenia, honesty, jasmine, lemon, lemon balm, lilac, lotus, moonflower, myrrh, nicotiana, pumpkin, sandalwood, wallflower, white rose

LEO (JULY 23 TO AUGUST 22; RULED BY THE SUN): bay, cinnamon, chrysanthemum, forsythia, frankincense, heliotrope, juniper, marigold, nutmeg, oak tree, orange, peony, palm tree, rosemary, rowan, sandalwood, sunflower, witch hazel

VIRGO (AUGUST 23 TO SEPTEMBER 22; RULED BY MERCURY): bergamot, clover, dill, fennel, hazel tree, hazelnut, lavender, lemon verbena, mace, mandrake, marjoram, mint, mulberry, parsley, peppermint, southernwood

LIBRA (SEPTEMBER 23 TO OCTOBER 22; RULED BY VENUS): apple, chamomile, catnip, heather, lilac, magnolia, marjoram, mugwort, orchid, rose, spearmint, sweet pea, tansy, thyme, tulip, vanilla, vervain, violet, yarrow

SCORPIO (OCTOBER 23 TO NOVEMBER 21; RULED BY PLUTO AND MARS): allspice, basil, holly, ginger, mandrake, mushroom, pine, poppies (*note:* Pluto resonates with Mars energy, so some of these plants of Scorpio are also Mars's herbs)

SAGITTARIUS (NOVEMBER 22 TO DECEMBER 21; RULED BY JUPITER): chestnut tree, cinquefoil, clove, dandelion, honeysuckle (woodbine), hyssop, linden tree, maple tree, meadowsweet, mugwort, nutmeg, salvia

THE MYSTERIES OF EARTH AND SKY

I say the whole earth and all
the stars in the sky are for religion's sake.
WALT WHITMAN

As we've discovered in this chapter, there are always new magickal lessons available to a seeker if they just look hard enough. Sometimes you have to get outside, hunker down, and make a thorough study of the plants and trees that surround you to gain access to those hidden lessons of nature. And occasionally, those of us who spend a lot of time in the world of plants and herbs need to remember to turn our gaze heavenwards and to silently contemplate the stars. For the stars are also a part of nature, and they have enchanting lessons for us as well. We all need a gentle reminder, now and then, that all of nature is indeed interconnected.

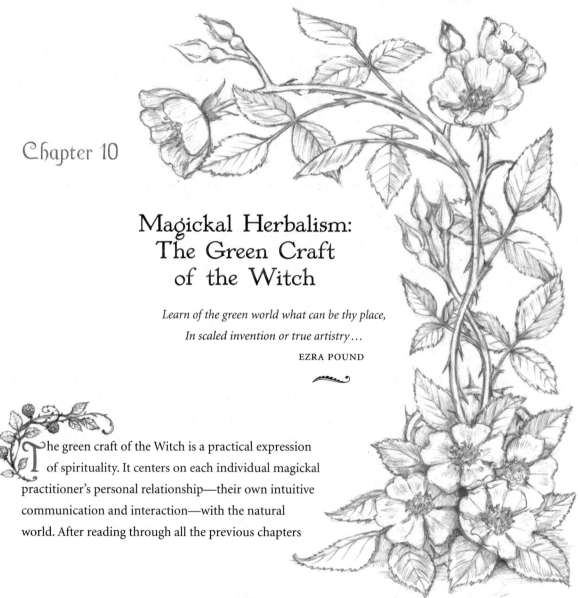

Chapter 10

Magickal Herbalism: The Green Craft of the Witch

Learn of the green world what can be thy place,
In scaled invention or true artistry…

EZRA POUND

The green craft of the Witch is a practical expression
of spirituality. It centers on each individual magickal
practitioner's personal relationship—their own intuitive
communication and interaction—with the natural
world. After reading through all the previous chapters

in this book, I sincerely hope that you now feel inspired and are raring to go and interact with nature. As Witches, this interconnectedness is essential for us.

Only you can choose to participate and to be present in your own religion. To do this, you must stay connected to the earth. As the children of the Lord and Lady, it is our privilege and our duty to care for the earth and to tend it well. Consider that the next time you are debating whether or not you want to log off the Internet or get up to go outside.

As I first suggested to readers in *Garden Witchery*, take a walk around your neighborhood, get some exercise, and really *look* at the trees, flora, and fauna that live nearby. See how many varieties of plants you can identify. What types of trees are indigenous to your area? What types of flowers and shrubs thrive in your neighborhood? Pay attention to the symbols and signs that are all around you in nature. Acknowledging these messages will help to heal your heart, and it will bring forth the magickal healer within you. Lastly, be open to all the possibilities of the natural world and green magick; they are an incredible source of wisdom. Change is the purpose of all magick, no matter what the theme of the spellwork. Imagine how much transformation you will allow into your life when you rejoice in the ever-changing natural world and your magickal connection to all of it.

There are seven classic themes of magickal work: harmony, health, love, happiness, peace, abundance, and protection. Each of these classifications, or genres, of enchantment is complementary with herbal magick (as you've seen by the variety of herbal spells that were presented within this book). The next step in your green journey is to roll up your sleeves and to get your hands dirty. Experiment with herbal magick, learn your basic correspondences, and make up your mind to grow your own herbs in pots and containers or in the garden. If you truly want to be connected to the natural world, then you have to be willing to enter it. To be a green practitioner, you simply must go outside and connect with nature.

Consider this a "Mystery" of the Craft, if you like. You must spend time outside in the natural world. It's not enough just to collect books on herbalism, you must practice the craft to become proficient. Where do you start? Well, you could plant a tree, start a community garden, grow a pot full of colorful and enchanting flowers, grow culinary herbs on a sunny deck or porch, or create a magickal garden of herbs, vegetables, and flowers in the yard. Just get out there! Try your hand at growing plants and tending to your garden. Yes, there is a lot of work preparing the soil, planting the herbs and flowers, watering, weeding, and pruning. However, it never fails to soothe the soul.

Each day spent in the garden will show you something new. Imagine all the insects, birds, and animals that live in the garden; they have enchantment as well. What do you suppose you would discover if you immersed yourself in the natural world? How much more potent do you imagine your magick would be if you used herbal ingredients that you have grown and tended to yourself? I can tell you from personal experience that those home-grown herbs and magickal flowers become extremely powerful tools in a Green Witch's hands.

And if you think about it, this makes a lot of sense. After all, your energy, love, and personal power has seeped into the herb every time you touched the plant. When you care for them, water and feed them, a connection grows between you and the plant. The plants thrive in your care and also soak up sunshine and moon magick from each lunar phase. Eventually, as you go to harvest a few leaves and blossoms for your magick, the plant happily passes on all of that energy to you. As you are its caretaker, in a very real way you become a magickal partner with the plant. You have cared for the plant and tended it well, and now it happily tends to your spells and magick in return.

Herbal Magick
and Lunar Enchantments

Know the green good,
Under the prayer-wheeling moon in the rosy wood
Be shielded by chant and flower and gay may you
Lie in grace.

DYLAN THOMAS

⌒

Herbal magick works at its best when it is performed in harmony with the coordinating days of the week and the complementary lunar phases. As the days of the week were discussed in chapter 9, now would be a good time to go over lunar phases and their uses in herbal magick. I bet you were wondering when I was going to work my way around to combining lunar phases and herbal magick. No matter how many years you have been practicing, it never hurts to brush up on the basics. There are layers within the most elementary of topics. Combining moon magick with herbalism takes some practice, and the only way to become proficient at any craft is to get in there and practice until it becomes second nature to you.

First Quarter
(from the new moon to the waxing half-moon)
In herbal magick, the waxing moon is represented by a flower that is in bud. This phase is classically associated with the Maiden Goddess. Look to the western sky to see this moon set in the early evenings. This lunar phase is a magickal time of beginnings, growth, and creativ-

ity. As the moon grows fuller each night, this is the lunar phase that is used to pull positive changes toward you.

The waxing first quarter moon is the occasion to celebrate freedom, growth, the learning process, youth, health, and to acknowledge your inner potential. Now is the time to pull positive changes, new friendships, and job opportunities into your life, for as the moon grows larger, your magickal goals will manifest.

Second Quarter
(from the waxing half-moon to the full moon)

In herbal enchantments, this lunar phase may be symbolized as a flower bud that is half-way open. This phase is associated with the Goddess as a huntress, pathfinder, spell spinner, and creator. This week-long phase is ripe with potential. During this lunar phase, herbal spells will come to fruition swiftly, especially if they are straightforward and heartfelt. All of the magickal topics listed in the first quarter are complementary to this lunar period as well. This magickal lunar interlude is all about possibilities. Also, keep in mind that the closer you can cast your spells to the actual date of the full moon, the more power and *oomph* your enchantments and charms will have.

Full Moon
(the full moon phase lasts for three days:
the night before the full moon, the night of, and the night after)

In herbal magick, this phase is signified by a flower in full and glorious bloom. The full moon is associated with the Mother aspect of the Goddess. Here, the Goddess is the loving and fertile mother. She is wise, beautiful, generous, and compassionate.

The full moon is an all-purpose lunar phase, and the sky is the limit. Here are a few magickal topics that are complementary to the full moon: spells to increase psychic powers, for health, wealth, abundance, protection of the home and job, fertility, pregnancy, family, home, marriage, and manifestation are best worked in this phase. Also, herbal spells and charms for passion, power, love, and life are complementary in this phase. The best magickal tip to remember is that the full moon is all about tapping into one of the biggest jolts of power that is available each month.

Third Quarter
(from the second night after the full moon to the waning half-moon)

In herbal magick, this may be symbolized as a blossom that is just starting to fade. Though that blossom is still lovely, now the energy of the plant turns inward. I associate this phase of the moon with the Goddess in her dark sorceress/bad-ass chick persona. When the moon begins to wane, it ushers in a powerful time of internal energy and an opportunity to quietly look within. This is also the best lunar phase to banish fears, to push away illness, and to smoothly dissolve relationships or friendships that you have outgrown.

Work magick in the third quarter to remove depression, disease, negativity, and any obstacles that you are facing. Now is also the time to carefully dissolve problems and to cast out troubles in the best way possible for all those concerned. Remember that as the moon wanes, so too will the situation or problem.

Fourth Quarter
(from the waning half-moon until the dark of the moon)

In herbal enchantments, this may be represented as a flower that has gone to seed. The flower appears to be declining, but in actuality it is setting seeds, ready to renew itself. As the moon becomes smaller in the evening sky, this time of the waning moon is associated with the Goddess as the wise and compassionate Crone. This is the lunar phase that is best employed to neutralize another person's manipulative spells. It is also complementary for personal spellwork that releases old self-images and that works to drive out bad or unhealthy habits from your life. Cast your spells now to push away, to release, or to banish problems.

Magickally, now is the occasion to tackle serious issues such as extreme protection magick, bindings, banishings, and keeping away criminals, prowlers, or stalkers. Casting your spells in the final days of the moon's cycle—when the moon is not visible at all—will increase the force behind your banishing and protective magick. This final phase of the moon is often linked to the darker aspects of the Crone Goddess, when she is a spiritual warrior.

BE CREATIVE:
THINKING OUTSIDE OF THE WINDOW BOX

Bloom where you are planted.

FAMILIAR SAYING

A good way to look at herbal magick is to picture it as a magickal toolbox. Inside of this box, you have your herbs and botanicals and your creativity. So now it is up to you to select the appropriate herb and combine that with your personal power and creativity and then bring forth a positive magickal change.

The best way to begin this process is to know your basics. Using a good basic (non-magickal) herb reference guide will be most beneficial. I prefer herb books with color photographs of the entire plant—root, stem, leaf, fruit, and flower. Also, start a gardener's journal and keep notes on your herbs and your magickal gardens. You can plan out future container gardens or plot out a new garden bed in this notebook. Gather little snippets of herb information from gardening magazines and paste them in. Make it colorful, creative, and uniquely yours, because this is a tool that you will refer to often as you practice your magickal herbalism.

When it comes to physical tools such as a gathering knife or basket, select yours carefully and with intention. You will need a gathering basket, a sickle or garden shears, a mortar and pestle, glass jars for herb storage, labels, and an herb-drying rack. Some Witches do prefer to bundle their herbs together, hang them upside down, and allow them to air-dry. There is just something quintessentially witchy about the image of bundles of aromatic herbs drying from the ceiling!

> **Garden Witch Tip:** To avoid the mess that hanging herbs can make and to protect the flowers from dust and the fading effects of sunlight, try this clever tip. Once the herbs are bundled together, take a simple brown paper lunch bag and cover the herbs with it, leaving the open end at the stem section of the bundle. Now fasten it loosely closed. This way, the herbs are protected from sunlight, air gets in, and if anything drops off the bundle during the drying process, it stays neatly within the bag. You may hang the bag-covered bundle in an out-of-the-way part of the house that has some air circulation such as the garage or basement. I don't recommend drying bundled herbs in the closet—there is no air moving around, and this may promote mold. For more information on tools of the herb magick trade, please refer to my book *Herb Magic for Beginners*.

Herbal Spell and
Green Magick Worksheet

O who can tell
The hidden power of herbs and might of magic spell?
EDMUND SPENSER, *THE FAERIE QUEENE*

～⌒

When you compose your own herbal spells and green magick, you may find it helpful to use a spell worksheet, which I will personally admit to using all the time. This way, you are plotting out the course of your magick and getting organized beforehand, because nothing blows the mood faster than having to stop working on your spell to go and gather a few missing components or supplies.

SPELL WORKSHEET

GOAL: _____

_____

_____

_____

MOON PHASE: _____

_____

DAY OF THE WEEK: _____

_____

ASTROLOGICAL/ MAGICKAL SYMBOLS USED: _____

_____

CANDLE COLOR (IF YOU ADD CANDLE MAGICK): _____

_____

_____

_____

HERBS USED: _____

_____

_____

_____

MAGICKAL SIGNIFICANCE OF THE HERBS: _____

_____

_____

_____

CRYSTALS OR STONES USED AND THEIR ASSOCIATIONS: _____

_____

_____

_____

CHARM OR VERSE: _____

_____

_____

_____

_____

_____

RESULTS: _____

_____

_____

_____

_____

_____

Finding Your Path
in the Green World

I walk unseen

On the dry smooth-shaven green,

To behold the wandering moon

Riding near her highest noon...

JOHN MILTON

At this point in your studies, you may be wondering what is next, and honestly, that is completely up to you. This herbal was designed to take a deeper look at botanicals, herbs, and green magick. Looking back at the topics covered, we have accomplished that, but now comes the tough part. You have to put down the book and dive into the gardens and the green world. Come on, you can do it. Get off the Internet for a while, and play outside! Remember when you were a child and your mother rousted you out of the house and told you to go outside and play? Well, that's a good thing. As Witches, we should be happiest when we are out and about in the natural world.

I don't expect you to step out your front door and be greeted by the babbling of a brook and the soft murmur of the forest; I expect you to work with what you have. For example, I live and practice my craft in the suburbs of the Midwestern United States. My family and I live in a mid-century ranch-style house, and there is a busy neighborhood street at the end of my front yard. However, to soften that, there are perennials, shrubs, flowers, and trees all over our front, back, and side yards. We put up a privacy fence, landscaped our little hearts out, and lavishly planted perennials and blooming shrubs.

This helped to create our own little magickal oasis right smack in the middle of the city. I assure you, not only does this green magick work, it works very well. Has it always been easy? No. We have dealt with our tragedies and triumphs, too. Sometimes nature is a bitch, and you learn to deal with whatever dramas she dishes out—for the only thing constant in nature is change, and sometimes you have to adapt to that change and discover along the way what new spiritual lessons there are to learn.

As I finish up this book, I'm looking back at everything my home, family, and gardens have experienced over the last calendar year. And in this past year, I have experienced change to both my home and my garden in very dramatic ways.

A Life Lesson from Mother Nature

In nature there are unexpected storms;
in life there are unpredictable changes.
CHINESE PROVERB

The summer of 2006 and the winter of 2007 were particularly tough on my home and gardens. It began with tornadoes in July 2006 that ripped our sixty-year-old trees apart. The storm winds tore off gutters, shingles, and sections of the garage roof. Eighty-mile-an-hour storm winds caused large tree limbs to snap and fall, punching holes in the roof and mashing established perennial beds full of magickal plants, herbs, and flowers.

So did I stand there and ring my hands and cry during the storm? No, I did not. Did I indulge in some squealing? I'll admit to that. When the storm hit, it was unlike any other storm I've seen. A roll cloud came through, and the wind picked up in an instant. There wasn't even time to think *hmmm, this looks nasty*. All of a sudden it was here.

My son Kyle and I were standing in the kitchen, as those windows face northwest, and we watched the storm come in. We knew there was a severe thunderstorm predicted, but in the Midwest that's not unusual. Where I live, everyone just says, "Oh, another storm. Well, I'll just go look outside and see how bad it is."

Suddenly it hit, fast and furious. This was no typical summer thunderstorm. I wanted to get both of us away from the kitchen windows and take cover in the hallway, since we don't have a basement. Of course, Kyle wouldn't budge. He was looking out the kitchen windows and yelling "Awesome!" as the neighborhood trees started to snap.

I grabbed him and tried to drag him into the hallway. As he is a buff six foot two inches tall, that was not easy to do. When one of our big elm trees snapped and then hit the house, he stopped arguing and then instead grabbed *me* to get in the hallway. I squealed like a little girl—I had no idea how loud of a *boom* that a tree makes when it falls on your house. Even my son was shouting.

Items began to fall off the shelves, and the pictures were rattling on the walls. It was a wild couple of minutes. Then, as quickly as it began, it passed. The thunder continued, but the meanness of the storm was over. We carefully went back into the kitchen to peer out the windows, and all we could see were downed electrical wires and leaf-covered tree branches against the windows.

After a bit of time, we cautiously went to the back door and looked out to discover the extent of the damage. I grabbed my cell phone and called my other son, who lives on his own, to make sure he was okay and ask him to bring us some ice. I knew we would be without power for days. In the twenty-plus years we had lived here, this was the worse storm damage ever. Then I called my husband, who was on an outing with my daughter, and left him a message to call me and then to come back home. Once the storm passed, I called my insurance company, reported the damage, and called the electric company and reported the downed wires—they got ripped right out of the side of the house. Kyle and I took pictures for the insurance people and then called my parents and asked them to bring over their chain saw.

Within an hour, we had begun the cleanup process. It took about a month to wait our turn to have the gutters and the roof repaired. I had most of the trees trimmed up to save them, but one had to come down. The shady perennial bed was mashed beyond repair, so I cut back the broken foliage and took it in stride. It would always bloom again the following year.

Six months later, in January of 2007, we got hit with a major ice storm. This storm was described as "catastrophic." The weight of the thick ice pulled down even more tree limbs, and those limbs tore down power lines all over the neighborhood. I did magick all night long to keep the family safe. No one slept. We heard the transformers on the utility poles blowing up all night long. They lit up the sky in weird colors of blue and green. Not to mention the sound of tree branches cracking, then the rush of ice as they fell and the occasional boom as they hit the house or somewhere close by. With no power, you could not see outside. It was a very long night punctuated by the sounds of explosions or trees falling down. Fire trucks and the police were everywhere, trying to put out fires and to make sure people were not hurt. Our neighborhood sounded like a war zone.

This ice storm decimated most of the large trees in the area and snapped off huge sections from the trees in our yard, which had fallen on top of the house and punched holes in our roof again. This time we lost power for five days—which is a long damn time to be without power in frigid temperatures.

We knew we were in trouble the following morning when the sun came up, and we saw the damage for ourselves. You could not go out and look, you could only safely peer out the windows. It was too dangerous to poke around in the yard as ice-covered limbs were still falling. Later in the morning, we heard a rumble and looked out the living-room windows to see troops of National Guard soldiers walking down our street in their camouflage. They cleared out downed trees and ice-covered limbs as they worked their way down the street.

It was surreal to see soldiers and a Humvee rolling down our block. But Goddess bless them, the guardsmen went to every house and checked on people and handed out flyers for warming shelters and other emergency information. I won't even mention the CNN national news van or the local news. My mind basically snapped to survival mode once I saw the soldiers.

That afternoon, my husband climbed up on the ice-covered roof, much to my dismay, to cover the holes in the roof with waterproof tarps. He was up there with a battery-operated drill, a pocket full of large screws, a few two-by-fours, and ropes. We tied off the edges of the tarps to bricks and large branches on the ground to keep the tarp down so it would not flap in the wind. It's amazing what you can do when you have to. We cleaned up the tree debris in the yard ourselves to save money, and my husband had covered up the roof so well that the insurance company gave us a break on our deductible. Having our neighborhood declared a disaster area by the governor didn't hurt, either.

We had thought that the tornado damage was bad. By the time the ice melted and people began the cleanup, there were more branches down on the ground then left up in the trees. Besides the roof damage, our shed in the backyard was completely mashed, our privacy fence was damaged, and the patio furniture was in pieces. We ended up with so much damage to the house that the local paper interviewed us, and we ended up on the front page. It was a real adventure.

After making the repairs to the roof (they ripped half of the roof off to the rafters and rebuilt it) and cleaning up the damage to the yard each time, the landscape and layout of my garden took a striking turn. Gone were two of my largest trees, one lost to the tornado and yet another to that horrific winter ice storm. What was at one time a mysterious shade garden was now laid bare and exposed to bright sunshine.

On Imbolc day in 2007, three weeks after the ice storm, I walked out in the backyard to regard the area where the big old maple tree had been cut down the day before. Even though I knew it was going to make a huge difference in the yard's landscape, I was still shocked to realize just how dramatic of a change it was. All of those shady perennials, which were at the moment safely sleeping away the winter underground, were going to have to be dug up and moved come spring. My well-ordered and established beds were a wreck, and I knew I had massive amounts of work to do, both to heal the land and to reclaim our gardens.

But with all the change laid out before me and the realization of months of hard work ahead, a little seed of hope began to sprout in me. What better chance to dig a little deeper and to personally explore the wonders of the magick of herbalism and of the garden? That spring, we tore down the flattened shed and rebuilt a better one in a different location in the backyard. This gave us the opportunity to expand one of the patios, and it made the garden look much more open. I transplanted all my shady perennials, which took about a week's worth of hard work, and started over. We left the bed open where the maple tree had stood. We did amend the soil and plant a few annuals, but I watched it to see how much sunshine it would receive—it got a ton. So, since we had so much money tied up in landscaping and rebuilding the fence and the shed, I filled the space full of pots and containers and plotted the reestablishing of my enchanted garden for the following year.

Some of the magickal shady plants didn't survive. A few of my foxgloves didn't make it. My lady's mantle, columbine, ferns, and sweet woodruff were all transplanted into what I figured would be shade but turned out to be sun. Oops. Well, come August, they and my hostas had taken a beating. So I watered, tried to keep them alive, and watched the sun and shade patterns. I kept notes all summer and fall and then considered my options. In a moment of dark humor, I said to my husband as we realized we had yet again more transplanting to do, "A lot of good perennials died this summer … I wonder how many didn't have to."

GARDEN CHALLENGES AND STARTING OVER

To make a great garden,
one must have a great idea or a great opportunity.
SIR GEORGE SITWELL

Now, as I sit in my office, it's late January, a year later. Imbolc is coming in a week, and in my mind (and on paper) I have been working out where all those shady perennials will be moved to for the second time. As for that spot where the maple used to be, it is going to be planted full of sun-loving magickal herbs and perennials: monarda, coneflowers, butterfly bush, tall phlox, roses, yarrow, and lavender. So not only will it be a reclaimed and lovely spot again, it will also pull in butterflies and birds, and hopefully the faeries will return. With all the hoopla of rebuilding, transplanting, and salvaging what we could in the garden, we didn't notice that tingle or tug that let us know they were there. But after a few group sabbat rituals were performed out in the garden area and patio this autumn, I knew we would get them to return. I learned quite a bit about the garden and green magick while we rebuilt the backyard. Now, if I go outside in the back, I can feel that sense of expectancy. Spring is on the way, and the garden is waiting to be rebuilt.

All I have to do is wait until spring, and then I'm diving in. I will replant, nurture, create, and bless a brand-new magickal garden. While it won't be the mysteriously magickal and shady haven it once was, it will be bright, open, fragrant, and full of enchanting possibilities.

So yes, as a magickal herbalist, a Witch, and a Green Magician, you will face challenges, both in how and where you practice. However, it shows who you truly are when you can make it work despite what is going on around you—or when you can turn a garden misfortune into a gardening triumph.

CLOSING THOUGHTS

Nature has her own best mode of doing each thing,
and she has somewhere told it plainly, if we will keep
our eyes and ears open. If not, she will not be slow in
undeceiving us, when we prefer our own way to hers.
RALPH WALDO EMERSON

By exploring this particular path of magick and by listening to our own hearts, we gain a deep and meaningful sense of connection to nature and to the spirit world. This sense of reverence is but a tool and another magickal lesson to be learned. As we acknowledge the magickal forces and energies of nature while working with the green world, this puts us on a less-traveled route. However, it does offer the seeker a quiet sense of rightness and belonging. When we enter the wild places, looking for magick, we work hand-in-hand with nature.

So sit, pray, and practice your craft in your own sacred outdoor area, wherever it may be. Perhaps it will be in a sunny southwestern garden surrounded by succulents and bright herbs and wildflowers. Maybe that will be in your own backyard, surrounded by a witchy cottage-style garden of herbs, vegetables, and flowers. Perchance you are a clever urban Witch and have created a little oasis on the deck with hanging baskets and container gardens. Perhaps you go to the meadows, the woodlands, the mountains, or the beach to gain your sense of connection. No matter where you draw strength from the natural world, you must cultivate your relationship with nature and within your own magickal gardens.

Both green magick and herb magick are creative, physical activities. The longer you tend to and work in your enchanted gardens, the more you will notice that your use of the garden as a sacred space has indeed evolved, for the same divinity that is present in nature begins to transform you, too. Over the seasons and as you gain more experience, you will bloom into a more centered and spiritual magickal practitioner.

Individuals who honor the powers of nature, green magick, and the traditional ways of the wise woman and the cunning men gain a connection to the magickal world that is amazingly personal. Whether you are part of a large Pagan community or are all on your own, no matter if you work in a traditional coven, an open eclectic circle, or prefer to be a solitary, as a Green Practitioner (or Green Witch, if you prefer), you are truly never alone. Here, in the green world of the gardens, groves, wild places, hedgerows, forests, and woodlands, you are joined by the spirits of the wise ones throughout time.

The magick of the green world is waiting for you. Will you answer the call?

Glossary

Strive to realize your kinship with all life on Earth by discovering
more about the processes going on unnoticed in your garden.
MAUREEN GILMER, *THE GARDENER'S WAY*

ALKALOID: A nitrogen-based compound contained in a plant, usually capable of having a powerful effect on bodily systems such as painkilling or poisoning.

ALLERGEN: A substance that causes an allergic reaction.

AMULET: A type of herbal charm, ornament, or jewel that aids and protects its wearer.

ANNUAL: A plant that completes its life cycle in one growing season.

AUTUMN EQUINOX: A Pagan/Wiccan sabbat also known as Mabon. This festival is celebrated on the autumnal equinox, which falls on or around September 21. This is called the Witches' Thanksgiving. It is the second of three harvest festivals and the forerunner of the "harvest home" celebrations.

BANEFUL HERB: A toxic herb. A poisonous herb or plant that causes death if ingested.

BELTANE: A greater sabbat celebrated by Wiccans and Pagans. Beltane begins at sundown on April 30. May Day, or Beltane Day, is May 1. This sabbat is considered the union of the God and Goddess. It is celebrated as a time of fertility, frivolity, and sexuality. Faerie magick is popular at Beltane, as it is also a time when the veil between our world and the world of faerie is thin, and anything can happen. Wreaths, baskets of flowers, and the Maypole are all part of the celebration.

BIENNIAL: A plant that grows vegetatively the first year and then is fruiting/ blooming or dormant the second year. Foxglove, hollyhocks, and Queen Anne's lace are prime examples of this type of plant.

BRACT: A modified or specialized leaf. They are usually smaller in size than the foliage leaves, or a different color or texture from the plant's green foliage. Bracts may be brightly colored as compared to the foliage of the plant; good examples of a brightly colored bract are the Scarlet Indian paintbrush and the poinsettia.

CASSIEL: The archangel of Saturn. His sacred flower is the snowdrop, and his day of the week is Saturday. He governs good luck, temperance, and creativity.

CHAPLET: A crown of flowers, herbs, and greenery that is worn on the head.

CHARM: A rhyming series of words (a simple spell) used for specific magickal purposes.

CHARM BAG: Similar to a sachet, a charm bag is a small cloth bag filled with aromatic herbs, charged crystals, and other magickal ingredients. Charm bags may be carried for any magickal purpose: health, safe travel, protection, to increase your confidence, and so on.

CRAFT, THE: The Witches' name for the old religion and practice of Witchcraft.

CULTIVAR: A cultivar is a variant of a plant that has particular characteristics such as a leaf or flower variation. This new variant is developed and maintained under cultivation. The name of the cultivar is printed in Roman type, within single quotation marks, and is capitalized. An example would be this popular and hearty variety of lavender: Lavandula x angustifiolia 'Munstead'. Munstead is the name of the cultivar.

CUNNING MAN: An old term, traditionally meaning a male practitioner of magick and natural or holistic healing.

DECIDUOUS: A tree or shrub that loses its leaves annually in the autumn. The plants go dormant during the winter months and regrow their foliage the following spring.

DIOECIOUS: A plant that produces male and female flowers on different plants. There are male and female versions of these plants. Examples would be holly, bittersweet, and the yew tree.

DRUPE: A fleshy fruit with one or more seeds enclosed in a stony casing.

DRYAD: A tree spirit, usually associated with one tree.

ELEMENTALS: Nature spirits, or energies, that coordinate with each element. Earth elementals are brownies and gnomes. Air elementals are faeries and sylphs.

Fire elementals are dragons, drakes, and djinns. Finally, water elementals are undines and sirens.

ELEMENTS: The four classic natural elements are earth, air, fire and water. These are the components of reality; without any one of these natural elements, human life would not be possible on our planet.

ENCHANT: The classic definition is "to sing to." To enchant something means that you load, or charge, an object with your personal power and positive intention.

ENCHANTMENT: A spell, an act of magick. This word is often used interchangeably for the word *spell*.

FAERIE: A nature spirit, usually an earth or air elemental. May also be the spirit of a particular plant or flower.

FLORIGRAPHY: The language of flowers.

FLOWER FASCINATION: *Fascination* is the art of directing another's consciousness or will toward you—to command or bewitch. Flower fascinations are elementary flower spells and floral charms used for various magickal purposes.

GARDEN WITCH: A practical, down-to-earth magickal practitioner. A Witch who is well versed in herbal knowledge and its uses and is a magickal gardener.

GENUS: A genus contains one species or several related species. The name appears in italic type and is designated by a capitalized Latin singular noun such as the genus for yarrow: *Achillea*.

GLOCHID: A short hair, bristle, or spine having a barbed tip.

GREEN MAGICK: A practical, nature-based system of the Craft that focuses on a reverence for the natural world, the individual's environment, and the plants and herbs that are indigenous to the practitioner's own area. Herbal and natural magick are essential to green magick.

HAWK MOTH: Any of numerous moths of the family *Sphingidae*, known for their very swift flight and ability to hover while sipping nectar from flowers. Also called sphingid, sphinx moth, and the hummingbird moth. Some hawk moths, like the hummingbird hawk moth, hover in midair while they feed on nectar from flowers. They are sometimes mistaken for hummingbirds.

HERB: A plant that is used for medicine, food, flavoring, or scent. Any part of the plant—the roots, stem, bark, leaves, seeds, or flowers—may be used for such purposes. An herb may be a tree, shrub, woody perennial, flower, annual, or fern.

HERBACEOUS PERENNIAL: A plant that is nonwoody and whose aboveground parts usually die back to the ground each winter. These plants survive by means of their vigorous root systems.

HERBALISM: The use of herbs in conjunction with magick to bring about positive change and transformation.

HYBRID: A hybrid plant is created when two dissimilar plant species are crossed. Hybridized roses usually spring to mind, but mints, echinacea, lavender, columbine, and other herbs such as yarrow may be hybrids too. A hybrid is indicated by a multiplication sign, e.g., *Achillea x lewisii*. The specific cultivar name of this variety of blooming yarrow plant is 'King Edward'.

IMBOLC: A Pagan/Wiccan sabbat. A cross-quarter day and the halfway point of winter and spring. The light is returning, and spring is not far away. This sabbat is celebrated on February 2 and is also known as Brigid's day, Candlemas, and Oimelc.

LUGHNASADH: A greater sabbat that is celebrated on August 1. The first of three harvest festivals, it is also known as Lammas. This is the celebration of fruits, grains, and veggies from the gardens and the fields.

MAGICK: The combination of your own personal power used in harmony with natural objects such as herbs, crystals, and the elements. Once these are combined and your goal is focused upon, typically by the act of repeating the spell verse and the lighting of a candle or the creation of an herbal charm, the act of magick then creates a positive change.

MIDSUMMER: The summer solstice and a Pagan/Wiccan sabbat that occurs on or around June 21. This is the point of the year when the sun is at its highest in the sky, and it is the longest day and shortest night. It is interesting to note that flowering herbs and perennials that bloom after the summer solstice will bloom for shorter time spans. This sabbat is also known as Litha, and it is a prime time to bless the garden and to commune with the faeries.

OSTARA: The vernal equinox and a Pagan/Wiccan sabbat that falls on or around March 20. This is a spring celebration of the Norse goddess Eostre, whose symbols include spring flowers, the hare of fertility, and colored eggs. This is a festival that celebrates spring and the earth's fertility in all its possibilities. It is a time to rejoice in life and new beginnings.

PERENNIAL: A perennial plant is one that lives three or more years. Herbaceous perennials are plants that are nonwoody and whose aboveground parts usually die back to the ground each winter. They survive by means of their vigorous root system.

RACEME: An unbranched flower cluster, usually pyramid-shaped, with stalked blossoms on a lengthened axis.

SABBAT: A sabbat is one of eight Pagan festivals and holy days of the Witch's year.

SACHET: A small cloth bag filled with aromatic herbs and spices.

SACHIEL: The archangel of Jupiter. His sacred flower is the violet, his day of the week is Thursday. He governs justice, law, wealth, and victory.

SAMHAIN: Also known as Halloween, the Witches' New Year. The day when the veil between our world and the spirit world is at its thinnest. This greater sabbat is celebrated at sundown on October 31. A popular holiday for children and adults, this is the time of year to honor and to remember your loved ones who have passed and to celebrate the coming year.

SEPAL: A petal-like leaf. A ring of sepals surrounds and protects the flower bud, forming the calyx.

SIMPLE: A simple is a basic element—a charm or spell that features only one ingredient, such as an enchanted herb.

SIMPLING: The art of simpling consists of working with one select magickal herb or flower. These spells and charms are quick and, well, simple.

SPELL: A spell is a series of rhyming words that announces the spellcaster's intention verbally. These spoken words are combined with specific actions such as lighting a candle, creating an amulet, or gathering an herb. This is then worked in harmony with the tides of nature, and combined with the spellcaster's personal energy, thus making the magickal act endowed with the power to create positive change.

STAMEN: The pollen-producing reproductive organ of a flower, usually consisting of a filament and an anther.

STOMATA: This is a tiny opening, or pore, found mostly on the underside of a plant leaf and used for gas exchange.

STREWING HERB: An herb or aromatic plant that was spread out on floors along with rushes during medieval times. This helped both to keep down insect infestation and perfume the room. The herbs were literally strewn on the floor and thus came to be known as "strewing herbs."

SUCCULENT: A plant that is thick, cellular, and fleshy. Good examples are portulaca and sedums.

TENDER PERENNIAL: A tender perennial is a plant that, while listed as a perennial, will not likely survive the winter season unless steps are taken to protect it from the cold. Many varieties of basil, rosemary, and lavender are tender perennials.

TRANSPIRATION: This is the evaporation of water from the aerial parts of plants, especially leaves but also stems, flowers, and roots. Leaf transpiration occurs through stomata. As the stomata opens, it allows the diffusion of carbon dioxide gas from the air for photosynthesis.

TUSSIE-MUSSIE: A small bouquet, also called a nosegay or posy.

UMBEL: An umbrella-shaped flower cluster.

VARIEGATED: Leaves with secondary markings.

VEIL: A mushroom membrane that encloses the young fruit-body. An example of this is the fly agaric mushroom.

WICCA: The contemporary name for the religion of the Witch. Wicca takes its roots from the Anglo-Saxon word *wicce*, which may mean "wise." It is also thought to mean "to shape or to bend." Wicca is a Pagan religion based on the cycles of nature and the belief in karma, reincarnation, and the worship of both God and Goddess.

WILDFLOWER: A wildflower is a plant that has not undergone any change or improvement by humans and is usually still found growing natively somewhere in the region where it is being cultivated.

WISE WOMEN: The first Witches; the custodians of the old herbal knowledge of benevolent spells and charms.

WITCHCRAFT: The craft of the Witch.

WORT: An old Anglo-Saxon word that means "herb."

WORT CUNNING: Herb craft.

YULE: The Wiccan sabbat celebrated on or around December 21, on the day of the winter solstice. This is the longest night and shortest day of the year. From this point on, the daylight hours will increase. Traditionally a time when Pagans celebrate the return of light and the birth of the Sun God from the Mother Goddess. Decorated pine trees, the Yule log, mistletoe, and evergreen wreaths feature prominently in our decorations.

Bibliography

These trees shall be my books.
SHAKESPEARE

Arrien, Angeles. *The Four-Fold Way: Walking the Paths of the Warrior, Teacher, Healer, and Visionary.* San Francisco: Harper Collins, 1993.

Barash, Cathy Wilkinson. *Kitchen Gardens: How to Create a Beautiful and Functional Culinary Garden.* New York: Houghton Mifflin Company, 1998.

Beth, Rae. *The Wiccan Way: Magickal Spirituality for the Solitary Practitioner.* Blaine, WA: Phoenix Publishing, 2001.

Bird, Richard. *Annuals: A Complete Guide to Successful Growing.* London: Lorenz Books, 1999.

Burrell, C. Colston. *A Gardener's Encyclopedia of Wildflowers*. Emmaus, PA: Rodale Press, 1997.

Conway, D. J. *Ancient and Shining Ones: World Myth, Magick & Religion*. St. Paul, MN: Llewellyn, 1993.

Cornell, Joseph. *Listening to Nature*. Nevada City, CA: Dawn Publications, 1987.

Cotterell, Arthur, and Rachel Storm. *The Ultimate Encyclopedia of Mythology*. London: Hermes House, 2004.

Culpeper's Color Herbal. Potterson, David, ed. New York: Sterling Publishing Company, 1983.

Cunningham, Scott. *Cunningham's Encyclopedia of Magical Herbs*. St. Paul, MN: Llewellyn, 1985.

———. *Magical Aromatherapy*. St. Paul, MN: Llewellyn, 1993.

———. *The Complete Book of Incense, Oils & Brews*. St. Paul, MN: Llewellyn, 1998.

Cunningham, Scott, and David Harrington. *The Magical Household*. St. Paul, MN: Llewellyn, 2000.

Danaan, Clea. *Sacred Land*. Woodbury, MN: Llewellyn, 2007.

Denison, Edgar. *Missouri Wildflowers*. Jefferson City, MO: Missouri Department of Conservation, 2001.

Dugan, Ellen. "Urban Herbal Gardening," *Llewellyn's 2003 Herbal Almanac*. St. Paul, MN: Llewellyn, 2002.

———. *Garden Witchery: Magick from the Ground Up*. St. Paul, MN: Llewellyn, 2003.

———. *7 Days of Magic: Spells, Charms & Correspondences for the Bewitching Week*. St. Paul, MN: Llewellyn, 2004.

———. *Herb Magic for Beginners*. Woodbury, MN: Llewellyn, 2006.

———. *Natural Witchery: Intuitive, Personal & Practical Magick*. Woodbury, MN: Llewellyn, 2007.

Dunwich, Gerina. *The Pagan Book of Halloween*. New York: Penguin/Putnam, 2000.

Franklin, Anna. *Midsummer: Magical Celebrations of the Summer Solstice*. St. Paul, MN: Llewellyn, 2002.

Gardening in the Shade. Des Moines, IA: Better Homes and Gardens Books, 1996.

Gilmer, Maureen. *The Gardener's Day: A Day Book of Acts and Affirmations*. Chicago: Contemporary Books, 2001.

Gordon, Lesley. *Green Magic: Flowers, Plants & Herbs in Lore & Legend*. New York: Viking Press, 1977.

Green, Marian. *A Witch Alone*. San Francisco: Aquarian Press, 1991.

Grimassi, Raven, and Stephanie Taylor. "The Wheel of the Year" class notes. July 2007.

Hall, Gill. *The Feng Shui Garden*. Pownal, VT: Storey Books, 1998.

Hopman, Ellen Evert. *A Druid's Herbal for the Sacred Earth Year*. Rochester, VT: Destiny Books, 1995.

Houdret, Jessica. *Practical Herb Garden*. London: Anness Publishing Limited, 2003.

Illes, Judika. *The Element Encyclopedia of 5000 Spells*. London: HarperElement, 2004.

———. *The Element Encyclopedia of Witchcraft*. London: HarperElement, 2005.

King, John. *The Celtic Druid's Year*. New York: Sterling Publishing Company, 1994.

Knight, Sirona. *Exploring Celtic Druidism*. Franklin Lakes, NJ: New Page Books, 2001.

———. *Faerie Magick*. Franklin Lakes, NJ: New Page Books, 2003.

Laufer, Geraldine Adamich. *Tussie-Mussies: The Victorian Art of Expressing Yourself in the Language of Flowers*. New York: Workman Publishing Company, 1993.

Matthews, Caitlin. *The Celtic Tradition*. Rockport, MA: Element, 1995.

Moura, Ann. *Green Witchcraft II*. St. Paul, MN: Llewellyn, 2001.

———. *Green Witchcraft III*. St. Paul, MN: Llewellyn, 2002.

Muller-Ebeling, Claudia, and Christian Ratsch. *Pagan Christmas: The Plants, Spirits and Rituals at the Origins of Yuletide*. Rochester, VT: Inner Traditions, 2006.

Muller-Ebeling, Claudia, Christian Ratsch, and Wolf-Dieter Storl. *Witchcraft Medicine: Healing Arts, Shamanic Practices & Forbidden Plants*. Rochester, VT: Inner Traditions, 2003.

Murphy-Hiscock, Arin. *The Way of the Green Witch*. Avon, MA: Provenance Press, 2006.

Nahmad, Claire. *Earth Magic: A Wise Woman's Guide to Herbal, Astrological and Other Folk Wisdom*. Rochester, VT: Destiny Books, 1994.

———. *Garden Spells: An Enchanting Collection of Victorian Wisdom*. Philadelphia: Running Press, 1994.

———. *Summoning Angels: How to Call on Angels in Every Life Situation.* London: Watkins Publishing, 2004.

Norfolk, Donald. *The Soul Garden: Creating Green Spaces for Inner Growth and Spiritual Renewal.* Woodstock, NY: Overlook Press, 2002.

O' Rush, Claire. *The Enchanted Garden.* New York: Gramercy Books, 2000.

Patterson, Jacqueline Memory. *Tree Wisdom.* London: Thorsons, 1996.

Penczak, Christopher. *The Temple of Shamanic Witchcraft.* St. Paul, MN: Llewellyn, 2005.

Pennick, Nigel. *Celtic Sacred Landscapes.* London: Thames and Hudson Publishers, 1996.

Randolph, Vance. *Ozark Magic and Folklore.* New York: Dover, 1964.

Ravenwolf, Silver. *Angels: Companions in Magick.* St. Paul, MN: Llewellyn, 2006.

Sanders, Jack. *The Secrets of Wildflowers.* Guilford, CT: Lyons Press, 2003.

Scoble, Gretchen, and Ann Field. *The Meaning of Herbs: Myth, Language & Lore.* San Francisco, CA: Chronicle Books, 2001.

Skolnick, Solomon M. *The Language of Flowers.* White Plains, NY: Peter Pauper Press, 1995.

Stevens, Elaine. *The Creative Container Gardener.* Berkeley, CA: Ten Speed Press, 1995.

Streep, Peg. *Spiritual Gardening: Creating Sacred Space Outdoors.* Alexandria, VA: Time-Life Books, 1999.

Talbot, Rob, and Robin Whiteman. *Brother Cadfael's Herb Garden*. New York: Bulfinch Press, 1997.

Telesco, Patricia. *The Victorian Grimoire*. St. Paul, MN: Llewellyn, 1993.

Vitale, Alice Thoms. *Leaves: In Myth, Magic & Medicine*. New York: Stewart, Tabori & Chang, 1997.

Walker, Barbara J. *The Woman's Dictionary of Symbols & Sacred Objects*. Edison, NJ: Castle Books, 1988.

Wizards and Witches (The Enchanted World Series). Alexandria, VA: Time-Life Books, 1984.

Wydra, Nancilee. *Feng Shui in the Garden*. Chicago: Contemporary Books, 1997.

Websites

http://www.ars.usda.gov/Services/docs.htm?docid=9950—Lupine/Lupinus USDA information (January 2008)

http://www.bellaonline.com/articles/art15737.asp—Poinsettia folklore (November 2007)

www.fortunecity.com/greenfield/tigris/567/id94.htm—Planetary correspondences (December 2007)

www.hedgerows.com.uk—Hedgerow plant information (August 2007)

www.isisbooks.com/tblcrspnd.asp—Table of planetary correspondences (December 2007)

http://www.leics.gov.uk/index/community/museums/holly_hayes/celebrating_ wildlife_old/chi_surveys/chi_hedge_intro/chi_hedgerow.htm—Leicestershire County Council Community Heritage Initiative "What is a Hedgerow?" (August 2007)

Index

Sea Salt
Soak

---

1 c Epsom Salts
1/4 c Coarse sea salt
1½ tbsp. fresh herb

Lavender - Relax
Rosemary / Mint - Energize
Sage / Lemon Verbena - Purifying Calm

---

1 Lavender
Rosemary
Lemon Verbena